Series Editor

PAOLO BERTINETTI

*Professor of English Literature,
University of Turin*

JAMES JOYCE

JAMES JOYCE
A selection from
Dubliners

Introduction by
MARGARET ROSE
University of Milan

Notes by
ANDREW THOMPSON
University of Genoa

Activities by
MAUD JACKSON
Syracuse University, Florence

CIDEB

Introduction, notes and activities

© Cideb Editrice Genoa, 1992
© Cideb Editrice Genoa, 1995

Edited by Ian Harvey

10 9 8 7 6 5 4 3 2 1

The photographs have been reproduced courtesy of Peter Costello/James
Joyce Archive Dublin and John Wyse Jackson & Bernard McGinley
Collection; The Irish Tourist Board; The National Gallery of Ireland.

Every effort has been made to trace copyright, but in the event of any
accidental infringement where it has proved untraceable, we shall be pleased
to come to a suitable arrangement with the righful owner.

ISBN 88-7754-232 2

Printed in Italy by Istituto Grafico Bertello, Borgo San Dalmazzo (CN)

Contents

Drawing by Wyndham Lewis, 1921.

VIII

PHONETIC SYMBOLS

Vowels

[ɪ]	*as in*	six
[i]	"	happy
[iː]	"	see
[e]	"	red
[æ]	"	hat
[ɑː]	"	car
[ɒ]	"	dog
[ɔː]	"	door
[ʊ]	"	put
[uː]	"	food
[ʌ]	"	cup
[ə]	"	about
[ɜː]	"	girl

Diphthongs

[eɪ]	*as in*	made
[aɪ]	"	five
[aʊ]	"	house
[ɔɪ]	"	boy
[əʊ]	"	home
[ɪə]	"	beer
[eə]	"	hair
[ʊə]	"	poor

Consonants

[b]	*as in*	**b**ed
[k]	"	**c**at
[tʃ]	"	**ch**ur**ch**
[d]	"	**d**ay
[f]	"	**f**oot
[g]	"	**g**ood
[dʒ]	"	pa**ge**
[h]	"	**h**ow
[j]	"	**y**es
[l]	"	**l**eg
[m]	"	**m**u**m**
[n]	"	**n**i**n**e
[ŋ]	"	si**ng**
[p]	"	**p**en
[r]	"	**r**ed
[s]	"	**s**oon
[z]	"	**z**oo
[ʃ]	"	**sh**ow
[ʒ]	"	mea**s**ure
[t]	"	**t**ea
[θ]	"	**th**in
[ð]	"	**th**is
[v]	"	**v**oice
[w]	"	**w**ine

['] represents primary stress in the syllable which follows

[ˌ] represents secondary stress in the syllable which follows

[r] indicates that the final "r" is only pronounced before a
word beginning with a vowel sound (British English).
In American English, the "r" is usually pronounced
before both consonants and vowel sounds.

Joyce with (from left) Lucia, an unidentified woman, his brother Stanislaus, and Stanislaus's wife, Nelly, in Salzburg, 1928.

INTRODUCTION

A Joyce Bio-bibliography

Today James Joyce's life and works can be interpreted in a different way thanks to recent research in the area of cross-cultural studies and the growing number of contemporary authors, like Timothy Mo, Kazuo Ishiguro and Winsome Pinnock, who are based in a country – in their specific case Great Britain – whose language and culture are not their original ones. While Joyce was born 2 February 1882 in Rathgar, a suburb south of Dublin, the city which was to leave an indelible mark on all his writing, in 1904 he left Ireland to spend the rest of his life in self-imposed exile, staying for long periods in Trieste, Zürich and Paris. Even if Joyce's wanderings cannot be said to parallel exactly those of other 'migrant' artists, like Joseph Conrad and later Samuel Beckett, today he can be considered as an early example of a displaced artist. His particular case is that of an Irishman whose native Anglo-Irish culture was a mixed one, who wrote in an English which was heavily marked by Irish (see section on Language in *Dubliners*), and whose extraordinary talent as a linguist allowed him to assimilate with ease the languages and cultures of those foreign countries where he lived and worked.

Joyce was the eldest son of ten children whose parents, John Stanislaus Joyce (1849-1931) and Mary Jane Murray (1859-1903) were middle-class, but came down in the world during his early life. Joyce's childhood and adolescence were unsettled since his restless and flamboyant father, after being made to take early retirement from his position in the Civil Service in 1891, never stayed in a job or a house long enough for the family to feel at home. The young Joyce received a sound Catholic education from two Jesuit colleges. From 1888-91 he attended the finest Catholic preparatory school in Ireland, Clongowes Wood College in County

Kildare. Joyce's talent as a writer revealed itself early in life: in 1891, to commemorate the death of Charles Stewart Parnell ('the uncrowned king of Ireland') on 6 October – from then on to be known as 'Ivy Day' – the nine-year-old Joyce composed a poem in honour of Ireland's hero: "Et Tu, Healy".

In 1892, due to John Joyce losing his job, the family experienced serious financial difficulties and moved first to Blackrock and then to the city of Dublin itself. After a brief period at the Christian Brothers' School, Joyce resumed his Jesuit schooling at Belvedere College, from 1893 to 1898, where he proved a model student who succeeded in winning scholarships in order to supplement the family income.

In 1898, at the age of sixteen, he enrolled at University College, Dublin, where he read Italian, French and English. He had been contemplating entering the Jesuit Order but decided against it in favour of another and evidently stronger vocation, that of art as a way to self-fulfilment. By this time he had become something of a rebel and nonconformist and his examination results were not brilliant. On 1 April 1900, *The Fortnightly Review* published his article "Ibsen's New Drama", which brought a swift reply of approval from the Norwegian dramatist. Joyce's next article "The Day of the Rabblement" (rejected by the magazine to which it was submitted due to opposition from several Irish nationalists) attacked the current Irish Literary Movement led by W.B. Yeats and Lady Gregory. In Joyce's opinion, the Irish Literary Renaissance supporters were too provincial and backward-looking and therefore unable to save Ireland from the state of paralysis which he perceived everywhere.

In 1902, having graduated from university, Joyce began his wanderings abroad with a trip to Paris where he studied medicine for a short time before returning to Dublin. His second trip to the French capital was cut short in April when he received a telegram, "Mother dying come home. Father". Mary Joyce died in August.

The year 1904 was an eventful one. Joyce started work on the first draft of the novel *Stephen Hero* (published posthumously in 1944) as well as on *Dubliners*. In 1904, he fell in love with Nora Barnacle, a simple girl from Galway, who was working at the time as a maid in a hotel. She was to become his life-long companion. Nora, like many real-life people of Joyce's acquaintance, proved a significant inspiration for his work. He took her out for the first time on 16 June 1904, which became the "Bloomsday" of his novel *Ulysses*. On 13 August, he published the first story of *Dubliners*, "The Sisters", in AE's (George Russell's) review, *Irish Homestead*. In October, Joyce invited Nora to leave "to spend a hazardous life together" in Europe. He was hoping to teach at the Berlitz School of Languages, but the position was no longer available when he arrived in Trieste, and he accepted a job in nearby Pola.

In 1905, he was appointed to a teaching post in Trieste where he continued with the composition of *Dubliners*. On 27 July 1905, the Joyces' first son, Giorgio, was born. Soon after the family were joined by Joyce's brother Stanislaus, on whom they were heavily dependent financially for many years. In December of that year Joyce took twelve stories of *Dubliners* to the publisher Grant Richards. While the manuscript was quickly accepted, difficulties subsequently arose with Richards which delayed publication until 1914.

In 1906, Joyce was in Rome working in a bank, a job and a city he disliked intensely. In 1907 he moved back to Trieste. The same year a collection of his poems, entitled *Chamber Music*, was published, and his daughter Lucia Anna was born.

The next six years were marked by the beginning of Joyce's eye troubles which were to leave him almost blind in his fifties. During the period he made his last two trips to Ireland: to Dublin in 1909 and to Dublin and Galway in 1912. In 1914 the autobiographical fiction *A Portrait of the Artist as a Young Man*, belonging to an established genre, namely the novel of adolescent awakenings, was published in serial form in the avant-garde review *The Egoist* (and in book form in 1916). *A Portrait* is the tale of a young artist-intellectual, Stephen Dedalus, whom we follow during his adolescent years and his search for an authentic identity. We watch him as he experiences his first love, refuses to

James Joyce with Sylvia Beach outside her bookshop, Shakespeare and Co. in 1920.

become a Jesuit and begins to believe in art as a way of transcending the narrowness and suffocation of his religious upbringing.

In 1915, during the First World War, Joyce moved to Zürich in neutral Switzerland, since as a British citizen his position in Trieste was that of an enemy alien. After the war, in 1919, the Joyces returned to Trieste, a city which by this time they found rather provincial. In 1920 they left for London; their plan was to stop over in Paris on the way but they ended up staying there for twenty years. In the French capital, Joyce became something of a cult figure at the centre of an international group of writers and artists. It was at this time that his cause as an uncommercial writer and as an exponent of Modernism was embraced by fellow writers, like Ezra Pound and T.S. Eliot.

Joyce's only play *Exiles* was published in 1918 in London and New York, where *The Little Review* began serially publishing his magnum opus, *Ulysses*. In 1922, the novel appeared in book form in Paris due to problems of censorship in English-speaking countries, and a French translation, which Joyce cooperated on, followed in 1929. *Ulysses,* like Fielding's *Joseph Andrews*, might be considered a comic epic poem in prose. As in *Dubliners*, the author's concern is with Dublin, and we follow its central character, Leopold Bloom, during sixteen hours of a single day, on 16 June 1904. Joyce succeeds magnificently in mixing realism with epic qualities. On the one hand, it is a book about real people living in Dublin; the city is presented with the love for detail that characterises the best writers of Naturalism and becomes a microcosmic representation of certain recurring themes and patterns in human life. Yet Leopold Bloom, middle-aged and unheroic, is at the same time Homer's Ulysses, the Wanderer, an archetypal Father searching for a Son, an exile in an unfamiliar world. Joyce made every chapter in *Ulysses* – which is nothing less than a modern-day *Odyssey* – correspond to one of Ulysses' adventures. It was in this novel that the Irish author first seriously experimented with the "stream of consciousness method" – the attempt to find a

Joyce in Lucerne with Nora, Hans Curjel
and Carola Giedion-Welcker (late 1930s).

verbal equivalent for the inner thought processes of an individual. The method allowed him to present his characters' subconscious minds, a territory which had previously remained largely unexplored. At the end of the novel, for example, Molly Bloom's half-awake reveries, significantly written without punctuation, express both conscious and unconscious thoughts and feelings.

Joyce's second collection of poems, *Pomes Penyeach*, was published in 1927. On 4 July 1931, Joyce and Nora married in London "for testamentary reasons". The same year their son Giorgio was married to Helen Kaster Fleischmann and a grandson Stephen was born in 1932. That year Lucia's mental health began to deteriorate and she was placed in a mental hospital. On 29 December, Joyce's father died in Dublin. By 1933 Joyce was nearly blind and had to be helped to read by friends, including the young Samuel Beckett. In the same year *Ulysses* was ruled to be not obscene by the authorities in New York, and an American version was authorised.

In 1936 Joyce's *Collected Poems* were published, followed by *Finnegans Wake* (1939), undoubtedly his most difficult book. Once again, Joyce employed the stream of consciousness technique, and this time he sought to explore the subconscious processes of a sleeping individual and to weave into this pattern various symbolic, psychological and mythological concepts. To appreciate the novel, the reader must enter the realm of psychic activity and take part in Joyce's linguistic games. The writing techniques are associative, linking multiple dream images in an innovative language, made up prevalently of English, but including other foreign languages. The linguistic games, the frequent foregrounding of sounds, rhythm and patterning rather than referential meaning make *Finnegans Wake* a significant precursor of Postmodernist writing.

In December 1940, Joyce and Nora fled from the perils of 'Vichy' France to take refuge in Switzerland. Joyce died on 13 January 1941 in Zürich from a perforated ulcer.

Organisation

According to Joyce's own indications, the stories of *Dubliners* may be arranged in four categories:

a) *Stories of childhood*
   "The Sisters"; "An Encounter"; "Araby"

b) *Stories of adolescence*
   "Eveline"; "After the Race"; "Two Gallants" (added later); "The Boarding House"

c) *Stories of mature life*
   "A Little Cloud"; "Counterparts" (both dealing with married life); "Clay" (concerned with an unmarried woman's life); "A Painful Case" (dealing with an intimate affair)

d) *Stories of public life*
   "Ivy Day in the Committee Room"; "A Mother"; "Grace". The fifteenth story, "The Dead", represents a case apart, no longer dealing simply with the life of Dublin and its people but, as the title suggests, also with their death and perhaps their resurrection.

The present volume contains ten stories chosen in order to include all four sections.

Background to *Dubliners*

All Joyce's works, it has frequently been said, express the paradoxical situation of an author who chose to abandon his native land, culture and religion, but for the rest of his life wrote about nothing else. This paradox is especially true of his first important work, *Dubliners*, written between 1904 and 1907. It is worth remembering that the stories were composed by a young and inexperienced writer, with a great admiration for Flaubert and to a lesser degree Maupassant, who still had to make the acquaintance of his Modernist contemporaries and the innovative European movements which evolved in the first three decades of the twentieth century. The young Joyce, therefore, deliberately wrote about what he knew and had personally experienced. During his life he remained faithful to this precept as the following statement proves: "You must write what is in your blood not what is in your brain", and he continues that he always wrote about Dublin because "If I can get to the heart of Dublin, I can get to the heart of all the cities in the world. In the particular is contained the universal".[1]

The Function of Art

Like Eliot and Pound, Joyce was an inheritor of Aestheticism. While not going so far as to believe in the concept of "Art for Art's sake", he and his contemporary writers upheld that art was not a branch of ethics, nor was it obliged to give a didactic message. Joyce's correspondence with his publishers, however, reveals that he thought his stories would have a definite effect on the reader. He told Grant Richards in 1906 that his "intention was to write a chapter of the moral history of my country and I chose Dublin for the scene because that city seemed to me the centre of paralysis." (Ellmann, *Letters*, p. 83) Joyce strongly urges Richards to publish *Dubliners* because he has offered the Irish "one good look at themselves in my nicely polished looking-glass". (Ellmann, *Letters*, pp. 63-4) He was particularly determined to make the Irish take a more truthful look at themselves, since, to his mind, Irish art had tended to distort rather than accurately reflect reality. In *Ulysses*, Dedalus describes the art of Joyce's homeland as "the cracked looking-glass of a servant", suggesting that British colonialism and poverty had so far prevented Irish writers from doing what Joyce believed was their duty.

Joyce saw his writing as a way of transforming and deepening his readers' awareness of the pettiness of his characters' lives and way of thinking. The artist's task was not to tell people what to believe, but to persuade them to perceive reality differently. For this reason he thought a work of art should be impersonal, ideally without an explicit authorial presence. So in the case of *Dubliners* Joyce remains essentially outside the tales since he does not give himself an authorial voice that intervenes in the narrative. Nonetheless, through the way each story is structured and through the author's judicious use of point of view (see section on Narrative Techniques), the reader is brought to an understanding of the moral paralysis of those people who practise a constant evasion from the world. Joyce clearly likes or dislikes certain characters and places more than others: see, for example, his sympathy for Eveline, the protagonist of the eponymous tale or his antipathy for the bullying mother in "The Boarding House", attitudes which one gleans from the text's use of structure, language, plot, allusion and irony.

This method of writing produces a different relationship between text and reader since it gives the latter more responsibility; s/he is actually called upon to use his/her interpretative skills rather than being told or advised what to think.

Realism and Symbolism

The style of *Dubliners*, compared to Joyce's later work, is much closer to the Realist mode of writing, the aim of which was the detailed observation of real people and events. As Joyce told Grant Richards, in *Dubliners* he was aiming at a "a style of scrupulous meanness" (Ellmann, *Letters*, p. 83), which implied his rejection of a complicated plot, a ruthless paring away of all superfluous details, and rigorous selection, all objectives which his keen sense of artistic form allowed him to attain.

While still living in Dublin the young author observed and made notes about the people and events familiar to him, and these provided the raw material for the tales. Once in Trieste Joyce regularly corresponded with his brother Stanislaus, asking him to confirm many details about Dublin life which he was to channel into the stories. In the tales,

Dublin place names abound, like the General Post Office, George's Street, and the Christian Brothers' School, enabling the reader who is acquainted with the city to revisit it in her/his mind's eye. Joyce's characters are vividly and authentically painted since they use linguistic registers that closely reflect their social situation and psychological state.

This accuracy of detail was one of the reasons why publishers hesitated so long about bringing out the volume. The fact that the characters were shown in real pubs and cafés, walking down real streets, and using idiomatic and sometimes bawdy expressions was just too audacious. Publishers doubtless felt that, given the strict censorship laws in Ireland at the time, Joyce's exacting realism laid them wide open to the risk of law suits.

The stories, though, are not wholly realistic. Even in this early period Joyce is already a writer of the twentieth century and the Realist mode does not satisfy him completely. Like the works of the late nineteenth-century Symbolists and Ibsen in his more Symbolist vein, *Dubliners* blends the real and the unreal. Symbolic levels continually creep into the minute everyday descriptions of events and people. It should, however, be remembered that these early stories lack the overall patterning of *Ulysses* and *Finnegans Wake*. Joyce made little effort to build a symbolic system in *Dubliners* such as William Butler Yeats attempted in his poetry and theatre.

Joyce's symbolism is apparent at several levels. The names of certain objects are very carefully chosen and stand out from the naturalistic context in which they are placed. The choice of the term, "broken harmonium", in "Eveline", in contrast to the everyday words for the rest of the furniture in the sitting room, takes on symbolic resonance. It appears to point to the general disharmony in Eveline's family, where the dead mother was a victim of her aggressive husband and Eveline now shares the same fate. People's names can also have symbolic connotations: for example, Gabriel Conroy and Michael Furey (the archangels, Gabriel and Michael) in "The Dead", Eveline (Eve), Maria (Mary, Mother of Jesus) in

"Clay" and Kathleen (suggesting Kathleen Ni Houlihan, the legendary Irish countess and a key symbol in Yeats' Irish Literary Revival) in "The Mother". Colour symbolism is also at work, with brown and yellow frequently suggesting the pervading atmosphere of paralysis. In the following description from "Araby" yellow joins with several other adjectives to conjure up the idea of immobility and decay: "The former tenant of our house, a priest, had died in the back drawing-room. Air, musty from having been long enclosed, hung in all the rooms, and the waste room behind the kitchen was littered with old useless papers. Among these I found a few paper-covered books, the pages of which were curled and damp: *The Abbot*, by Walter Scott, *The Devout Communicant* and *The Memoirs* of Vidocq. I liked the last best because the leaves were yellow" (p. 27). Joyce often pays particular attention to the colour of his characters' eyes as indicators of their personality. In "A Little Cloud" Gallaher's eyes are "of bluish-slate colour, [which] relieved his unhealthy pallor" (p. 114). In "An Encounter" (not in the present volume) the strange man the two boys meet is said to have "a pair of bottle green eyes" and his suit is "greenish-black", green being a colour which may symbolise a shifty and unreliable person (Gifford, C. 23, p. 39). A character's complexion can also be significant: for example, Mr Duffy's face in "A Painful Case", which is said "to carry the entire tale of his years, was of the brown tint of the Dublin streets" (p. 157).

Other symbols are borrowed from the Celtic tradition, such as the hazel stick which Mr Duffy carries; the hazel is the "poet's tree, simultaneously bearing the nut of wisdom and the flower of beauty" (Gifford, C. 108, p. 84). In the story the hazel stick functions ironically since Mr Duffy would seem to possess neither of these attributes. Religious symbolism can also be found, like the chalice (in the sacrament of the Eucharist this denotes the ceremonial cup holding the wine) which is mysteriously broken and is crucial to the meaning of "The Sisters".

Joyce once described the way he hoped his reader would respond to the symbolism. He thought of the process in religious terms. Writing to a friend in August 1904, he called *Dubliners* "a series of epicleti" (in the Greek Orthodox Church epicleti refer to invocations to the Holy Ghost to transform the bread and wine into the body and blood of Christ). (Ellmann, *Letters*, p. 55) In a letter to Stanislaus, Joyce was even more precise:

> Don't you think there is a certain resemblance between the mystery of the Mass and what I am trying to do? I mean I am trying ... to give people some kind of intellectual pleasure or spiritual enjoyment by converting the bread of everyday life into something that has a permanent life of its own ... for their mental moral and spiritual uplift ...

Through the particular, then, the reader is invited to reach a more universal level. This process has also been termed an "epiphany", meaning a revelation. So through an art dealing with everyday things Joyce sought to reveal essential truths. At these revelatory moments the reader's attention is arrested and s/he is made to focus on the implications of the narrative which are suddenly and surprisingly made manifest. There are many examples of epiphanies, such as the description of Mrs Kearney at the end of "The Mother": "She stood at the door haggard with rage, arguing with her husband and daughter, gesticulating with them. ... She stood still for a moment like an angry stone image ..." (pp. 199-200) Here, after witnessing the woman's battle to promote her daughter's talent, we are confronted with the ire of a defeated warrior. Another startling epiphany comes at the end of "Two Gallants", when Corley, without uttering a single word, unexpectedly reveals the small gold coin in his palm, confirming his own moral degradation since he has presumably succeeded in extracting the money from the girl who he has disparagingly called a "slavey".

The Short-Story Tradition

The short-story form which Joyce chose for *Dubliners* is part of both a European tradition with which he was acquainted – he had read and admired short stories by Maupassant (1850-93) and Chekhov (1860-94) – as well as an Irish tradition, whose exponents include Joseph Sheridan le Fanu (1814-73), Fitzjames O'Brien (1828-62) and Oscar Wilde (1856-1900), to name just a few of the more important ones. In Ireland this genre enjoys an ancient heritage, taking its origin from the Gaelic tradition of the oral tale told by professional storytellers. The form developed slowly, first in Gaelic then in English, from legend to the modern short story (Rafroidi, p. 7).

As Frank O'Connor has pointed out, from a sociological point of view the short story would seem particularly suited to give expression to "submerged population groups". O'Connor conceives of the novel as adhering to the classical concept of civilised society, of man as a member of a community, an idea supported by the novels of Jane Austen and Anthony Trollope. On the other hand, the short story remains by its very nature distant from the community, in the words of O'Connor, "romantic, individualistic and intransigent".[2] So Joyce, who had recently become a voluntary exile in Italy and was writing about a people whose cultural and linguistic identity had been continually repressed by the English, chose an extremely apt vehicle of expression.

Furthermore, the demands of the marketplace certainly persuaded the young author to try his hand at the short – story form. At the turn of the century commercially minded publishers realised there was a great call for short stories in the many magazines and newspapers. These publications often featured short tales, sketches, impressions of places and people, the sort of reading that might help a city commuter enjoy his journey home into the suburbs. At a popular level, in the *Strand Magazine* Conan Doyle enjoyed great success with the stories of his detective Sherlock

Holmes, whereas a more elitist journal like the *Yellow Book* published more experimental short prose pieces. No less a figure than Henry James voiced his warm approval of the short-story form, praising its specific merits over the novel. While still at school Joyce produced a number of sketches called "Silhouettes", some of which anticipate themes he would later address in *Dubliners*. So in his early writing he already experimented with this form in miniature.

Themes

In *Dubliners* Joyce treats several different but interlocking themes, like paralysis, religion, Irish politics, autobiography and man-woman relationships.

Paralysis

The most crucial and pervasive concern is certainly that of paralysis. We see Joyce's Dubliners confined by the restrictions of nationality, language and religion. At the same time, though, the word "life" occurs very often in *Dubliners,* signalling the attempt on the part of many of his characters to escape from their immobility.

In 1903, the author used the medical term for paralysis in his frequently quoted remark to his brother Stanislaus: "What's the matter with you is that you are afraid to live. You and people like you. The city is suffering from hemiplegia of the will." (S. Joyce, p. 248) In another letter he specified, "I call the series *Dubliners* to betray the soul of that hemiplegia or paralysis which many people consider a city". (Ellmann, *Letters*, p. 55)

The theme of paralysis has psychological, spiritual, social as well as physical implications and is felt on several levels: many of the characters suffer from a physical and spiritual paralysis. This is true, for example, of the recently deceased Reverend James Flynn in "The Sisters". The man's physical paralysis is expressed in the opening lines: "There was no

hope for him this time; it was his third stroke" (p. 3). From
the narrator's reverie Flynn emerges as a gruesome figure:
"I imagined that I saw again the heavy grey face of the
paralytic... . I felt my soul receding into some pleasant and
vicious region; and there again I found it waiting for me. It
began to confess to me in a murmuring voice and I wondered
why it smiled continually and why the lips were so moist
with spittle. But then I remembered that it had died of
paralysis and I felt that I too was smiling feebly as if to
absolve the simioniac of his sin". The implication is that
Flynn has rejected spiritual values in favour of material ones
(Gifford, C. 9, pp. 29-30). Furthermore, other forces would
seem to be at work, in which the boy narrator is mysteriously
caught up and which have brought about the priest's
misfortune. His sister claims "his life was crossed" and "It
was that chalice he broke... (...) They say it was the boy's
fault" (p. 17). In some strange way, the chalice, which has
been placed on the priest's breast as he lies in his coffin,
has exerted a profound influence on his life and destiny.

In "Eveline" a paralysis of action can be detected which
is once again accompanied by a kind of physical paralysis.
This time, though, a strong counter-movement can be felt in
the figure of Frank, who urges Eveline to break the bounds
of her confinement by marrying him and going to live in
South America. Prior to meeting Frank, Eveline has spent
her life engaged in routine tasks like the daily dusting and
cleaning and a monotonous job as a shop assistant.
Significant is the repetition of the adverb "regularly" in the
following passage: "She had hard work to keep the house
together and to see that the two young children who had
been left in her charge went to school regularly, got their
meals regularly" (pp. 50-51). The very atmosphere of the
house weighs the young woman down and prevents her from
leaving: "Her time was running out but she continued to sit
by the window, leaning her head against the window curtain,
inhaling the odour of dusty cretonne" (p. 54). In the final
passage, finding herself unable to make the decision to leave
with Frank, her body itself undergoes a gradual physical

paralysis. In contrast to Frank, who represents life and energy and is described with verbs like "steaming away", "rushing" and "moving", about Eveline we learn that "she stands" and "her distress awakened a nausea in her body and she kept moving her lips in silent fervent prayer" (p. 55). In the final image, her paralysis becomes total since even her eyes have grown numb: "She set her white face to him, passive, like a helpless animal. Her eyes gave him no sign of love or farewell or recognition" (p. 56).

Religion

Dubliners is steeped in religious concerns. As has been seen Joyce was educated by the Jesuits and considered becoming a priest before he eventually renounced his faith. Notwithstanding, especially the Catholic religion and its consequences for Irish society remained close to Joyce's heart. As an adult he saw religion as an oppressive and disabling force, something that could be pertinently paralleled to the negative authority of English rule in Ireland. He is reported to have said: "I do not see what good it does to fulminate against the English tyranny while the Roman tyranny occupies the palace of the soul" (J. Joyce, *Critical Writings*, p. 173). But this did not mean that he totally dismissed the positive aspects of religion, since in "Araby" he describes the figure of "a charitable priest" (p. 27).

Dubliners is brimming with details of church buildings, church institutions, sacred practices and traditions, religious attitudes, and repeated references to the Catechism. Even the atheist Mr Duffy in "A Painful Case" has a copy of the Catechism among his collection of books.

Some stories do more than simply contain religious details and actually have religion as their primary subject. Flynn's former life as a priest and his religious practices and malpractices are central to "The Sisters". Furthermore, the young boy's development has been mysteriously influenced by his relationship with the priest. In "Clay" one is brought to feel that Maria's religious education is crucial to understanding why she has led such a subservient existence, helping and tending to the needs of others, without expecting anything for herself. In "The Boarding House" Mr Doran's decision to marry Polly would appear to be largely dictated by the advice he has received from the priest during confession. But coupled to this are the mother's religiously motivated demands which make it necessary for him to "make reparation for his sins".

In *Dubliners*, it seems to me, some religious experiences verge on the mystical. In "Araby" the young boy describes a sort of ecstasy upon entering the dead priest's back drawing-room: "Some distant lamp or lighted window gleamed below me. I was thankful I could see so little. All my senses seemed to desire to veil themselves and, feeling that I was about to slip from them, I pressed the palms of my hands together until they trembled, murmuring: *O love! O love!* many times" (p. 30). Immediately after this Mangan's sister begins speaking to him and it is unclear if her words are part of this trance or not.

Irish Politics

The stories also touch upon Irish politics and the country's inferior position to England at the turn of the century. Joyce did not belong to any of the Nationalist groups, nor did he take an active part in politics. Joyce was an outsider who did not approve of the Irish Ireland Movement founded by Arthur Griffith in 1900 or the Irish Literary Revival created by Yeats and Lady Gregory as early as the 1880s, both of which sought to revive the Gaelic language and culture. But at the same time he was certainly no supporter of British Rule in Ireland. He condemned colonisation as one of the motives for Irish paralysis but did not think that either Yeats or Griffith had hit upon the solution to the problem. In "The Dead", for example, Miss Ivors is obviously a promoter of Gaelic and Irish culture. She is shown as mischief making and radiating puritan ardour when she accuses Gabriel Conroy of being a "West Briton", namely somebody who was more loyal to Britain than to Ireland, and provincial when she tells Gabriel he should take his holidays in Ireland rather than on the Continent.

Further reference is made to the strained relations between England and Ireland in "A Little Cloud". The journalist Gallaher has in fact left Ireland in order to live and work in London, capital and centre of power. Joyce first underlines his "travelled air" and "fearless accent" but later unveils the total wreck of the man beneath the mask. At the same time Joyce's dislike of Yeats' Irish Literary Revival is embodied in the failed literary ambitions of the frustrated poet, Little Chandler, who is paralysed by his life in Dublin. As Joyce puts it, Chandler is living "under the shadow of the gaunt spectral mansions in which the old nobility of Dublin had roistered" (pp. 108-9).

Autobiography

The stories contain autobiographical elements concerning events Joyce had experienced and characters he had known: "An Encounter" and "A Mother" are based on direct personal experience. In "The Dead" the characters of the Misses Morkan are based on Joyce's own great aunts who ran a finishing school on Usher's Island, while Gretta's story of her love for Michael Furey derived from Nora Barnacle's attachment to Michael Bodkin, who suffered a similar fate to Michael Furey. The figure of Mr Duffy in "A Painful Case" is closely based on the personality of Stanislaus, Joyce's bachelor brother, who Joyce feared would never get married.

Man-Woman Relationships

Joyce pays especial attention to close relationships between men and women, showing the specific suffering of women who were socially and legally inferior to men in the Dublin of his day (see section: Critical Views). He also explores male sexuality showing how men rarely manage to express their emotions and how, like women, they are also influenced by a strict religious dogma. Eveline, for example, within this patriarchal system, is expected to take on her mother's role, and among the reasons for her not leaving with Frank are a sense of duty and the promise she has made her mother to look after her father and younger brothers. In the relationship with Frank, it is he who sets the rules, offering her marriage only once they are in South America, hardly a conventional arrangement at the time. In "A Painful Case" Joyce concentrates on Mrs Sinico's lack of self-fulfilment and self-definition. Her husband has not only ceased to love her but as Joyce ironically informs us: "Captain Sinico had dismissed his wife so sincerely from his gallery of pleasures that he did not suspect that anyone else would take an interest in her" (p. 162). This woman appears to lack an identity of her own and when Duffy rejects her she commits suicide.

Joyce's men also have their share of problems. Mr Duffy, for example, decides to finish the relationship with Mrs Sinico in response to a voice telling him: "We cannot give ourselves, it said: we are our own" (p. 164). Only at the end when he learns of the woman's suicide does he recognise the "rectitude of his life" and bemoan the fact that he has been "outcast from life's feast" (p. 172). In "The Boarding House", Mr Doran, who has had extra-marital sex with the landlady's daughter, decides to marry her against his better judgement, because "The sin was there; even his sense of honour told him that reparation must be made for sin" (p. 96). Finally, Gabriel Conroy is likewise out of touch with his emotions as is apparent in his difficult relationship with Gretta, his wife.

Background to the City of Dublin

Dublin had been an important city during the eighteenth century, until the Act of Union in 1801 when the British Government transferred Parliament back to London. At the turn of the century it was still a beautiful city of some three hundred thousand inhabitants. Architecturally, its prestigious past could still be seen in the two medieval cathedrals, two universities (the first, Trinity College, founded during the Elizabethan period), the magnificent eighteenth-century Georgian buildings, and its fine squares like St Stephen's Green and Merrion Square. Yet for the whole of the nineteenth century the city had experienced a steady decline, both economically (the city lacked a real productive industrial base) and culturally. Even the once thriving Port of Dublin by the beginning of the twentieth century stood second to Cork and Belfast. In addition in rural Ireland there was a similar lack of dynamism.

In Dublin itself there was much inequality between the Protestant (17 per cent) and Catholic (83 per cent) sections of the population, the latter suffering much more from the economic recession. In *Dubliners* Joyce makes no attempt to give an overall analysis of Dublin society. The ruling class of Protestant professionals and politicians is rarely touched upon, and the same holds true for the growing underclass of Catholics living in great poverty in the slum tenements of the city (in "Araby" Joyce mentions "the rough tribes from the cottages"). Joyce concentrates his attention instead on the people from the lower middle class whom he knew best, the world of shopkeepers and tradesmen, functionaries of every kind, bank officials and salesmen. Mr Doran's fears of losing his job as clerk in the wine merchant's office where he has worked for thirteen years, reflect the real situation in Dublin at a time of mass unemployment. The people on the margins of society, eking out a dubious existence, are embodied in the figures of Corley and Lenehan in "Two Gallants".

Language in *Dubliners*

In modern literary criticism, linguistic questions occupy a central position. In *Ulysses* and particularly in *Finnegans Wake*, Joyce succeeded in forging a startlingly new language from his knowledge not just of English and Irish, but also of several European languages. Already in *Dubliners*, though, the language cannot fail to fascinate the attentive reader. One is constantly aware of Standard English being mixed with what is often termed Hiberno-English, a designation which exactly describes its two component parts. It is English, heavily coloured by Irish in its vocabulary, syntax, idiom and, naturally, its pronunciation.[3]

The language in *Dubliners* can better be appreciated if it is viewed from a historical perspective. The formative period for modern Hiberno-English was the seventeenth century when steadily more Irish people learned English in order to negotiate with the English ruling class. As English rule became more stable during the eighteenth century the trend in favour of English continued. In 1800 the Act of Union removed the Irish Parliament to Westminster, and this further reinforced the supremacy of English over Gaelic. In the early years of the nineteenth century, important native leaders, like Daniel O'Connell, chose to use English in their political speeches, thus contributing to the spread of English in the public sphere. In 1831 a system of primary education was established and the new syllabus stipulated English as the first language and medium of instruction. The Great Famine (1845 onwards), during which thousands of Irishmen died and many others were forced to emigrate, had disastrous effects on the Irish language. The number of Irish language speakers declined and those who emigrated were forced to learn English.

Consequently when Joyce received his early schooling in the 1880s English held a decidedly supreme position. At the same time, the English spoken and written by Irish people had – and still has today – a unique flavour distinguishing it from British English. In *Dubliners* Joyce uses Hiberno-English judiciously, and one can detect its presence on several levels.

From the point of view of vocabulary, there are many examples, such as "barmbracks" ("Clay"), a kind of Irish cake; "omadauns" ("Grace"), Irish for fool; "smahan" ("Counterparts"), meaning a small amount.

Syntactically, Irish English is distinct from British English in several ways. Examples of indirect questions following Irish syntax can be found. In Irish the inversion of subject and verb in the direct question is retained in the indirect question. In "An Encounter", we find "The man asked me how many had I" (Standard English would require

"The man asked me how many I had").

On other occasions, an Irish word or idiom is disguised behind the English, as in the following example: "I was great with him at the time" ("The Dead"). In this case, 'great' corresponds to the Irish "mór" which can mean friendly. Or "he would get his death" (ibid). In Irish, "to die" is expressed with the verb "bás a fháil" (literally, "to get one's death").

Irish English pronunciation differs greatly from British English. Anthony Burgess reminds us that when an Irish person uses the words "home, Christ, ale, master", the words are English, but the vowels and consonants are realised as if they were Irish (Anthony Burgess, p. 28). This gives Irish prose a particular flavour and musical quality when read aloud. Sometimes the Irish pronunciation is indicated in *Dubliners*: in "A Mother" we are told that Mr Fitzpatrick pronounces the word "ball" in an Irish way: "Mrs Kearney rewarded his very flat final syllable with a quick stare of contempt" (p. 185).

Joyce uses Hiberno-English appropriately to characterise certain individuals and at times to create humour. For example, the uncle's advice to the narrator in "The Sisters": "Let him learn to box his corner. That's what I'm always saying to that Rosicrucian there: take exercise. Why, when I was a nipper every morning of my life I had a cold bath, winter and summer. And that's what stands to me now. Education is all very fine and large... . Mr Cotter might take a pick of that leg of mutton, he added to my aunt" (p. 6). Joyce's use of Irish English, though, is far more restrained than, for example, Sean O'Casey in plays like *Juno and the Paycock* or *The Plough and the Stars*, whose characters generally speak in heavy Dublinese.

Narrative Techniques

As was previously indicated there is very little authorial intervention in *Dubliners*. Joyce like many modernist writers intended to diminish the role played by the omniscient narrator. He wished to achieve very different tecniques from those found in the novels of Realist writers like Balzac, George Eliot and Tolstoy, who tended to comment on their characters' lives and behaviour in an attempt to guide the reader's response.

Of course Joyce was not living and working in a vacuum. At the beginning of the twentieth century radical changes were taking place in the way man saw the world. Ideas concerning consciousness, time and space, and the nature of knowledge were reformulated by major figures like Croce, Bergson, Nietzsche, Freud and Einstein. In the fields of science and philosophy the idea of a single truth was called into question and consequently writers, too, found a single voice or point of view unacceptable. They claimed that reality was something shifting and relative which could only be authentically described from a multiple perspective.

In the first group of stories about childhood, Joyce begins experimenting. In "The Sisters", for instance, a first person narrator, who is a fictional persona of the author himself, describes events from the point of view of the young boy. This allows the reader to penetrate the young boy's mind and understand him better. First person narration, however, is combined with direct speech that introduces a variety of different voices characterised by a range of linguistic registers. We are directly presented with the speech patterns of Old Cotter, Flynn's sisters, the boy's aunt and uncle.

On the other hand, in the group of stories about adolescence Joyce adopts the free indirect style in which the narrative tends to reflect the language and sensitivity of the person being described. To use Stephen Dedalus' phrase from *A Portrait* the author has been "refined out of existence". In the case of "Eveline" the unidentified narrator tells the tale from Eveline's point of view. He obviously knows her well, entering her train of thought and revealing to us her very intimate thoughts about her family and Frank. At the same time, through, the focus moves in and out of Eveline's consciousness. While her point of view is present in the text (creating empathy), at the same time another unspecified point of view remains outside (creating irony and greater objectivity). It is clear that the narrator has not completely merged with the heroine by the kind of language and patterning which is of his own invention and independent of this uneducated woman. This is apparent in the following passage: "She sat at the window watching the evening invade the avenue. Her head was leaned against the window curtains and in her nostrils was the odour of dusty cretonne. She was tired. Few people passed. The man out of the last house passed on his way home; she heard his footsteps clacking along the concrete pavement and afterwards crunching on the cinder path before the new red houses" (p. 47). The use of the metaphor of the invading evening, the literary word "odour" and the onomatopoeic "clacking" and "crunching", make us aware of a presence which is different from that of Eveline, and which seeks to highlight her paralysis and inactivity. In the final passage, as Eveline becomes physically and psychologically paralysed, we are presented with another point of view: Frank's anguished voice is allowed to emerge in direct speech that contrasts sharply with Eveline's inability to speak and further underlines the tragic nature of the woman's situation.

In "The Dead", the last of these short stories, written in 1907, Joyce cleverly uses the technique of multiple points of view (a technique he later perfected in *Ulysses*) with greater flexibility since several different narrators, who adopt a wide range of linguistic registers, are constantly at work, describing the scene from different angles.

Tone

It is worth devoting a final word to the tone of *Dubliners*. Humorous situations and the tragi-comic vicissitudes of human beings rarely escape Joyce. Notwithstanding the main theme of paralysis (or maybe because of it!) the general tone of the stories is tragi-comic. Particularly after the childhood stories, where irony rather than comedy prevails, the comic elements come to the fore. The situation of "A Little Cloud" is amusing, thanks to the way the narrator relates the meeting between Gallaher and Little Chandler; there is a ridiculous clash between the two very different personalities: on the one hand, Little Chandler, who has remained in Dublin and wishes to flee, and on the other, Gallaher, who has escaped the paralysis and wishes to project a new image of himself as a dashing man of the world. The physical description of an ageing and rather unhealthy individual, however, which the narrator provides, stands in sharp contrast to how Gallaher would like to be seen, thereby provoking tragi-comic overtones: "Ignatius Gallaher took off his hat and displayed a large closely cropped head. His face was heavy, pale and clean-shaven. His eyes, which were of bluish slate-colour, relieved his unhealthy pallor and shone out plainly above the vivid orange tie he wore. Between these rival features the lips appeared very long and shapeless and colourless. He bent his head and felt with two sympathetic fingers the thin hair at the crown" (p. 114).

Comedy is also of a verbal kind. Gallaher, for instance, introduces touches of Gaelic and French into his English, making himself look ridiculous since his snobbery and pedantry are thereby revealed. At the beginning of "Grace" (not included in this selection), much of the humour derives from Kernan's virtually incomprehensible speech ("I'an't, 'an, he answered, 'y tongue is hurt") and his frequent repetition of "Sha, s'nothing", which sharply contradicts the pathetic state he finds himself in. Mrs Kernan's colourful Irish English is also very entertaining: as she enters the kitchen, having attended to her drunken husband, she exclaims: "Such a sight! Oh, he'll do for himself one day and that's the holy alls of it. He's been drinking since Friday".

Critical Views

Joyce on *Dubliners*

"As for my part and share in the book I have already told all I have to tell. My intention was to write a chapter of the moral history of my country and I chose Dublin for the scene because that city seemed to me to be the centre of paralysis. I have tried to present it to the indifferent public under four of its aspects: childhood, adolescence, maturity and public life. The stories are arranged in this order. I have written it for the most part in a style of scrupulous meanness and with the conviction that he is a very bold man who dares to alter in the presentment, still more to deform, whatever he has seen and heard. I cannot do any more than this. I cannot alter what I have written."

An excerpt from a letter Joyce wrote to his publisher Grant Richards (Ellmann, *Letters*, p. 83.).

On the Dubliners in *Dubliners*

"Joyce obeyed what he called 'the call of life' when he left Dublin. In *Dubliners* we see what happened to those who stayed behind, to the timid and conventional protagonists of these stories. One can argue endlessly as to whether these characters cannot escape their environment because they are timid, or whether their timidity has been engendered by the environment. Joyce does not explain and comment: he presents.

(C. A. Bitter, "Introduction" to *Dubliners*, Macmillan, London, 1974, p. 6).

On Style

"The prose never draws attention to itself except at the end of "The Dead", and by then it has been earned: throughout, it enters our imaginations as stealthily as the evening invading the avenue in "Eveline". Its classical balance allows no room for self expression: all the seas of the world may be tumbling in Eveline's heart, but her eyes give no sign of love or farewell or recognition.

Joyce does not judge. His characters live within the human constraints in space and time and within their own city. The quality of the language is more important than any system of ethics or aesthetics. Material and form are inseparable. So happy is the union of subject and object that they never become statements of any kind, but in their richness and truth are representations of particular lives – and of all life."

(John McGahern, "Dubliners" in *The Artist and the Labyrinth*, p. 71.)

On Religion

"Whether we take the entire first story, "The Sisters"; the educational background of "An Encounter"; Saint Marguerite Marie Alacoque presiding over the destinies of "Eveline"; the respect, ability and religious practice of the mother in "The Boarding House"; "Grace" which offers a vast knowledge of religion in general and the worldliness for which the Jesuits were reproved; or "The Dead" with its evocation of Cistercian monks who slept in their coffins – everything points to a type of upbringing and to a specific mood whose Irishness need not be stressed.

The obsessive recurrence of religious references is particularly striking in one who is supposed to have abandoned the faith of his fathers. "It is a curious thing," Cranley tells Stephen in *A Portrait of the Artist*, "how your mind is supersaturated with the religion in which you say you disbelieve."

(Rafroidi, p. 13)

On Marriage

"Marriage itself was by no means something that could be expected in due course. After the Great Famine of the 1840s the population of Ireland declined and continued to decline. The marriage rate declined; the average age at which people married rose towards the mid-1930s, and the birth rate declined. In Ireland in 1901 52.7 percent of the women of marriageable age in the population (16 years of age and older) were unmarried; 37.7 percent were married; 9.6 percent widowed ... these are high rates. What they mean is that Frank's offer to marry Eveline in the story "Eveline", is the exception rather than the rule, and it is quite probable that when Eveline turns away from Frank she turns away towards a celibate future, a fate like that of Maria in "Clay"."

(Gifford, p. 12.)

NOTES

1. Quoted by Arthur Power in his book, *From an Old Waterford House* in Rafroidi, p. 12.

2. See Frank O'Connor, *The Lonely Voice* (New York: Bantam Books, 1968), p. 23.

3. See T.P. Dolan "The Language of Dubliners", pp. 25-40 in *James Joyce: the Artist and the Labyrinth* (ed.) Augustine Martin, (London: Ryan Publishing, 1990) for a more exhaustive treatment of this topic.

James Joyce, Paris, 1937.

Select Bibliography

The Text of *Dubliners*

The original version was published by Grant Richards, London, 1914.

GIFFORD, Don, *Joyce Annotated: Notes for "Dubliners" and "A Portrait of the Artist as a Young Man"* (Berkeley and London: University of California Press, 1982) provides an indispensable commentary on *Dubliners* and *A Portrait*.

Other Works by Joyce

Chamber Music (London: Elkin Matthews, 1907).

A Portrait of the Artist as a Young Man (New York: Huebsch, 1916; the best modern edition: New York: The Viking Press, 1964).

Exiles (London: Grant Richards, 1918; London: Triad Panther Books, 1979).

Ulysses (Paris: Shakespeare and Co., 1922; Harmondsworth: Penguin, 1969).

Pomes Penyeach (Paris: Shakespeare and Co., 1927).

Collected Poems (New York: Black Sun Press, 1936).

Finnegans Wake (London: Faber and Faber, 1939 and 1971).

Posthumous Publications

GILBERT, Stuart, (vol. 1, 1957) and ELLMANN, Richard, (vols. 2 and 3, 1966) (eds.), *Letters* (New York: The Viking Press).

MASON, Ellsworth and ELLMANN, Richard (eds.),
  Critical Writings (New York: The Viking Press, 1959).

SILVERMAN, Oscar (ed.), *Epiphanies* (University of
  Buffalo, 1956).

SPENCER, Theodore (ed.), *Stephen Hero* (Norfolk Conn.:
  New Directions, 1944; London: Triad, Panther Books, 1977).

General Critical Studies on Joyce

BENSTOCK, Bernard, *James Joyce: The Undiscovered Country*
  (Dublin: Gill and Macmillan, 1977).

BISHOP, John, *Joyce's Book of the Dark* (Madison: University of
  Wisconsin Press, 1986).

BOLT, Sydney, *A Preface to James Joyce* (London: Longman, 1981).

BRIVIC, Sheldon R., *Joyce Between Freud and Jung* (Port
  Washington and London: Kennikat Press, 1980).

BURGESS, Anthony, *Joysprick: An Introduction to the
  Language of James Joyce*, The Language Library
  (London: André Deutsch, 1973).

CRONIN, Anthony, *A Question of Modernity* (London: Secker and
  Warburg, 1966).

ELLMANN, Richard, *Eminent Domain* (New York: Oxford
  University Press, 1967).

GROSS, John, *James Joyce* (New York: Viking Press, 1970).

HERRING, Philip F., *Joyce's Uncertainty Principle* (Princeton:
  Princeton University Press, 1987).

HODGART, Matthew, *A Student's Guide* (London: Routledge
  and Kegan Paul, 1978).

KENNER, Hugh, *Joyce's Voices* (London: Faber and Faber, 1978).

LEVIN, Harry, *James Joyce: A Critical Introduction* (Norfolk:
  New Direction Press, 1960).

LITZ, Walter A., *James Joyce* (Boston: Twayne, 1966).

MACCABE, Colin, *James Joyce and the Revolution of the World*
  (London: Macmillan, 1979).

MAGANIELLO, Dominic, *Joyce's Politics* (London: Routledge and
  Kegan Paul, 1980).

SENN, Fritz, *Joyce Dislocutions: Essays on Reading as Translation* (Baltimore: The Johns Hopkins University Press, 1984).

TINDALL, William Y., *James Joyce. His Way of Interpreting the Modern World* (New York: Scribner's, 1950).

TINDALL, William Y., *A Reader's Guide to James Joyce* (London: Thames and Hudson, 1959).

Criticism on *Dubliners*

ATTRIDGE, Derek and FERRER, Daniel (eds.), *Post-structuralist Joyce: Essays from the French* (Cambridge: Cambridge University Press, 1984).

ATTRIDGE, Derek (ed.), *The Cambridge Companion to James Joyce* (Cambridge: Cambridge University Press, 1990).

BEJA, Morris, *James Joyce: "Dubliners" and "A Portrait"* (London: Macmillan, Casebook Series, 1973).

BENSTOCK, Bernard, "Narrative Strategies: Tellers in *Dubliners* Tales." *Journal of Modern Literature*, (Philadephia, 1989, Spring, 15:4, pp. 541-559).

BLOOM, Harold (ed.), James Joyce's "Dubliners" (New York: Chelsea, 1988).

DOLAN, T.P. "The Language of *Dubliners*" in Martin Augustine (ed.) *James Joyce: The Artist and the Labyrinth* (London: Ryan, 1990).

FUGER, Wilhelm (ed.), *Concordance to James Joyce's "Dubliners"* (New York: George Olms and Hildersteim, 1980).

HART, Clive (ed.), *James Joyce's "Dubliners"* (London: Faber and Faber, 1969).

JOHNSEN, William A.,"Joyce's "*Dubliners*" and the Futility of Modernism" in McCormack, W.J. (ed.); Stead, Alistair (ed.), *James Joyce and Modern Literature* (London: Routledge, 1982).

MCGAHERN, John, "*Dubliners*" in Martin Augustine (ed.) *James Joyce: The Artist and the Labyrinth* (London: Ryan, 1990).

RAFROIDI, Patrick, "*Dubliners*" York Notes, (Essex: Longman, 1985).

TORCHIANA, Donald, T., *Backgrounds for Joyce's "Dubliners"* (Boston: Allen and Unwin, 1986).

Biographies and Bibliographies

DEMING, Robert H., *A Bibliography of James Joyce Studies* (Lawrence: University of Kansas Libraries, 1964); to be updated by reading *Modern Fiction Studies*, 15 (Spring 1969) and recent issues of *The James Joyce Quarterly* (University of Tulsa).

ELLMANN, Richard, *James Joyce*, (New York and Oxford: Oxford University Press, 1959; new and revised edition, 1982).

JACKSON, Stanley Thomas, *James Joyce: A Guide to Research* (Brighton: Harvester, 1989).

JOYCE, Stanislaus, *My Brother's Keeper: James Joyce's Early Years* (ed.), R. Ellmann, preface by T. S. Eliot, (New York: The Viking Press, 1958).

A selection of critical works in Italian

BOSINELLI, Rosa Maria (ed.); Pugliatti, Paola (ed.); Zacchi Romana (ed.), Kemeny Tomaso (introduction), *Myriadminded Man: Jottings on Joyce* (Bologna: Cooperativa Lib. Uni. Ed., 1986).

CIANCI, Gianni, *La fortuna di Joyce in Italia* (Bari: Adritica, 1974).

ECO, Umberto, *Le poetiche di Joyce* (Milano: Bompiani, 1982).

MELCHIORI, Giorgio, *I funamboli: il manierismo nella letteratura inglese contemporanea* (Torino: Einaudi, 1963, includes an interesting chapter on Joyce).

PACI, Francesca Romana, *Vita ed opere di James Joyce* (Bari: Laterza, 1968).

PATEY, Caroline, *Tempi difficili su Joyce e Proust* (Milano: Marcos y Marcos, 1991).

VAGLIO MARENCO, Carlo, *Introduzione alla lettura di James Joyce*, (Milano: Mursia, 1979).

CHRONOLOGY

1882	Born 2 February in Rathgar, a Dublin suburb. He was the oldest of ten children born to John Stanislaus Joyce and Mary Jane Murray.
1884	Birth of Stanislaus Joyce, Joyce's brother.
1888	Begins Clongowes Wood College, one of the best preparatory schools in Ireland.
1891	On the death of the "uncrowned King of Ireland", Charles Stuart Parnell, Joyce writes his first published work, "Eh Tu, Healy". Leaves Clongowes Wood College.
1893	The Joyces are forced to move to a house in Dublin due to their poor financial circumstances. Joyce attends the Jesuit Belvedere College, where he wins several scholarships.
1898	Decides against entering the Jesuit Order and enrolls instead at University College, Dublin, where he reads Italian, French and English. (Beginning of the Boer War)
1900	Joyce's article "Ibsen's New Drama" appears in *Fortnightly Review*. He uses the money he

earns from this article to visit London. This is the trip that begins his exile from Ireland.

(Sigmund Freud's *Interpretation of Dreams*)

1901

Writes the article "The Days of the Rabblement" attacking the current Irish Literary Movement, headed by W.B. Yeats and Lady Gregory.

(Death of Queen Victoria)

1902

Graduates from University and goes to Paris. Enrolls as a medical student at the Sorbonne, but soon abandons these studies.

(Foundation of Irish Literary Society)

1903

Returns to Dublin. Death of his mother.

1904

Starts work on the first draft of the novel *Stephen Hero* (published posthumously in 1944) as well as beginning *Dubliners*. Meets Nora Barnacle and falls passionately in love. Takes her out on 16 June, which was to bcome the "Bloomsday" of *Ulysses*. The two decide to elope to Europe.

(Abbey Theatre founded)

1905

Joyce and Nora move to Trieste, where he takes up a teaching post at the Berlitz School of Languages. They are joined by Stanislaus Joyce. Birth of a son, Giorgio on 27 July. Submits 12 *Dubliners* stories to publisher Grant Richards.

(Founding of Sinn Fein Movement)

1906 They move to Rome, where Joyce accepts a post as a bank clerk. Richards accepts *Dubliners* in February, then rejects it in September.

1907 The Joyces return to Trieste. A collection of Joyce's poetry, under the title of *Chamber Music*, is published. Birth of a daughter, Lucia Anna.

  (Cubist Exhibition in Paris)

1909 Pays two visits to Dublin. Negotiates contracts for publishing *Dubliners*. Publication of *Dubliners* delayed.

1910 Returns to Trieste.

  (Futurist Manifesto)

1912 Last visit to Dublin; printing sheets for *Dubliners* destroyed.

1913 Meets Ezra Pound, who with great conviction begins to support Joyce's writing in the literary world. Richards asks to see *Dubliners* again.

1914 *A Portrait of the Artist as a Young Man* is published in serial form in the avant-garde review, *The Egoist*. Richards decides to publish *Dubliners*. Writes a play *Exiles* and sets to work on *Ulysses*.

  (Outbreak of World War I)

Joyce in his thirties.

1915	The Joyces are forced to leave Trieste and go to Zürich since their position as British Nationals in Austrian-occupied Trieste leaves them no alternative.
1916	Publication of *A Portrait of the Artist as a Young Man* in New York.
	(Dadaist Manifesto in Zürich)
1917	Undergoes the first of several eye operations.
	(The Russian Revolution)
1918	*Exiles* is published in London and New York. Serial publication of *Ulysses* begins in the *Little Review*.
	(End of World War I)
1919	The Joyces return to Trieste.
1920	The Joyces settle in Paris, where Joyce meets many literary celebrities, including Wyndham Lewis, Marcel Proust, Ernest Hemingway and Gertrude Stein.
1922	*Ulysses* is published by Sylvia Beach's Shakespeare and Company in Paris on 2 February, Joyce's fortieth birthday.
	(Foundation of the Irish Free State; T.S. Eliot's *The Waste Land*; André Breton's Surrealist Manifesto in 1924)
1923-30	Begins "Work in Progress" (later published as *Finnegans Wake*). Fragments of it appear in *Transition*.

1927	*Pomes Penyeach*, a second collection of poems, is published.
1931	Joyce and Nora marry for "testamentary reasons". Death of Joyce's father in Dublin. Lucia's mental health gets worse and she has to be placed in an institution.
1932	Birth of a grandson, Stephen.
1933	New York court decides *Ulysses* is not pornographic.
1934	*Ulysses* is published in the United States after the ban on it is lifted in all English-speaking countries. Joyce is by now almost blind.
1939	*Finnegans Wake* is published in London by Faber and Faber.
	(Outbreak of World War II)
1940	Moves to Zürich in neutral Switzerland.
1941	Dies of a perforated ulcer following a stomach operation. He is buried at the Fluntern Cemetery in Zürich.
1945	(End of World War II)
1951	Nora Barnacle Joyce dies in Zürich.

James Joyce towards the end of his life.

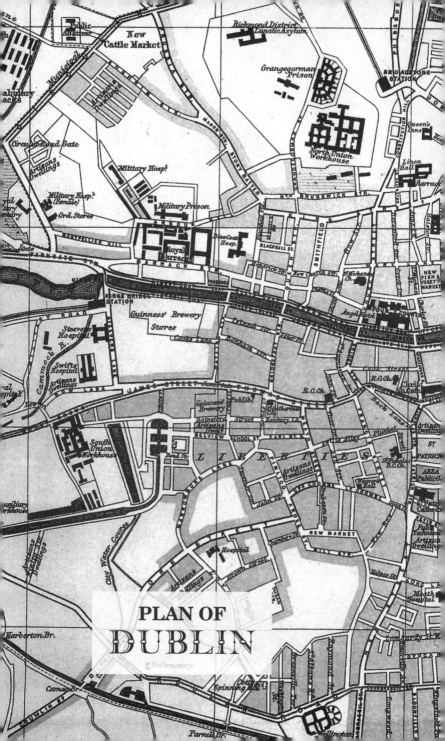

PLAN OF
DUBLIN

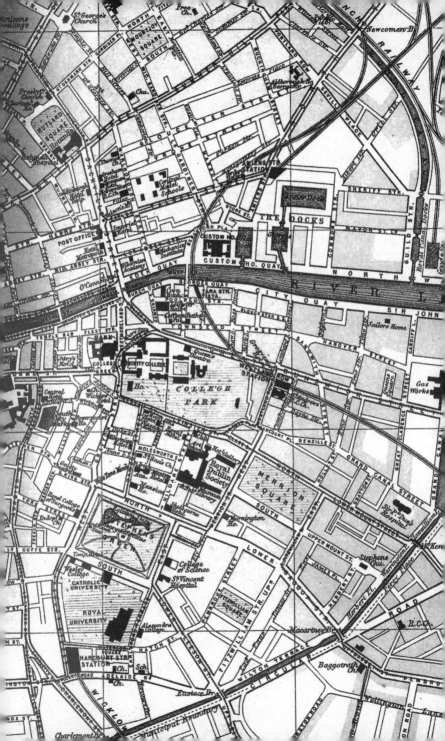

Pre-reading Activities

1. *Dubliners* is a collection of short stories. What other short stories have you read? What do you expect of a short story?

2. It is not, however, a random collection. Each story stands on its own, but *Dubliners* as a whole is more than the sum of the stories. This kind of text is called a 'short-story cycle'. Have you read any other short-story cycles? What do you expect of a short-story cycle?

3. James Joyce is a modernist. Have you read any other modernist fiction? What do you expect of modernist writing?

4. As its title suggests, *Dubliners* is about a city and its inhabitants. Have you read other works of literature in which the setting is a central concern?

THE SISTERS

These symbols indicate the beginning and end of the four stories recorded on the cassette.

THE SISTERS [1]

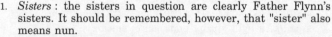

THERE WAS NO HOPE for him this time: it was the third stroke. Night after night I had passed the house (it was vacation time) and studied the lighted square of window: and night after night I had found it lighted in the same way, faintly and evenly. If he was dead, I thought, I would see the reflection of candles on the darkened blind for I knew that two candles must be set at the head of a corpse. He had often said to me: *I am not long for this world*, and I had thought his words idle. Now I knew they were true. Every night as I gazed up at the window I said softly to myself the word *paralysis*. [2] It had always sounded strangely

1. *Sisters* : the sisters in question are clearly Father Flynn's sisters. It should be remembered, however, that "sister" also means nun.

2. *paralysis* : Father Flynn has suffered three strokes, and is thus physically paralysed. Here, however, Joyce is introducing us to the main theme of the book: the religious, social and moral paralysis of turn-of-the-century Dublin.

in my ears, like the word *gnomon*[1] in the Euclid
and the word *simony*[2] in the Catechism. But now
it sounded to me like the name of some maleficent
and sinful being. It filled me with fear, and yet I
longed to be nearer to it and to look upon its
deadly work.

Old Cotter was sitting at the fire, smoking, when
I came downstairs to supper. While my aunt was
ladling out[3] my stirabout[4] he said, as if returning to
some former remark of his:

—No, I wouldn't say he was exactly . . . but there
was something queer . . . there was something
uncanny[5] about him. I'll tell you my opinion. . . .

He began to puff[6] at his pipe, no doubt arranging
his opinion in his mind. Tiresome old fool! When we
knew him first he used to be rather interesting,
talking of faints and worms;[7] but I soon grew tired
of him and his endless stories about the distillery.

—I have my own theory about it, he said. I think
it was one of those . . . peculiar cases. . . . But it's
hard to say. . . .

---

1. *gnomon* [ˈnəʊmɒn] : the Greek geometrician Euclid (circa 300
   B.C.) defines a gnomon as what is left of a parallelogram when
   a similar parallelogram containing one of its corners is removed.
2. *simony* [ˈsaɪmənɪ] : traffic in sacred things, such as the buying
   or selling of ecclesiastical offices, pardons or emoluments.
3. *ladling* [ˈleɪdlɪŋ] *out* : distributing with a large spoon.
4. *stirabout* [ˈstɜːrəbaʊt]: Anglo-Irish for "porridge".
5. *uncanny* [ʌnˈkænɪ] : disturbingly strange or weird.
6. *puff* : a light abrupt emission of smoke.
7. *faints and worms* : "faints" are impure spirits which come
   through first and last during the process of distillation;
   "worms" are the long spiral tubes which are connected to the
   head of a still.

He began to puff again at his pipe without giving us his theory. My uncle saw me staring [1] and said to me:

—Well, so your old friend is gone, you'll be sorry to hear.

—Who? said I.

—Father Flynn.

—Is he dead?

—Mr Cotter here has just told us. He was passing by the house.

I knew that I was under observation so I continued eating as if the news had not interested me. My uncle explained to old Cotter.

—The youngster and he were great friends. The old chap taught him a great deal, mind you; and they say he had a great wish for him. [2]

—God have mercy on his soul, said my aunt piously. Old Cotter looked at me for a while. I felt that his little beady [3] black eyes were examining me but I would not satisfy him by looking up from my plate. He returned to his pipe and finally spat rudely into the grate. [4]

—I wouldn't like children of mine, he said, to have too much to say to a man like that.

—How do you mean, Mr Cotter? asked my aunt.

—What I mean is, said old Cotter, it's bad for children. My idea is: let a young lad run about and play with young lads of his own age and not be. . . .

---

1. *staring* [steərɪŋ]: looking fixedly with eyes wide open.
2. *a great wish for him* : "great esteem" - from the Irish "meas".
3. *beady* : round and glittering.
4. *grate* [greɪt] : the frame of metal bars on which the fire is lit in the fireplace.

Am I right, Jack?

—That's my principle, too, said my uncle. Let him learn to box his corner.[1] That's what I'm always saying to that Rosicrucian[2] there: take exercise. Why, when I was a nipper[3] every morning of my life I had a cold bath, winter and summer. And that's what stands to me now. Education is all very fine and large. . . . Mr Cotter might take a pick of[4] that leg of mutton, he added to my aunt.

—No, no, not for me, said old Cotter.

My aunt brought the dish from the safe[5] and laid it on the table.

—But why do you think it's not good for children, Mr Cotter? she asked.

—It's bad for children, said old Cotter, because their minds are so impressionable. When children see things like that, you know, it has an effect. . . .

I crammed[6] my mouth with stirabout for fear I might give utterance to my anger. Tiresome old red-nosed imbecile!

It was late when I fell asleep. Though I was angry with old Cotter for alluding to me as a child I puzzled

---

1. *to box his corner* : to take care of himself, stand up for himself.
2. *Rosicrucian* [ˌrəʊzɪˈkruːʃn] : a member of the fraternity of religious mystics, the Ancient Order Rosae Crucis, revived in the fifteenth century by Christian Rosenkreuz (possibly a legendary figure). The order was revived in England in the nineteenth century when people became fascinated with the occult. It was generally associated with a dreamy withdrawal from worldly cares.
3. *nipper* [ˈnɪpər] (slang) : boy, lad.
4. *take a pick of* : eat some of.
5. *safe* : a meat safe - a ventilated cupboard in which meat is kept to keep it fresh and cool.
6. *crammed* : filled to excess.

my head to extract meaning from his unfinished sentences. In the dark of my room I imagined that I saw again the heavy grey face of the paralytic. I drew the blankets over my head and tried to think of Christmas. But the grey face still followed me. It murmured; and I understood that it desired to confess something. I felt my soul receding into some pleasant and vicious region; and there again I found it waiting for me. It began to confess to me in a murmuring voice and I wondered why it smiled continually and why the lips were so moist[1] with spittle. But then I remembered that it had died of paralysis and I felt that I too was smiling feebly as if to absolve the simoniac of his sin.

The next morning after breakfast I went down to look at the little house in Great Britain Street. It was an unassuming[2] shop, registered under the vague name of *Drapery*. The drapery consisted mainly of children's bootees and umbrellas; and on ordinary days a notice used to hang in the window, saying: *Umbrellas Re-covered*. No notice was visible now for the shutters[3] were up. A crape[4] bouquet was tied to the door-knocker with ribbon. Two poor women and a telegram boy were reading the card pinned on[5] the crape. I also approached and read:

---

1. *moist* [mɔist] *with spittle*: slightly wet with saliva
2. *unassuming* [ˌʌnə'sjuːmɪŋ]: modest.
3. *shutters* ['ʃʌtəz] : moveable panels fixed to the window for security.
4. *crape* [kreip]: (modern English "crepe") a black, semi-transparent material with a wrinkled or folded surface.
5. *pinned on* : attached to with a pin.

July 1st, 1895
The Rev. James Flynn (formerly of S. Catherine's
Church, Meath Street), aged sixty-five years.
R.I.P.

The reading of the card persuaded me that he was dead and I was disturbed to find myself at check.[1] Had he not been dead I would have gone into the little dark room behind the shop to find him sitting in his arm-chair by the fire, nearly smothered in his great-coat. Perhaps my aunt would have given me a packet of High Toast[2] for him and this present would have roused him from his stupefied doze.[3] It was always I who emptied the packet into his black snuff-box for his hands trembled too much to allow him to do this without spilling half the snuff about the floor. Even as he raised his large trembling hand to his nose little clouds of smoke dribbled[4] through his fingers over the front of his coat. It may have been these constant showers of snuff which gave his ancient priestly garments their green faded look for the red handkerchief, blackened, as it always was, with the snuff-stains of a week, with which he tried to brush away the fallen grains, was quite inefficacious.

I wished to go in and look at him but I had not the courage to knock. I walked away slowly along the sunny side of the street, reading all the theatrical advertisements in the shop-windows as I went. I

---

1. *at check* : taken by surprise.
2. *High Toast* : the name of a brand of snuff (tobacco to be inhaled through the nose).
3. *doze* [dəʊz] : light sleep.
4. *dribbled* ['drɪbld] : escaped.

The interior of St Catherine's, Meath Street.

found it strange that neither I nor the day seemed in a mourning mood and I felt even annoyed at discovering in myself a sensation of freedom as if I had been freed from something by his death. I wondered at this for, as my uncle had said the night before, he had taught me a great deal. He had studied in the Irish college in Rome[1] and he had taught me to pronounce Latin properly. He had told me stories about the catacombs and about Napoleon Bonaparte, and he had explained to me the meaning of the different ceremonies of the Mass and of the different vestments worn by the priest. Sometimes he had amused himself by putting difficult questions to me, asking me what one should do in certain circumstances or whether such and such sins were mortal or venial or only imperfections. His questions showed me how complex and mysterious were certain institutions of the Church which I had always regarded as the simplest acts. The duties of the priest towards the Eucharist and towards the secrecy of the confessional seemed so grave to me that I wondered how anybody had ever found in himself the courage to undertake them; and I was not surprised when he told me that the fathers of the Church had written books as thick as the *Post Office Directory* and as closely printed as the law notices in the newspaper, elucidating all these intricate questions. Often when I thought of this I could make no answer or only a very foolish and halting[2] one upon which

---

1. *Irish college in Rome* : seminaries were forbidden in Ireland until the foundation of Maynooth in the late eighteenth century. Subsequently, Irish colleges were set up in Louvain, Lille, Douai, Paris and Rome. Some of these still exist.
2. *halting* [hɒltɪŋ] : unsure, lacking in confidence.

he used to smile and nod his head twice or thrice. Sometimes he used to put me through the responses of the Mass which he had made me learn by heart; and, as I pattered,[1] he used to smile pensively and nod his head, now and then pushing huge pinches[2] of snuff up each nostril alternately. When he smiled he used to uncover his big discoloured teeth and let his tongue lie upon his lower lip – a habit which had made me feel uneasy in the beginning of our acquaintance before I knew him well.

As I walked along in the sun I remembered old Cotter's words and tried to remember what had happened afterwards in the dream. I remembered that I had noticed long velvet curtains and a swinging lamp of antique fashion. I felt that I had been very far away, in some land where the customs were strange – in Persia,[3] I thought. . . . But I could not remember the end of the dream.

In the evening my aunt took me with her to visit the house of mourning.[4] It was after sunset; but the window-panes of the houses that looked to the west reflected the tawny gold[5] of a great bank of clouds. Nannie received us in the hall; and, as it would have been unseemly[6] to have shouted at her, my aunt

1. *pattered* : recited them.
2. *pinch* [pɪntʃ] : the quantity of something (e.g. snuff, salt) it is possible to pick up between the thumb and forefinger.
3. *Persia* : an important theme in *Dubliners* is that of the attraction of the East. Joyce himself went East to Zürich and Trieste, in order to escape from the paralysis of life in Dublin. Remember, too, that Christianity has its roots in the East.
4. *mourning* [mɔːnɪŋ] : the expression of mental anguish for a person's death.
5. *tawny gold* : reddish gold colour.
6. *unseemly* [ʌnˈsiːmli] : impolite.

shook hands with her for all. The old woman pointed upwards interrogatively and, on my aunt's nodding, proceeded to toil up[1] the narrow staircase before us, her bowed head being scarcely[2] above the level of the banister-rail. At the first landing she stopped and beckoned[3] us forward encouragingly towards the open door of the dead-room.[4] My aunt went in and the old woman, seeing that I hesitated to enter, began to beckon to me again repeatedly with her hand.

I went in on tiptoe.[5] The room through the lace end of the blind was suffused with dusky[6] golden light amid which the candles looked like pale thin flames. He had been coffined.[7] Nannie gave the lead and we three knelt down at the foot of the bed. I pretended to pray but I could not gather my thoughts because the old woman's mutterings[8] distracted me. I noticed how clumsily[9] her skirt was hooked at the back and how the heels of her cloth boots were trodden down[10] all to one side. The fancy[11] came to me that the old priest was smiling as he lay there in his coffin.

1. *toil up* ['tɔɪl 'ʌp]: mount with difficulty.
2. *scarcely* ['skeəsli] : only just.
3. *beckoned* : made a summoning sign.
4. *the dead-room* : the room where the corpse lay.
5. *on tiptoe* ['tɪptəʊ] : with the back part of the feet (the heels) raised to enable him to go in very quietly.
6. *dusky* ['dʌski] : dark or obscure in colour.
7. *coffined* : put in his coffin.
8. *mutterings* : low indistinct utterances.
9. *clumsily* : awkwardly, without grace.
10. *trodden down* : damaged, worn away through use.
11. *The fancy* : the idea.

But no. When we rose and went up to the head of
the bed I saw that he was not smiling. There he lay,
solemn and copious, vested as for the altar, his large
hands loosely retaining a chalice. His face was very
truculent,[1] grey and massive, with black cavernous
nostrils and circled by a scanty[2] white fur. There was
a heavy odour in the room – the flowers.

We blessed ourselves and came away. In the little
room downstairs we found Eliza seated in his
arm-chair in state. I groped my way[3] towards my usual
chair in the corner while Nannie went to the sideboard
and brought out a decanter of sherry[4] and some
wine-glasses. She set these on the table and invited us
to take a little glass of wine. Then, at her sister's
bidding,[5] she poured out the sherry into the glasses
and passed them to us. She pressed me to take some
cream crackers[6] also but I declined because I thought
I would make too much noise eating them. She
seemed to be somewhat disappointed at my refusal
and went over quietly to the sofa where she sat down
behind her sister. No one spoke: we all gazed at[7] the
empty fireplace.

My aunt waited until Eliza sighed and then said:
—Ah, well, he's gone to a better world.

Eliza sighed[8] again and bowed her head in assent.

---

1. *truculent* ['trʌkjʊlənt] : aggressive, fierce.
2. *scanty* : very small quantity of.
3. *groped* [grəʊpt] *my way* : felt my way blindly.
4. *sherry* : sherry wine, rather like Marsala.
5. *bidding* : an order or invitation to do something.
6. *cream crackers* : dry biscuits. Possibly a symbol for the host
   in the Eucharist.
7. *gazed* [geɪzd] *at* : looked vacantly at.
8. *sighed* [saɪd] : made a long, audible exhalation expressing sadness.

My aunt fingered the stem of her wine-glass before sipping[1] a little.

—Did he ... peacefully? she asked.

—Oh, quite peacefully, ma'am,[2] said Eliza. You couldn't tell when the breath went out of him. He had a beautiful death, God be praised.

—And everything ...?

—Father O'Rourke was in with him a Tuesday[3] and anointed him and prepared him and all.

—He knew then?

—He was quite resigned.

—He looks quite resigned, said my aunt.

—That's what the woman we had in to wash him said. She said he just looked as if he was asleep, he looked that peaceful and resigned. No one would think he'd make such a beautiful corpse.

—Yes, indeed, said my aunt.

She sipped a little more from her glass and said:

—Well, Miss Flynn, at any rate it must be a great comfort for you to know that you did all you could for him. You were both very kind to him, I must say.

Eliza smoothed her dress over her knees.

—Ah, poor James! she said. God knows we done [4]

---

1. *sipping* : drinking a very small quantity.
2. *ma'am* [mɑːm] : "Madam" – a respectful form of address (now rarely used).
3. *a Tuesday* : Irish usage for "on Tuesday".
4. *we done* : a non-standard form associated with lack of education. Joyce characterises Eliza through her speech.

all we could, as poor as we are – we wouldn't see him want anything[1] while he was in it.[2]

Nannie had leaned her head against the sofa-pillow and seemed about to fall asleep.

—There's poor Nannie, said Eliza, looking at her, she's wore out.[3] All the work we had, she and me, getting in the woman to wash him and then laying him out and then the coffin and then arranging about the Mass in the chapel. Only for Father O'Rourke I don't know what we'd have done at all. It was him brought us all them flowers and them two candlesticks out of the chapel and wrote out the notice for the *Freeman's General*[4] and took charge of all the papers for the cemetery and poor James's insurance.

—Wasn't that good of him? said my aunt.

Eliza closed her eyes and shook her head slowly.

—Ah, there's no friends like the old friends, she said, when all is said and done, no friends that a body can trust.

—Indeed, that's true, said my aunt. And I'm sure now that he's gone to his eternal reward he won't forget you and all your kindness to him.

—Ah, poor James! said Eliza. He was no great trouble to us. You wouldn't hear him in the house any more than now. Still, I know he's gone and all to that. . . .

1. *we wouldn't see him want anything* : we would have made sure he had everything.
2. *while he was in it* : while he was still alive.
3. *she's wore out* : she's extremely tired ("worn out" in Standard English).
4. *Freeman's General* : "General" is a malapropism (a mistaken use of a wrong word which sounds similar to the one intended) for "Journal": the *Freeman's Journal* was an important daily newspaper in Dublin.

—It's when it's all over that you'll miss him, said my aunt.

—I know that, said Eliza. I won't be bringing him in his cup of beef-tea[1] any more, nor you, ma'am, sending him his snuff. Ah, poor James!

She stopped, as if she were communing with the past and then said shrewdly:[2]

—Mind you, I noticed there was something queer coming over him latterly.[3] Whenever I'd bring in his soup to him I'd find him with his breviary fallen to the floor, lying back in the chair and his mouth open.

She laid a finger against her nose and frowned:[4] then she continued:

—But still and all he kept on saying that before the summer was over he'd go out for a drive one fine day just to see the old house again where we were all born down in Irishtown[5] and take me and Nannie with him. If we could only get one of them new-fangled[6] carriages that makes no noise that Father O'Rourke told him about – them with the rheumatic wheels[7] – for the

---

1. *beef-tea* : clear soup made from the juice of beef.
2. *shrewdly* [ˈʃruːdli] : cleverly, astutely.
3. *latterly* [ˈlætəli] : recently, in the later stages of his life.
4. *frowned* [fraʊnd] : brought the eyebrows together so that lines appeared on the forehead: often an expression of displeasure, anger or concentrated thought.
5. *Irishtown* : a poor area of Dublin.
6. *new-fangled* [ˈnjuːˌfæŋɡld] : implies that the speaker finds this latest invention rather bewildering.
7. *rheumatic wheels* : for "pneumatic wheels". Again a typical mistake in Eliza's speech, but perhaps not without significance. A possible allusion to an impotent, "rheumatic" Holy Ghost. There are in fact many references in *Dubliners* to objects which need air in order to function properly. See, for example, the rusty pump in "Araby", or the broken harmonium in "Eveline".

day cheap, he said, at Johnny Rush's over the way [1] there and drive out the three of us together of a Sunday evening. He had his mind set on [2] that. . . . Poor James!

—The Lord have mercy on his soul! said my aunt.

Eliza took out her handkerchief and wiped her eyes with it. Then she put it back again in her pocket and gazed into the empty grate for some time without speaking.

—He was too scrupulous always, she said. The duties of the priesthood was too much for him. And then his life was, you might say, crossed. [3]

—Yes, said my aunt. He was a disappointed man. You could see that.

A silence took possession of the little room and, under cover of it, I approached the table and tasted my sherry and then returned quietly to my chair in the corner. Eliza seemed to have fallen into a deep revery. [4] We waited respectfully for her to break the silence: and after a long pause she said slowly:

—It was that chalice he broke. . . . That was the beginning of it. Of course, they say it was all right, that it contained nothing, [5] I mean. But still. . . . They say it was the boy's fault. But poor James was so nervous, God be merciful to him!

—And was that it? said my aunt. I heard something. . . .

---

1. *over the way* : on the other side of the road.
2. *He had his mind set on* : he had decided to, he intended to.
3. *crossed* : not in accordance with his desires, afflicted.
4. *revery* ['revəri] : pleasant thoughts and dreams while awake.
5. *it contained nothing* : the chalice was either empty, or the wine had not yet been transubstantiated into the blood of Christ, according to Catholic ritual.

Eliza nodded.

—That affected his mind, she said. After that he began to mope [1] by himself, talking to no one and wandering about by himself. So one night he was wanted for to go on a call [2] and they couldn't find him anywhere. They looked high up and low down; and still they couldn't see a sight of him anywhere. So then the clerk suggested to try the chapel. So then they got the keys and opened the chapel and the clerk and Father O'Rourke and another priest that was there brought in a light for to look for him.... And what do you think but there he was, sitting up by himself in the dark in his confession-box, wide-awake and laughing-like softly to himself?

She stopped suddenly as if to listen. I too listened; but there was no sound in the house: and I knew that the old priest was lying still in his coffin as we had seen him, solemn and truculent in death, an idle [3] chalice on his breast.

Eliza resumed:

—Wide-awake and laughing-like to himself.... So then, of course, when they saw that, that made them think that there was something gone wrong with him....

---

1. *mope* [məʊp] : be in low spirits.
2. *go on a call*: visit someone.
3. *idle* ['aɪdl] : empty, useless, not being used.

Characters

1.   Fill in the table below, placing adjectives from the list opposite the character they describe.

serious	uneducated	sensitive	slow-moving
opinionated	silent gossipy	polite	humble
affectionate	active	reflective	sympathetic
observant	treacherous	robust	knowledgeable

CHARACTERS	ADJECTIVES
the boy	
his aunt	
his uncle	
old Cotter	
the priest	
Eliza	
Nannie	

2.   What purpose does old Cotter serve in the narrative?

3.   The boy experiences a 'sensation of freedom' as a result of the priest's death. What is he freed from? Do any of the other characters seem to have the same reaction?

Settings

1. The various scenes have different settings. Fill in the chart below, placing the right setting opposite each scene. The first has been done for you as an example.

in the house of the boy's aunt and uncle	inside the priest's house	outside the priest's house

SCENES	SETTINGS
The opening description of what the narrator did 'night after night'	*outside the priest's house*
Old Cotter's conversation with the narrator's aunt and uncle.	
The narrator recalls the old priest (from 'The next morning' to 'the end of the dream')	
The long final scene (from 'In the evening' to the end of the story)	

2. Circle the adjectives in the following list that describe the atmosphere created by the settings of the story:

bright	dark	glamorous	gloomy	luxurious
natural	urban	rural	seedy	exciting
oppressive	bleak	cosy	airy	suffocating

Structure

We learn about the priest's life through **flashback** (when the narrator recounts events before the time of the story) or **dialogue** (when characters discuss the past). In the table below, place flashback or dialogue in the right-hand column as appropriate. The first has been done as an example.

INFORMATION ABOUT THE PAST	WE LEARN THIS THROUGH ...
During the priest's illness, the boy used to watch the window of the priest's house.	*flashback*
The priest had 'a great wish' for the boy.	
There was something strange about the priest.	
Old Cotter used to be interesting.	
The priest told the boy stories of Napoleon.	
The priest had broken a chalice.	

Symbolism

Find all the references to the 'chalice'. What is their symbolic significance?

Narrator

1. **a.** Complete the following sentences by marking the most appropriate of the endings provided in the right-hand column:

    The story is narrated by
    - ☐ a third-person narrator
    - ☐ several narrators
    - ☐ James Joyce
    - ☐ a first-person narrator

    The narrator is
    - ☐ omniscient
    - ☐ unreliable
    - ☐ objective
    - ☐ naive

    b. Find evidence in the text to support your view.

2. How does this particular kind of narrative voice affect your reading of the story? (Before answering this question, it would be useful to imagine how other kinds of narrators might have told the story differently.)

Themes

1. Why is this story called "The Sisters"?

2. How is the Catholic Church represented in the story?

3. Joyce claimed that a central theme of *Dubliners* was 'paralysis'. List the references to paralysis (both physical and moral) in "The Sisters".

ARABY

ARABY [1]

NORTH RICHMOND STREET, being blind,[2] was a quiet street except at the hour when the Christian Brothers' School[3] set the boys free. An uninhabited house of two storeys stood at the blind end, detached from its neighbours in a square ground. The other houses of the street, conscious of decent lives within them, gazed at one another with brown[4] imperturbable faces. The former tenant of our house, a priest, had died in the back drawing-room. Air, musty[5] from having been long enclosed, hung in all the rooms, and the waste

1. *Araby* : Araby refers to the "Grand Oriental fête" given in aid of the Jervis Street Hospital in Dublin in May 1894. The title is also suggestive of the sensuous romanticism of popular stories set in the Middle East. Remember, too, that the Christian church has its roots in that region.
2. *blind* : a dead-end street.
3. *Christian Brothers' School* : a teaching order supported by public funds. The Christian Brothers charged very low fees and provided a practical rather than an academic education.
4. *brown* : one of the colours Joyce uses to indicate paralysis.
5. *musty* ['mʌsti] : no longer fresh.

No 12 North Richmond Street.

The upstairs windows of No 13 North Richmond St.

room behind the kitchen was littered with old useless papers. Among these I found a few paper-covered books, the pages of which were curled and damp: *The Abbot*,[1] by Walter Scott, *The Devout Communicant*[2] and *The Memoirs of Vidocq*.[3] I liked the last best because its leaves were yellow. The wild garden behind the house contained a central apple-tree and a few straggling bushes under one of which I found the late tenant's rusty bicycle-pump. He had been a very charitable priest; in his will he had left all his money to institutions and the furniture of his house to his sister.

When the short days of winter came dusk fell before we had well eaten our dinners. When we met in the street the houses had grown sombre. The space of sky above us was the colour of ever-changing violet and towards it the lamps of the street lifted their feeble lanterns. The cold air stung us[4] and we played till our bodies glowed.[5] Our shouts echoed in the silent street. The career of our play[6] brought us through the dark muddy lanes behind the houses where we ran the gantlet[7] of the rough tribes from

1. *The Abbot* : a historical novel by Walter Scott, published in 1820.
2. *The Devout Communicant* : a religious tract written by the Franciscan friar, Pacificus Baker, in 1813.
3. *The Memoirs of Vidocq* : a French criminal who eventually became head of the police force. *The Memoirs* had been translated into English by the Irishman, William Maginn (1794-1842).
4. *stung us* (sting, stung, stung): we felt a painful sensation.
5. *our bodies glowed* [gləʊd] : our bodies became hot with the energy expended.
6. *The career of our play* : the direction of our games.
7. *ran the gantlet* [ˈgɑːntlɪt]: defied. (A more common spelling is "gauntlet").

the cottages,[1] to the back doors of the dark dripping[2]
gardens where odours arose from the ashpits,[3] to the
dark odorous stables where a coachman smoothed
and combed the horse or shook music from the
buckled harness.[4] When we returned to the street
light from the kitchen windows had filled the areas.[5]
If my uncle was seen turning the corner we hid in
the shadow until we had seen him safely housed. Or
if Mangan's sister came out on the doorstep to call
her brother in to his tea we watched her from our
shadow peer[6] up and down the street. We waited to
see whether she would remain or go in and, if she
remained, we left our shadow and walked up to
Mangan's steps resignedly. She was waiting for us,
her figure defined by the light from the half-opened
door. Her brother always teased[7] her before he
obeyed and I stood by the railings[8] looking at her.
Her dress swung as she moved her body and the soft
rope of her hair tossed from side to side.

Every morning I lay on the floor in the front
parlour watching her door. The blind was pulled

---

1. *the cottages* : small dwellings for the poor off North Richmond
   Street.
2. *dripping* : the water falling in drops from the leaves of the
   plants, perhaps after rain.
3. *ashpits* : rubbish dumps.
4. *buckled* ['bʌkld] *harness* : an apparatus for controlling a horse
   and securing it to a wheeled vehicle (e.g. a cart), held together
   with metal fasteners ("buckles").
5. *areas* : spaces between the fronts of houses and the street:
   these are below ground level in many Dublin houses.
6. *peer* : look very carefully or hard.
7. *teased* [tiːzd] : laughed at or made jokes about.
8. *railings* ['reɪlɪŋz] : fence or barrier often made of metal bars
   ("rails").

down to within an inch of the sash[1] so that I could
not be seen. When she came out on the doorstep my
heart leaped. I ran to the hall, seized[2] my books and
followed her. I kept her brown figure always in my
eye and, when we came near the point at which our
ways diverged, I quickened my pace[3] and passed her.
This happened morning after morning. I had never
spoken to her, except for a few casual words, and yet
her name was like a summons to all my foolish blood.

Her image accompanied me even in places the
most hostile to romance. On Saturday evenings when
my aunt went marketing I had to go to carry some
of the parcels. We walked through the flaring
streets,[4] jostled[5] by drunken men and bargaining
women, amid the curses of labourers, the shrill[6]
litanies of shop-boys who stood on guard by the
barrels of pigs' cheeks, the nasal chanting of
street-singers, who sang a *come-all-you* about
O'Donovan Rossa,[7] or a ballad about the troubles in
our native land. These noises converged in a single

---

1. *sash* : window frame.
2. *seized* [siːzd]: took hold of forcefully.
3. *pace* [peɪs] : speed of walking.
4. *flaring streets*: streets bright with the light from the street lamps and the houses.
5. *jostled* ['dʒɒsld] : pushed or knocked against.
6. *shrill* [ʃrɪl] : high and sharp sounding.
7. *a come-all-you about O'Donovan Rossa* : a topical ballad starting with these words, sung on the streets and in public houses. Jeremiah O'Donovan (1831-1915) was a Fenian leader who advocated violent measures in the struggle for Irish independence. Born in Ross Carberry in County Cork, he was nicknamed Dynamite Rossa.

sensation of life for me: I imagined that I bore my chalice safely[1] through a throng[2] of foes. Her name sprang to my lips at moments in strange prayers and praises which I myself did not understand. My eyes were often full of tears (I could not tell why) and at times a flood from my heart seemed to pour itself out into my bosom. I thought little of the future. I did not know whether I would ever speak to her or not or, if I spoke to her, how I could tell her of my confused adoration. But my body was like a harp and her words and gestures were like fingers running upon the wires.

One evening I went into the back drawing-room in which the priest had died. It was a dark rainy evening and there was no sound in the house. Through one of the broken panes I heard the rain impinge upon the earth, the fine incessant needles of water playing in the sodden[3] beds. Some distant lamp or lighted window gleamed below me. I was thankful that I could see so little. All my senses seemed to desire to veil themselves and, feeling that I was about to slip from them, I pressed the palms of my hands together until they trembled, murmuring: *O love! O love!* many times.

At last she spoke to me. When she addressed the first words to me I was so confused that I did not know what to answer. She asked me was I going to *Araby.* I forgot whether I answered yes or no. It would be a splendid bazaar, she said; she would love

---

1. *I bore my chalice safely* : the context echoes nineteenth-century versions of the quest for the Holy Grail.
2. *throng* [θrɒŋ]: a large crowd.
3. *sodden* : very wet.

to go.

—And why can't you? I asked.

While she spoke she turned a silver bracelet round and round her wrist. She could not go, she said, because there would be a retreat that week in her convent. Her brother and two other boys were fighting for their caps and I was alone at the railings. She held one of the spikes,[1] bowing her head towards me. The light from the lamp opposite our door caught the white curve of her neck, lit up her hair that rested there and, falling, lit up the hand upon the railing. It fell over one side of her dress and caught the white border of a petticoat,[2] just visible as she stood at ease.

—It's well for you,[3] she said.

—If I go, I said, I will bring you something.

What innumerable follies laid waste my waking and sleeping thoughts after that evening! I wished to annihilate the tedious intervening days. I chafed against[4] the work of school. At night in my bedroom and by day in the classroom her image came between me and the page I strove[5] to read. The syllables of the word *Araby* were called to me through the silence in which my soul luxuriated and cast an Eastern enchantment over me.[6] I asked for leave to go to the

---

1. *spikes* [spaɪks] : pointed tops of the railings (see note 8, p. 28).
2. *petticoat*: a piece of women's clothing worn under the skirt.
3. *It's well for you* : "You're lucky". The Irish expression, however, often has undertones of envy or bitterness.
4. *chafed* [tʃeɪft] *against* : became impatient and annoyed with.
5. *strove* [strəʊv] (strive, strove, striven) : tried hard to.
6. *cast ... over me* : induced a feeling of ... in me.

Araby Bazaar.

bazaar on Saturday night. My aunt was surprised and hoped it was not some Freemason affair.[1] I answered few questions in class. I watched my master's face pass from amiability to sternness;[2] he hoped I was not beginning to idle. I could not call my wandering thoughts together. I had hardly any patience with the serious work of life which, now that it stood between me and my desire, seemed to me child's play, ugly monotonous child's play.

On Saturday morning I reminded my uncle that I wished to go to the bazaar in the evening. He was fussing[3] at the hallstand, looking for the hat-brush, and answered me curtly:[4]

—Yes, boy, I know.

As he was in the hall I could not go into the front parlour and lie at the window. I left the house in bad humour and walked slowly towards the school. The air was pitilessly raw[5] and already my heart misgave me.[6]

When I came home to dinner my uncle had not yet been home. Still it was early. I sat staring at the clock for some time and, when its ticking began to irritate me, I left the room. I mounted the staircase and gained the upper part of the house. The high cold empty gloomy rooms liberated me and I went from room to room singing. From the front window I saw

1. *some Freemason affair* : the Freemasons were regarded as enemies of the Roman Catholic Church.
2. *sternness* : severity, inflexibility.
3. *fussing* : being excessively busy with trivial things.
4. *curtly* ['kɜːtli]: briefly and discourteously.
5. *raw* [rɔː] : painfully cold.
6. *and already my heart misgave me* : I had a kind of negative premonition.

The exotic transports of the east.

my companions playing below in the street. Their
cries reached me weakened and indistinct and,
leaning my forehead against the cool glass, I looked
over at the dark house where she lived. I may have
stood there for an hour, seeing nothing but the
brown-clad figure cast by my imagination, touched
discreetly by the lamplight at the curved neck, at the
hand upon the railings and at the border below the
dress.

When I came downstairs again I found Mrs Mercer
sitting at the fire. She was an old garrulous[1] woman,
a pawnbroker's[2] widow, who collected used stamps for
some pious purpose. I had to endure the gossip of the
tea-table. The meal was prolonged beyond an hour
and still my uncle did not come. Mrs Mercer stood
up to go: she was sorry she couldn't wait any longer,
but it was after eight o'clock and she did not like to
be out late, as the night air was bad for her. When
she had gone I began to walk up and down the room,
clenching[3] my fists. My aunt said:

—I'm afraid you may put off your bazaar for this
night of Our Lord.

At nine o'clock I heard my uncle's latchkey[4] in the
hall-door. I heard him talking to himself and heard
the hall stand rocking[5] when it had received the weight
of his overcoat. I could interpret these signs. When he
was midway through his dinner I asked him to give

1. *garrulous* ['gærələs]: very talkative on trivial matters.
2. *pawnbroker* ['pɔːnˌbrəukə] : a person who lends money on the
    security of an article "pawned" (left in the possession of the
    moneylender).
3. *clenching* [klentʃɪŋ]: closing the fingers tightly together.
4. *latchkey* ['lætʃkiː] : key to the main (usually front) door.
5. *rocking* : moving from side to side.

me the money to go to the bazaar. He had forgotten.

—The people are in bed and after their first sleep [1] now, he said.

I did not smile. My aunt said to him energetically:

—Can't you give him the money and let him go? You've kept him late enough as it is.

My uncle said he was very sorry he had forgotten. He said he believed in the old saying: *All work and no play makes Jack a dull boy*. He asked me where I was going and, when I had told him a second time he asked me did I know *The Arab's Farewell to his Steed*.[2] When I left the kitchen he was about to recite the opening lines of the piece to my aunt.

I held a florin [3] tightly in my hand as I strode [4] down Buckingham Street towards the station. The sight of the streets thronged with buyers and glaring with gas recalled to me the purpose of my journey. I took my seat in a third-class carriage of a deserted train. After an intolerable delay the train moved out of the station slowly. It crept onward among ruinous [5] houses and over the twinkling river. At Westland Row Station a crowd of people pressed to the carriage doors; but the porters moved them back, saying that it was a special train for the bazaar. I remained alone in the bare carriage. In a few minutes the train drew up beside an improvised

1. *after their first sleep* : have just gone to sleep.
2. *The Arab's Farewell to his Steed* : a poem by Caroline Norton (1808-77), said to be the original of George Meredith's "Diana of the Crossways" (1885).
3. *florin* : two shillings (10 new pence).
4. *strode* [strəʊd] (stride, strode, stridden) : walked with long steps.
5. *ruinous* ['ruːɪnəs] : decayed, dilapidated.

wooden platform. I passed out on to the road and saw by the lighted dial of a clock that it was ten minutes to ten. In front of me was a large building which displayed the magical name.

I could not find any sixpenny entrance and, fearing that the bazaar would be closed, I passed in quickly through a turnstile, handing a shilling to a weary-looking man. I found myself in a big hall girdled [1] at half its height by a gallery. Nearly all the stalls were closed and the greater part of the hall was in darkness. I recognised a silence like that which pervades a church after a service. I walked into the centre of the bazaar timidly. A few people were gathered about the stalls which were still open. Before a curtain, over which the words *Café Chantant* [2] were written in coloured lamps, two men were counting money on a salver. [3] I listened to the fall of the coins.

Remembering with difficulty why I had come I went over to one of the stalls and examined porcelain vases and flowered tea-sets. At the door of the stall a young lady was talking and laughing with two young gentlemen. I remarked their English accents and listened vaguely to their conversation.

—O, I never said such a thing!

—O, but you did!

—O, but I didn't!

---

1. *girdled* ['gɜːdld] : surrounded.
2. *Café Chantant* [ˌkæfeɪˈʃɑ̃ːntɑ̃ːŋ] : a kind of pub with entertainment. Note however, the near homophony of 'Café Chant(ant)' and 'confession', particularly in the light of other religious references in the passage.
3. *two men were counting money on a salver* : a possible reference to the moneylender passage in the Bible (Matthew, 21:12-13).

—Didn't she say that?

—Yes. I heard her.

—O, there's a . . . fib![1]

Observing me the young lady came over and asked me did I wish to buy anything. The tone of her voice was not encouraging; she seemed to have spoken to me out of a sense of duty. I looked humbly[2] at the great jars that stood like eastern guards at either side of the dark entrance to the stall and murmured:

—No, thank you.

The young lady changed the position of one of the vases and went back to the two young men. They began to talk of the same subject. Once or twice the young lady glanced[3] at me over her shoulder.

I lingered[4] before her stall, though I knew my stay was useless, to make my interest in her wares[5] seem the more real. Then I turned away slowly and walked down the middle of the bazaar. I allowed the two pennies to fall against the sixpence in my pocket. I heard a voice call from one end of the gallery that the light was out. The upper part of the hall was now completely dark.

Gazing up into the darkness I saw myself as a creature driven and derided by vanity; and my eyes burned with anguish and anger.

1. *fib* : small lie.
2. *humbly* ['hʌmbli] : in a deferential way.
3. *glanced* : looked quickly.
4. *lingered* ['lɪŋgəd] : waited because reluctant to go away.
5. *wares* [weəz]: merchandise, the things being sold.

Characters

1. You will notice that very few characters are actually named. What effect does this have on the reader?

2. Look at the passage on pp. 30-1 beginning, 'At last she spoke' and ending 'I will bring you something'. What does it tell you about Mangan's sister and her situation?

3. Look at the last two paragraphs of the story. What do they tell you about the boy and his situation?

Settings

1. **a.** Fill in the table below, placing in the right-hand column adjectives from the story that, in your opinion, most appropriately describe the settings in the left-hand column. The first has been done for you as an example.

SETTINGS	ADJECTIVES
North Richmond Street	*blind, quiet, decent, brown, sombre, cold.*
The narrator's house	
The building that houses 'Araby'	

b. Bearing in mind your answers to the above question, complete the following sentence with one or more of the nouns offered in the list below (or with other nouns of your own, if you prefer):
The overall atmosphere created by the settings of the story is one of _____.

| despondency | cheerfulness | | dejection | gaiety |
| oppression | alienation | romance | frivolity | sensuality |

Symbolism

1. Why is this story called "Araby"?

2. On pp. 29-30, the narrator tells us 'I imagined that I bore my chalice safely through a throng of foes.' What is the symbolic significance of this? And how does it link "Araby" to "The Sisters"?

3. Make a list of references, literal or metaphorical, to sight, eyes, and blindness (they are particularly frequent at the beginning and the end of the story). What is their significance?

SIGHT	**EYES**	**BLINDNESS**

Narrator

Fill in the chart below with the similarities and differences between the boy-narrator of "Araby" and that of "The Sisters".

Similarities in their Characters and Situations:

_____

_____

_____

_____

Differences:

_____

_____

_____

_____

Similarities in their Ways of Telling the Story:

_____

_____

_____

_____

Differences:

_____

_____

_____

_____

Themes

1. What would you say is the central theme of the story?

2. How are the frequent literal and metaphorical references to the Catholic Church (some of which are specified in earlier questions) connected to this central theme?

3. Does the story have any themes in common with "The Sisters"?

Eveline

EVELINE

SHE SAT AT THE WINDOW watching the evening invade the avenue. Her head was leaned against the window curtains and in her nostrils was the odour of dusty cretonne.[1] She was tired.

Few people passed. The man out of the last house passed on his way home; she heard his footsteps clacking[2] along the concrete pavement and afterwards crunching[3] on the cinder path before the new red houses. One time there used to be a field there in which they used to play every evening with other people's children. Then a man from Belfast[4]

---

1. *cretonne* ['kretɒn]: a strong fabric used for chair covers and curtains, often printed with a floral design.
2. *clacking*: the sharp noise of his footsteps.
3. *crunching*: the noise of his footsteps on the cinders; the same noise comes from walking on snow.
4. *a man from Belfast*: not really Irish, as far as a Dubliner is concerned, since his sympathies probably lie with the Protestant English establishment. Yet another reference to British rule in Ireland.

bought the field and built houses in it – not like their little brown houses [1] but bright brick houses with shining roofs. The children of the avenue used to play together in that field – the Devines, the Waters, the Dunns, little Keogh the cripple,[2] she and her brothers and sisters. Ernest, however, never played: he was too grown up. Her father used often to hunt them in out of the field with his blackthorn [3] stick; but usually little Keogh used to keep *nix* [4] and call out when he saw her father coming. Still they seemed to have been rather happy then. Her father was not so bad then; and besides, her mother was alive. That was a long time ago; she and her brothers and sisters were all grown up; her mother was dead. Tizzie Dunn was dead, too, and the Waters had gone back to England. Everything changes. Now she was going to go away like the others, to leave her home.

Home! She looked round the room, reviewing all its familiar objects which she had dusted once a week for so many years, wondering where on earth all the dust came from. Perhaps she would never see again those familiar objects from which she had never dreamed of being divided. And yet during all those years she had never found out the name of the priest whose yellowing photograph hung on the wall above the broken harmonium

---

1. *little brown houses* : see note 4, p. 25 ("Araby").
2. *cripple* : a person who cannot walk normally.
3. *blackthorn* ['blækθɔːn]: a small dark-coloured tree with sharp spines ("thorns").
4. *keep nix* [nɪks] : be on the alert.

beside the coloured print of the promises made to Blessed Margaret Mary Alacoque.[1] He had been a school friend of her father. Whenever he showed the photograph to a visitor her father used to pass it with a casual word:

—He is in Melbourne now.

She had consented to go away, to leave her home. Was that wise? She tried to weigh each side of the question. In her home anyway she had shelter[2] and food; she had those whom she had known all her life about her. Of course she had to work hard, both in the house and at business. What would they say of her in the Stores[3] when they found out that she had run away with a fellow? Say she was a fool, perhaps; and her place would be filled up by advertisement. Miss Gavan would be glad. She had always had an edge on her,[4] especially whenever there were people listening.

—Miss Hill, don't you see these ladies are waiting?

—Look lively, Miss Hill, please.

She would not cry many tears at leaving the Stores.

But in her new home, in a distant unknown country, it would not be like that. Then she would be married – she, Eveline. People would treat her with

---

1. *Blessed Margaret Mary Alacoque* : a French nun (1647-90) who had several visions of the Sacred Heart. Twelve promises were made through her to those who display a representation of the Sacred Heart in their homes, and receive the Eucharist on the first Friday of each month.
2. *shelter* : a place providing protection from the weather.
3. *Stores* : big shops selling a variety of goods in different departments.
4. *had an edge on her* : enjoyed having power and superiority over her.

respect then. She would not be treated as her mother had been. Even now, though she was over nineteen, she sometimes felt herself in danger of her father's violence. She knew it was that that had given her the palpitations. When they were growing up he had never gone for her,[1] like he used to go for Harry and Ernest, because she was a girl; but latterly[2] he had begun to threaten her and say what he would do to her only for her dead mother's sake. And now she had nobody to protect her. Ernest was dead and Harry, who was in the church decorating business, was nearly always down somewhere in the country. Besides, the invariable squabble[3] for money on Saturday nights had begun to weary[4] her unspeakably. She always gave her entire wages – seven shillings – and Harry always sent up what he could but the trouble was to get any money from her father. He said she used to squander the money, that she had no head, that he wasn't going to give her his hard-earned money to throw about the streets, and much more, for he was usually fairly bad of a Saturday night. In the end he would give her the money and ask her had she any intention of buying Sunday's dinner. Then she had to rush out as quickly as she could and do her marketing, holding her black leather purse tightly in her hand as she elbowed her way[5] through the crowds and returning home late under her load of provisions. She had hard work to

1. *had never gone for her* : had never attacked her.
2. *latterly* : see note 3, p. 16.
3. *squabble* ['skwɒbl] : dispute, quarrel.
4. *weary* ['wɪəri] : tire extremely.
5. *elbowed her way* : pushed herself ahead with her elbows.

keep the house together and to see that the two
young children who had been left to her charge [1] went
to school regularly and got their meals regularly. It
was hard work – a hard life – but now that she was
about to leave it she did not find it a wholly
undesirable life.

She was about to explore another life with Frank.
Frank was very kind, manly, open-hearted. She was
to go away with him by the night-boat to be his wife
and to live with him in Buenos Ayres [2] where he had
a home waiting for her. How well she remembered
the first time she had seen him; he was lodging in a
house on the main road where she used to visit. It
seemed a few weeks ago. He was standing at the
gate, his peaked cap pushed back on his head and
his hair tumbled [3] forward over a face of bronze. Then
they had come to know each other. He used to meet
her outside the Stores every evening and see her
home. He took her to see *The Bohemian Girl* and she
felt elated as she sat in an unaccustomed part of the
theatre with him. He was awfully [4] fond of music and
sang a little. People knew that they were courting
and, when he sang about the lass [5] that loves a sailor,
she always felt pleasantly confused. He used to call
her Poppens [6] out of fun. First of all it had been an

1. *to her charge* : for her to look after.
2. *Buenos Ayres* : capital of Argentina. Contrast the "good air"
   of Eveline's destination with the "bad air" of Dublin – the
   broken harmonium, the pump in "Araby" and the "rheumatic"
   wheels in "The Sisters".
3. *tumbled* ['tʌmbld]: fell down.
4. *awfully* ['ɔːfli]: very, extremely.
5. *the lass* : the girl.
6. *Poppens* : a term of endearment, from "poppet", dialect
   English for "small person".

excitement for her to have a fellow and then she had begun to like him. He had tales of distant countries. He had started as a deck boy [1] at a pound a month on a ship of the Allan Line going out to Canada. He told her the names of the ships he had been on and the names of the different services. He had sailed through the Straits of Magellan and he told her stories of the terrible Patagonians. He had fallen on his feet [2] in Buenos Ayres, he said, and had come over to the old country just for a holiday. Of course, her father had found out the affair and had forbidden her to have anything to say to him.

—I know these sailor chaps, he said.

One day he had quarrelled with Frank and after that she had to meet her lover secretly.

The evening deepened in the avenue. The white of two letters in her lap [3] grew indistinct. One was to Harry; the other was to her father. Ernest had been her favourite but she liked Harry too. Her father was becoming old lately, she noticed; he would miss her. Sometimes he could be very nice. Not long before, when she had been laid up [4] for a day, he had read her out a ghost story and made toast for her at the fire. Another day, when their mother was alive, they had all gone for a picnic to the Hill of Howth.[5] She remembered her father putting on her mother's bonnet to make the children laugh.

---

1. *deck boy* : ship-boy.
2. *fallen on his feet* : been very lucky.
3. *lap* : the front part of the body, from the waist to the knees, of a person who is sitting.
4. *laid up* : ill.
5. *Hill of Howth* : the northeast headland of Dublin Bay.

Old Buenos Aires.

North Wall.

Her time was running out but she continued to sit by the window, leaning her head against the window curtain, inhaling the odour of dusty cretonne. Down far in the avenue she could hear a street organ playing. She knew the air. Strange that it should come that very night to remind her of the promise to her mother, her promise to keep the home together as long as she could. She remembered the last night of her mother's illness; she was again in the close dark room at the other side of the hall and outside she heard a melancholy air of Italy. The organ-player had been ordered to go away and given sixpence. She remembered her father strutting back[1] into the sickroom saying:

—Damned Italians! coming over here![2]

As she mused[3] the pitiful vision of her mother's life laid its spell on the very quick[4] of her being – that life of commonplace sacrifices closing in final craziness. She trembled as she heard again her mother's voice saying constantly with foolish insistence:

—Derevaun Seraun![5] Derevaun Seraun!

She stood up in a sudden impulse of terror. Escape! She must escape! Frank would save her. He would give her life, perhaps love, too. But she wanted

1. *strutting back* : walking stiffly.
2. *Damned Italians! coming over here!* : Is there a reference to the power of the Roman Catholic Church in this Italian organ grinder?
3. *As she mused* : as she meditated.
4. *on the very quick* : to the depths.
5. *Derevaun Seraun* : there is no certain translation for this Gaelic expression. It might mean "the end of pleasure is pain", or "the end of song is raving madness".

to live. Why should she be unhappy? She had a right
to happiness. Frank would take her in his arms, fold
her in his arms. He would save her.

.   .   .   .

She stood among the swaying[1] crowd in the
station at the North Wall. He held her hand and she
knew that he was speaking to her, saying something
about the passage over and over again. The station
was full of soldiers with brown baggages. Through
the wide doors of the sheds[2] she caught a glimpse of
the black mass of the boat, lying in beside the quay
wall, with illumined portholes.[3] She answered
nothing. She felt her cheek pale and cold and, out of
a maze[4] of distress, she prayed to God to direct her,
to show her what was her duty. The boat blew a long
mournful whistle into the mist. If she went,
to-morrow she would be on the sea with Frank,
steaming towards Buenos Ayres. Their passage had
been booked. Could she still draw back after all he
had done for her? Her distress awoke a nausea in her
body and she kept moving her lips in silent fervent
prayer.[5]

A bell clanged[6] upon her heart. She felt him seize
her hand:

1. *swaying* [sweɪɪŋ] : here, moving backwards and forwards.
2. *sheds* : structures for storing or shelter.
3. *portholes* ['pɔːthəʊlz] : small round windows in a ship.
4. *maze* : labyrinth.
5. *prayed to God ... silent fervent prayer* : notice again the
    importance of the Church in the average Dubliner's life.
6. *clanged* [klæŋd] : made a loud resonant metallic sound.

—Come!

All the seas of the world tumbled about her heart.[1] He was drawing her into them: he would drown her. She gripped[2] with both hands at the iron railing.

—Come!

No! No! No! It was impossible. Her hands clutched[3] the iron in frenzy. Amid the seas she sent a cry of anguish!

—Eveline! Evvy!

He rushed beyond the barrier and called to her to follow. He was shouted at to go on but he still called to her. She set her white face to him,[4] passive, like a helpless animal. Her eyes gave him no sign of love or farewell or recognition.

1. *All the seas of the world tumbled about her heart* : an ironic reversal of what reportedly happened to Blessed Margaret Mary Alacoque, who "felt her breast alive with fire".
2. *gripped* [grɪpt] : held firmly or tightly.
3. *clutched* [klʌtʃt] : took hold of quickly and convulsively.
4. *She set her white face to him* : she turned her white face to him.

Characters

1. Describe Eveline's character, using brief quotations from the
    text to support your view.

2. Bearing in mind your answers to the above question, answer
    the following:
    a. What are her reasons for leaving?
    b. Why is she tempted to stay?
    c. Do you think she made the right decision?

3. Look at the passage on p. 52 beginning 'Her father was
    becoming old' and ending 'make the children laugh'. What
    does this tell us about the father's character? What does it
    tell us about Eveline's?

4. Describe the character of Eveline's lover. What is the
    significance of his name? Is there any reason to doubt his
    sincerity?

Settings

Describe the structure of the story in terms of its settings.

Symbolism

1. Towards the end of the story, we are told, 'She gripped
    with both hands at the iron railing'. Do you see any symbolic
    significance in this? Does it remind you of anything earlier
    in *Dubliners*?

2. Below are two quotations from the story. What are their
    symbolic meanings?
    'objects which she had dusted once a week for so many
    years, wondering where on earth all the dust came from.' (p. 48)
    '... a broken harmonium...' (p. 48)

Narrator

Complete the following sentences by marking the most appropriate of the endings provided in the right-hand column:

The story is narrated by

☐ a third-person narrator
☐ several narrators
☐ James Joyce
☐ a first-person narrator

The narrator is

☐ omniscient
☐ unreliable
☐ objective
☐ naive
☐ reticent

Themes

1. Discuss the themes of emigration and escape in "Eveline".

2. Do you see any relevance in the reference to Eve in Eveline's name?

3. How is the Catholic Church represented in the story?

4. Compare and contrast the theme of paralysis in "The Sisters" and "Eveline".

Two Gallants

TWO GALLANTS

T HE grey warm evening of August had descended upon the city and a mild warm air, a memory of summer, circulated in the streets. The streets, shuttered[1] for the repose of Sunday, swarmed[2] with a gaily coloured crowd. Like illumined pearls the lamps shone from the summits of their tall poles upon the living texture below which, changing shape and hue[3] unceasingly, sent up into the warm grey evening air an unchanging, unceasing murmur.

Two young men came down the hill of Rutland Square. One of them was just bringing a long monologue to a close. The other, who walked on the verge[4] of the path and was at times obliged to step on to the road, owing to his companion's rudeness,[5]

---

1. *shuttered* ['ʃʌtəd] : closed with shutters (see note 3, p. 7).
2. *swarmed* [swɔːmd] : were full of large numbers of people.
3. *hue* [hjuː] : colour.
4. *verge* [vɜːdʒ] : edge, border, margin.
5. *rudeness* [ruːdnəs] : impoliteness, discourtesy.

wore an amused listening face. He was squat [1] and
ruddy. A yachting cap was shoved far back from his
forehead and the narrative to which he listened
made constant waves of expression break forth [2] over
his face from the corners of his nose and eyes and
mouth. Little jets of wheezing [3] laughter followed one
another out of his convulsed body. His eyes,
twinkling with cunning enjoyment, glanced [4] at every
moment towards his companion's face. Once or twice
he rearranged the light waterproof which he had
slung [5] over one shoulder in toreador fashion. His
breeches, his white rubber shoes and his jauntily [6]
slung waterproof expressed youth. But his figure fell
into rotundity at the waist, his hair was scant and
grey and his face, when the waves of expression had
passed over it, had a ravaged [7] look.

When he was quite sure that the narrative had
ended he laughed noiselessly for fully half a minute.
Then he said:

—Well! . . . That takes the biscuit! [8]

His voice seemed winnowed [9] of vigour; and to

---

1. *squat* [skwɒt]: short and wide.
2. *break forth* : suddenly emerge, burst out.
3. *wheezing* [wiːzɪŋ]: a harsh or whistling sound caused by
    dryness in the throat.
4. *glanced* : see note 3, p. 39.
5. *slung* [slʌŋ] (sling, slung, slung) : thrown carelessly.
6. *jauntily* ['dʒɔːntɪli]: elegantly, stylishly.
7. *ravaged* ['rævɪdʒd] : devastated.
8. *takes the biscuit!* : That's the limit! Some critics have found
    allusions to the Eucharist in the biscuits, wine and stout
    which are frequently found in *Dubliners*.
9. *winnowed* ['wɪnəʊd] : (here) emptied (metaphorical − to
    "winnow" means to separate the edible part of the grain from
    the husk which surrounds it).

enforce his words he added with humour:

—That takes the solitary, unique, and, if I may so call it, *recherché* [1] biscuit!

He became serious and silent when he had said this. His tongue was tired for he had been talking all the afternoon in a public-house in Dorset Street. Most people considered Lenehan a leech [2] but, in spite of this reputation, his adroitness and eloquence had always prevented his friends from forming any general policy against him. He had a brave manner of coming up to a party of them in a bar and of holding himself nimbly [3] at the borders of the company until he was included in a round. [4] He was a sporting vagrant armed with a vast stock of stories, limericks [5] and riddles. He was insensitive to all kinds of discourtesy. No one knew how he achieved the stern [6] task of living, but his name was vaguely associated with racing tissues. [7]

—And where did you pick her up, Corley? he asked.

Corley ran his tongue swiftly along his upper lip.

—One night, man, he said, I was going along Dame Street and I spotted a fine tart [8] under Waterhouse's clock and said good-night, you know. So we went for a walk round by the canal and she

---

1. *recherché* [rəˈʃeəʃeɪ] : French for "rare, elegant".
2. *leech* : parasite.
3. *nimbly* [ˈnɪmbli] : (here) cleverly, skilfully.
4. *until ... in a round* : until somebody offered to buy everyone a drink.
5. *limericks* : nonsense verses, often of a licentious nature.
6. *stern* [stɜːn] : hard, difficult.
7. *racing tissues* : information sheets for horse racing.
8. *tart* (coll.) : prostitute.

told me she was a slavey[1] in a house in Baggot Street. I put my arm round her and squeezed her a bit that night. Then next Sunday, man, I met her by appointment. We went out to Donnybrook and I brought her into a field there. She told me she used to go with a dairyman.... It was fine, man. Cigarettes every night she'd bring me and paying the tram out and back. And one night she brought me two bloody fine cigars – O, the real cheese,[2] you know, that the old fellow used to smoke.... I was afraid, man, she'd get in the family way.[3] But she's up to the dodge.[4]

—Maybe she thinks you'll marry her, said Lenehan.

—I told her I was out of a job, said Corley. I told her I was in Pim's.[5] She doesn't know my name. I was too hairy[6] to tell her that. But she thinks I'm a bit of class, you know.

Lenehan laughed again, noiselessly.

—Of all the good ones ever I heard, he said, that emphatically takes the biscuit.

Corley's stride[7] acknowledged the compliment. The swing of his burly[8] body made his friend execute a few light skips[9] from the path to the roadway and back again. Corley was the son of an inspector of

1. *slavey* ['sleɪvi] : an all-purpose maid.
2. *the real cheese* : the real thing.
3. *in the family way* : pregnant.
4. *up to the dodge* : knows how to avoid getting pregnant.
5. *Pim's* : a large, respectable general store. (See note 3, p. 49).
6. *hairy* (slang) : astute, clever.
7. *stride* [straɪd] : the way he walked.
8. *burly* ['bɜːli] : big and strong.
9. *skips* : light jumping movements.

police and he had inherited his father's frame and gait.[1] He walked with his hands by his sides, holding himself erect and swaying his head from side to side. His head was large, globular and oily; it sweated in all weathers; and his large round hat, set upon it sideways, looked like a bulb which had grown out of another. He always stared straight before him as if he were on parade and, when he wished to gaze after some one in the street, it was necessary for him to move his body from the hips. At present he was about town.[2] Whenever any job was vacant a friend was always ready to give him the hard word. He was often to be seen walking with policemen in plain clothes, talking earnestly.[3] He knew the inner side of all affairs and was fond of delivering final judgments. He spoke without listening to the speech of his companions. His conversation was mainly about himself: what he had said to such a person and what such a person had said to him and what he had said to settle the matter.[4] When he reported these dialogues he aspirated the first letter of his name after the manner of Florentines.[5]

Lenehan offered his friend a cigarette. As the two young men walked on through the crowd Corley occasionally turned to smile at some of the passing

1. *frame and gait* [geɪt] : shape of body and way of walking.
2. *about town* : out of work, but it implies that he is making a living by doing things which are almost outside the law.
3. *He was often to be seen ... earnestly* : this implies that Corley is a police informer.
4. *settle the matter* : decide, come to a fixed decision on a question.
5. *he aspirated ... Florentines* : Corley thus becomes "Horley", or "Whorely". A whore is a prostitute.

girls but Lenehan's gaze was fixed on the large faint moon circled with a double halo. He watched earnestly the passing of the grey web of twilight across its face. At length he said:

—Well . . . tell me, Corley, I suppose you'll be able to pull it off[1] all right, eh?

Corley closed one eye expressively as an answer.

—Is she game[2] for that? asked Lenehan dubiously. You can never know women.

—She's all right, said Corley. I know the way to get around her, man. She's a bit gone on me.[3]

—You're what I call a gay Lothario,[4] said Lenehan. And the proper kind of a Lothario, too!

A shade of mockery[5] relieved the servility of his manner. To save himself he had the habit of leaving his flattery[6] open to the interpretation of raillery.[7] But Corley had not a subtle mind.

—There's nothing to touch a good slavey, he affirmed. Take my tip for it.[8]

—By one who has tried them all, said Lenehan.

—First I used to go with girls, you know, said

---

1. *pull it off* : succeed.
2. *game* : spirited enough.
3. *gone on me* (coll.) : infatuated with me.
4. *Lothario* : a young nobleman of Genoa in "The Fair Penitent" by Nicholas Rowe (1674-1718). The character in question is the archetypal libertine.
5. *shade* [ʃeɪd] *of mockery* : slight degree of ridicule or derision.
6. *flattery* : attempts to please or win favour by insincere compliments.
7. *raillery* ['reɪləri] : good-humoured ridicule.
8. *Take my tip for it* : take my word for it, you can be sure it's true.

Corley, unbosoming;[1] girls off the South Circular.[2] I used to take them out, man, on the tram somewhere and pay the tram or take them to a band or a play at the theatre or buy them chocolate and sweets or something that way. I used to spend money on them right enough, he added, in a convincing tone, as if he were conscious of being disbelieved.

But Lenehan could well believe it; he nodded gravely.

—I know that game, he said, and it's a mug's game.[3]

—And damn the thing I ever got out of it,[4] said Corley.

—Ditto[5] here, said Lenehan.

—Only off of one of them, said Corley.

He moistened his upper lip by running his tongue along it. The recollection brightened his eyes. He too gazed at the pale disc of the moon, now nearly veiled, and seemed to meditate.

—She was ... a bit of all right,[6] he said regretfully.

He was silent again. Then he added:

—She's on the turf[7] now. I saw her driving down Earl Street one night with two fellows with her on a car.

1. *unbosoming* [ˌʌnˈbʊzəmɪŋ]: confessing.
2. *girls off the South Circular* : the South Circular Road was a popular walking place for groups of unattached lower middle-class young women.
3. *a mug's game* : a game you can never win.
4. *damn the thing ... out of it* : implies that he never got anything out of it.
5. *Ditto* : the same.
6. *a bit of all right* : very attractive physically.
7. *on the turf* : working as a prostitute (euphemism – after the analogy with a racehorse).

—I suppose that's your doing, said Lenehan.

—There was others at her before me, said Corley philosophically.

This time Lenehan was inclined to disbelieve. He shook his head to and fro and smiled.

—You know you can't kid me,[1] Corley, he said.

—Honest to God! said Corley. Didn't she tell me herself?

Lenehan made a tragic gesture.

—Base betrayer! he said.

As they passed along the railings of Trinity College, Lenehan skipped out into the road and peered up at the clock.

—Twenty after, he said.

—Time enough, said Corley. She'll be there all right. I always let her wait a bit.

Lenehan laughed quietly.

—Ecod![2] Corley, you know how to take them, he said.

—I'm up to all their little tricks,[3] Corley confessed.

—But tell me, said Lenehan again, are you sure you can bring it off[4] all right? You know it's a ticklish job.[5] They're damn close on that point. Eh? . . . What?

His bright, small eyes searched his companion's face for reassurance. Corley swung his head to and fro as if to toss aside an insistent insect, and his brows gathered.[6]

—I'll pull it off, he said. Leave it to me, can't you?

---

1. *you can't kid me* (coll.) : you can't deceive me.
2. *Ecod* [iːˈkɒd] : a mild oath.
3. *I'm up to ... tricks* : I know all their little tricks.
4. *bring it off* : pull it off, succeed.
5. *a ticklish job* : a difficult job.
6. *his brows gathered* [ˈgæðəd] : he frowned (see note 4, p. 16).

Lenehan said no more. He did not wish to ruffle his friend's temper,[1] to be sent to the devil and told that his advice was not wanted. A little tact was necessary. But Corley's brow was soon smooth again. His thoughts were running another way.

—She's a fine decent tart, he said, with appreciation; that's what she is.

They walked along Nassau Street and then turned into Kildare Street. Not far from the porch of the club [2] a harpist stood in the roadway, playing to a little ring of listeners. He plucked at the wires heedlessly,[3] glancing quickly from time to time at the face of each new-comer and from time to time, wearily also, at the sky. His harp [4] too, heedless that her coverings had fallen about her knees, seemed weary alike of the eyes of strangers and of her master's hands. One hand played in the bass the melody of *Silent, O Moyle,* [5] while the other hand careered [6] in the treble after each group of notes. The notes of the air throbbed [7] deep and full.

The two young men walked up the street without speaking, the mournful [8] music following them. When they reached Stephen's Green they crossed the road. Here the noise of trams, the lights and the

1. *ruffle his friend's temper* : make his friend angry or annoyed.
2. *the club* : the Kildare Street Club was fashionable, Protestant and Anglo-Irish.
3. *heedlessly* : without noticing.
4. *harp* : the harp is a traditional symbol of Ireland's legendary past.
5. *Silent, O Moyle* : the first line of "The Song of Fionnuala", one of the "Irish Melodies" by Thomas Moore (1779-1852).
6. *careered* [kə'rɪəd] : move fast and wildly.
7. *throbbed* [θrɒbd] : vibrated rhythmically.
8. *mournful* ['mɔːnfl]: sad, dismal.

City Hall.

Looking towards Trinity College from the end of Nassau Street.

crowd released them from their silence.

—There she is! said Corley.

At the corner of Hume Street a young woman was standing. She wore a blue dress and a white sailor hat.[1] She stood on the curbstone,[2] swinging a sunshade in one hand. Lenehan grew lively.

—Let's have a squint[3] at her, Corley, he said.

Corley glanced sideways at his friend and an unpleasant grin appeared on his face.

—Are you trying to get inside me?[4] he asked.

—Damn it! said Lenehan boldly, I don't want an introduction. All I want is to have a look at her. I'm not going to eat her.

—O . . . A look at her? said Corley, more amiably. Well . . . I'll tell you what. I'll go over and talk to her and you can pass by.

—Right! said Lenehan.

Corley had already thrown one leg over the chains [5] when Lenehan called out:

—And after? Where will we meet?

—Half ten, answered Corley, bringing over his other leg.

—Where?

—Corner of Merrion Street. We'll be coming back.

---

1. *a blue dress and a white sailor hat* : blue and white are the colours of the virgin Mary. Compare the character of the slavey with Polly in "The Boarding House", and with Mangan's sister in "Araby".

2. *curbstone* ['kɜːbstəʊn] : stone laid at the edge of the pavement.

3. *squint* : (here) look.

4. *trying to get inside me* : trying to beat me to it, to get there before me.

5. *over the chains* : the chains, which were hung from bollards (low posts) made a low fence or barrier.

—Work it all right now, said Lenehan in farewell.

Corley did not answer. He sauntered[1] across the road swaying his head from side to side. His bulk,[2] his easy pace, and the solid sound of his boots had something of the conqueror in them. He approached the young woman and, without saluting, began at once to converse with her. She swung her sunshade more quickly and executed half turns on her heels. Once or twice when he spoke to her at close quarters she laughed and bent her head.

Lenehan observed them for a few minutes. Then he walked rapidly along beside the chains to some distance and crossed the road obliquely. As he approached Hume Street corner he found the air heavily scented[3] and his eyes made a swift anxious scrutiny of the young woman's appearance. She had her Sunday finery on. Her blue serge skirt was held at the waist by a belt of black leather. The great silver buckle of her belt seemed to depress the centre of her body, catching the light stuff of her white blouse like a clip. She wore a short black jacket with mother-of-pearl buttons and a ragged black boa.[4] The ends of her tulle collarette[5] had been carefully disordered and a big bunch of red flowers was pinned in her bosom[6] stems upwards.[7] Lenehan's eyes noted

---

1. *sauntered* ['sɔːntəd] : walked in a relaxed way.
2. *bulk* : large proportions of his body.
3. *scented* ['sentɪd] : smelling of perfume.
4. *ragged* ['rægɪd] *black boa* : a long black scarf with irregular edges, worn around the neck.
5. *tulle collarette* : an ornamental collar made of a fine, semi-transparent soft silk (tulle).
6. *bosom* ['bʊzəm] : breast.
7. *stems upwards* : the flowers were pointing downwards : this indicates her lack of sophistication.

approvingly her stout[1] short muscular body. Frank[2]
rude[3] health glowed in her face, on her fat red cheeks
and in her unabashed[4] blue eyes. Her features were
blunt.[5] She had broad nostrils, a straggling[6] mouth
which lay open in a contented leer,[7] and two
projecting front teeth. As he passed Lenehan took off
his cap and, after about ten seconds, Corley returned
a salute to the air. This he did by raising his hand
vaguely and pensively changing the angle of position
of his hat.

Lenehan walked as far as the Shelbourne Hotel
where he halted and waited. After waiting for a little
time he saw them coming towards him and, when
they turned to the right, he followed them, stepping
lightly in his white shoes, down one side of Merrion
Square. As he walked on slowly, timing his pace to
theirs, he watched Corley's head which turned at
every moment towards the young woman's face like
a big ball revolving on a pivot. He kept the pair in
view until he had seen them climbing the stairs of
the Donnybrook tram; then he turned about and
went back the way he had come.

Now that he was alone his face looked older. His
gaiety seemed to forsake[8] him, and, as he came by
the railings of the Duke's Lawn, he allowed his hand

---

1. *stout* : strong.
2. *Frank* : honest, open.
3. *rude* [ruːd] : simple.
4. *unabashed* [ˌʌnəˈbæʃt] : without shame. not disconcerted.
5. *blunt* : unrefined.
6. *straggling* : large and irregular.
7. *leer* [lɪər] : lascivious smile or look.
8. *forsake* [fəˈseɪk] : abandon.

to run along them. The air[1] which the harpist had played began to control his movements. His softly padded feet[2] played the melody while his fingers swept a scale of variations idly along the railings after each group of notes.

He walked listlessly[3] round Stephen's Green and then down Grafton Street. Though his eyes took note of many elements of the crowd through which he passed they did so morosely.[4] He found trivial all that was meant to charm him and did not answer the glances which invited him to be bold. He knew that he would have to speak a great deal, to invent and to amuse, and his brain and throat were too dry for such a task. The problem of how he could pass the hours till he met Corley again troubled him a little. He could think of no way of passing them but to keep on walking. He turned to the left when he came to the corner of Rutland Square and felt more at ease in the dark quiet street, the sombre look of which suited his mood. He paused at last before the window of a poor-looking shop over which the words *Refreshment Bar* were printed in white letters. On the glass of the window were two flying inscriptions: *Ginger Beer* and *Ginger Ale*.[5] A cut ham was exposed on a great blue dish while near it on a plate lay a segment of very light plum-pudding. He eyed this

---

1. *air* : melody, tune.
2. *His softly padded feet* : he was wearing comfortable shoes which protected ("padded") his feet.
3. *listlessly* ['lɪstləsli] : without any wish to exert himself or enthusiasm for his journey.
4. *morosely* [mə'rəusli] : in a dispirited or depressed way.
5. *Ginger Beer ... Ginger Ale* : non-alcoholic beverages, made with ginger.

food earnestly for some time and then, after glancing
warily[1] up and down the street, went into the shop
quickly.

He was hungry for, except some biscuits which he
had asked two grudging[2] curates[3] to bring him, he
had eaten nothing since breakfast-time. He sat down
at an uncovered wooden table opposite two
work-girls and a mechanic. A slatternly[4] girl waited
on him.

—How much is a plate of peas? he asked.

—Three halfpence, sir, said the girl.

—Bring me a plate of peas, he said, and a bottle
of ginger beer.

He spoke roughly in order to belie[5] his air of
gentility for his entry had been followed by a pause
of talk. His face was heated. To appear natural he
pushed his cap back on his head and planted his
elbows on the table. The mechanic and the two
work-girls examined him point by point before
resuming their conversation in a subdued voice. The
girl brought him a plate of hot grocer's peas,
seasoned with pepper and vinegar, a fork and his
ginger beer. He ate his food greedily and found it so
good that he made a note of the shop mentally. When
he had eaten all the peas he sipped his ginger beer
and sat for some time thinking of Corley's adventure.
In his imagination he beheld[6] the pair of lovers

1. *warily* ['wɪərɪli]: cautiously.
2. *grudging* ['grʌdʒɪŋ] : complaining, discontented.
3. *curates* ['kjʊərəts] : Irish slang for "bartenders", "barmen".
4. *slatternly* : untidy and of low character and manners.
5. *belie* [bɪ'laɪ] : contradict.
6. *beheld* : saw.

walking along some dark road; he heard Corley's voice in deep energetic gallantries and saw again the leer of the young woman's mouth. This vision made him feel keenly [1] his own poverty of purse and spirit. He was tired of knocking about,[2] of pulling the devil by the tail, of shifts and intrigues. He would be thirty-one in November. Would he never get a good job? Would he never have a home of his own? He thought how pleasant it would be to have a warm fire to sit by and a good dinner to sit down to. He had walked the streets long enough with friends and with girls. He knew what those friends were worth: he knew the girls too. Experience had embittered his heart against the world. But all hope had not left him. He felt better after having eaten than he had felt before, less weary of his life, less vanquished in spirit. He might yet be able to settle down [3] in some snug [4] corner and live happily if he could only come across some good simple-minded girl with a little of the ready.[5]

He paid twopence halfpenny to the slatternly girl and went out of the shop to begin his wandering again. He went into Capel Street and walked along towards the City Hall. Then he turned into Dame Street. At the corner of George's Street he met two friends of his and stopped to converse with them. He was glad that he could rest from all his walking. His friends asked him had he seen Corley and what was

---

1. *keenly* : strongly, intensely.
2. *knocking about* : wandering about.
3. *settle down* : make a permanent home.
4. *snug* : comfortable and well placed.
5. *a little of the ready* : some money (ready cash).

the latest. He replied that he had spent the day with
Corley. His friends talked very little. They looked
vacantly after some figures in the crowd and
sometimes made a critical remark. One said that he
had seen Mac an hour before in Westmoreland
Street. At this Lenehan said that he had been with
Mac the night before in Egan's.[1] The young man who
had seen Mac in Westmoreland Street asked was it
true that Mac had won a bit over a billiard match.
Lenehan did not know: he said that Holohan had
stood them drinks[2] in Egan's.

He left his friends at a quarter to ten and went
up George's Street. He turned to the left at the City
Markets and walked on into Grafton Street. The
crowd of girls and young men had thinned and on his
way up the street he heard many groups and couples
bidding one another good-night. He went as far as
the clock of the College of Surgeons: it was on the
stroke of ten. He set off briskly[3] along the northern
side of the Green, hurrying for fear Corley should
return too soon. When he reached the corner of
Merrion Street he took his stand in the shadow of a
lamp and brought out one of the cigarettes which he
had reserved and lit it. He leaned against the
lamp-post and kept his gaze fixed on the part from
which he expected to see Corley and the young
woman return.

His mind became active again. He wondered had
Corley managed it successfully. He wondered if he

1. *Egan's* : a Dublin pub.
2. *stood them drinks* : bought a round of drinks (see note 4, p. 63).
3. *He set off briskly* : he began walking quickly.

had asked her yet or if he would leave it to the last. He suffered all the pangs and thrills [1] of his friend's situation as well as those of his own. But the memory of Corley's slowly revolving head calmed him somewhat: he was sure Corley would pull it off all right. All at once the idea struck him that perhaps Corley had seen her home by another way and given him the slip. [2] His eyes searched the street: there was no sign of them. Yet it was surely half-an-hour since he had seen the clock of the College of Surgeons. Would Corley do a thing like that? He lit his last cigarette and began to smoke it nervously. He strained his eyes [3] as each tram stopped at the far corner of the square. They must have gone home by another way. The paper of his cigarette broke and he flung [4] it into the road with a curse.

Suddenly he saw them coming towards him. He started [5] with delight and, keeping close to his lamp-post, tried to read the result in their walk. They were walking quickly, the young woman taking quick short steps, while Corley kept beside her with his long stride. They did not seem to be speaking. An intimation of the result pricked [6] him like the point of a sharp instrument. He knew Corley would fail; he knew it was no go. [7]

They turned down Baggot Street and he followed

1. *pangs and thrills* : sudden strong feelings of pain and excitement.
2. *given him the slip* : escaped from him.
3. *strained his eyes* : tried hard to see.
4. *flung* [flʌŋ] (fling, flung, flung) : threw with force.
5. *started* : came awake suddenly.
6. *pricked* [prɪkt] : caused him pain or discomfort.
7. *he knew it was no go* : he knew the plan hadn't worked.

them at once, taking the other footpath. When they
stopped he stopped too. They talked for a few
moments and then the young woman went down the
steps into the area[1] of a house. Corley remained
standing at the edge of the path, a little distance
from the front steps. Some minutes passed. Then the
hall-door was opened slowly and cautiously. A
woman came running down the front steps and
coughed. Corley turned and went towards her. His
broad figure hid hers from view for a few seconds and
then she reappeared running up the steps. The door
closed on her and Corley began to walk swiftly
towards Stephen's Green.

Lenehan hurried on in the same direction. Some
drops of light rain fell. He took them as a warning
and, glancing back towards the house which the
young woman had entered to see that he was not
observed, he ran eagerly across the road. Anxiety
and his swift run made him pant.[2] He called out:

—Hallo, Corley!

Corley turned his head to see who had called him,
and then continued walking as before. Lenehan ran
after him, settling the waterproof on his shoulders
with one hand.

—Hallo, Corley! he cried again.

He came level with his friend and looked keenly
in his face. He could see nothing there.

—Well? he said. Did it come off?[3]

They had reached the corner of Ely Place. Still

---

1. *area* : see note 5, p. 28.
2. *pant* : breathe in quick short breaths.
3. *Did it come off?* : Did it work?

without answering Corley swerved[1] to the left and went up the side street. His features were composed in stern calm. Lenehan kept up with[2] his friend, breathing uneasily. He was baffled[3] and a note of menace pierced through his voice.

—Can't you tell us?[4] he said. Did you try her?

Corley halted at the first lamp and stared grimly[5] before him. Then with a grave gesture he extended a hand towards the light and, smiling, opened it slowly to the gaze of his disciple.[6] A small gold coin[7] shone in the palm.

1. *swerved* [swɜːvd] : deviated from his course.
2. *kept up with* : succeeded in walking as fast as.
3. *baffled* ['bæfld] : perplexed, confused.
4. *Can't you tell us?* : Can't you tell me? ("us" is a regional variation on "me").
5. *grimly* : resolutely and very seriously.
6. *disciple* [dɪ'saɪpl] : it is interesting that the "base betrayer" Corley should call Lenehan his "disciple".
7. *A small gold coin* : a sovereign.

Characters

1. Reread the passage on p. 62 beginning, 'His breeches' and ending 'a ravaged look'. What does it tell us about Lenehan?

2. Reread the passage on p. 65 beginning 'He knew the inner side' and ending 'to settle the matter'. Mark the nouns below that best describe Corley's attitude to other people (and, if you wish, add other nouns of your own):

contempt	compassion	egotism	deference	arrogance
cruelty	subtlety	humility	respect	sensitivity

3. Reread the passage on pp. 72-3 beginning 'She had her Sunday finery on' and ending 'projecting front teeth'. Mark the adverbs below that best describe the young woman's mode of dressing and her way of confronting the world (if you wish, add other adverbs of your own):

modestly	boldly	conservatively	jauntily
defiantly	carefully	carelessly	confidently

Settings

Where is the story set? And why is this setting particularly appropriate to the three characters of the story and their situations?

Structure

1. The story is built around the central question of whether or not Corley can get some money from the young woman. When does the reader discover this?

2. Before you found out what the question was, what did you think it might be?

3. Do you think Joyce created this confusion deliberately? If so, why and how?

Narrator

What is the narrator's attitude to:
◆ Lenehan?
◆ Corley?
◆ the young woman?

Themes

Below is a list of some possible themes of the story. Discuss each theme separately and decide which you think is the most important. Do you find any themes this story has in common with other stories in *Dubliners*?
◆ unemployment
◆ prostitution
◆ the abuse of women by men
◆ deception

THE BOARDING HOUSE

THE BOARDING HOUSE[1]

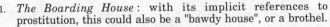

MRS MOONEY[2] was a butcher's daughter. She was a woman who was quite able to keep things to herself: a determined woman. She had married her father's foreman[3] and opened a butcher's shop near Spring Gardens. But as soon as his father-in-law was dead Mr Mooney began to go to the devil. He drank, plundered the till, ran headlong into debt. It was no use making him take the pledge:[4] he was sure to break out again a few days after. By fighting his wife in the presence of customers and by buying bad meat he ruined his business. One night he went for his wife with the cleaver[5] and she had to sleep in a neighbour's house.

1. *The Boarding House*: with its implicit references to prostitution, this could also be a "bawdy house", or a brothel.
2. *Mrs Mooney*: Mrs Mooney seems to be more interested in money than in her daughter's happiness.
3. *foreman* ['fɔːmən] : supervisor.
4. *take the pledge* : promise not to drink alcohol.
5. *cleaver* : a butcher's knife.

After that they lived apart. She went to the priest
and got a separation[1] from him with care of the
children. She would give him neither money nor food
nor house-room; and so he was obliged to enlist
himself as a sheriff's man.[2] He was a shabby stooped
little drunkard with a white face and a white
moustache and white eyebrows, pencilled above his
little eyes, which were pink-veined and raw; and all
day long he sat in the bailiff's room, waiting to be
put on a job. Mrs Mooney, who had taken what
remained of her money out of the butcher business
and set up a boarding-house in Hardwicke Street,
was a big imposing woman. Her house had a floating
population made up of tourists from Liverpool and
the Isle of Man and, occasionally, *artistes*[3] from the
music halls. Its resident population was made up of
clerks from the city. She governed her house
cunningly and firmly, knew when to give credit,
when to be stern and when to let things pass. All the
resident young men spoke of her as *The Madam*.[4]

Mrs Mooney's young men paid fifteen shillings a
week for board and lodgings (beer or stout at dinner
excluded). They shared in common tastes and
occupations and for this reason they were very
chummy[5] with one another. They discussed with one

1. *She went to the priest ... separation* : notice once again the
   role of the clergy in everyday life in Dublin.
2. *sheriff's man* : someone who runs errands for the bailiff.
3. *artistes* : the use of the French word conveys the idea of
   mediocre performers with pretensions to the status of serious
   artists.
4. *The Madam* : a term also used for the woman who runs a
   brothel.
5. *chummy* : friendly, intimate.

A fast couple from the Isle of Man.

Hardwicke Street and St George's.

another the chances of favourites and outsiders. Jack
Mooney, the Madam's son, who was clerk to a
commission agent in Fleet Street, had the reputation
of being a hard case. He was fond of using soldiers'
obscenities: usually he came home in the small
hours. When he met his friends he had always a good
one to tell them and he was always sure to be on to
a good thing – that is to say, a likely horse or a likely
artiste. He was also handy with the mits [1] and sang
comic songs. On Sunday nights there would often be
a reunion in Mrs Mooney's front drawing-room. The
music-hall *artistes* would oblige; and Sheridan
played waltzes and polkas and vamped [2]
accompaniments. Polly [3] Mooney, the Madam's
daughter, would also sing. She sang:

> *I'm a . . . naughty girl* [4]
> *You needn't sham:* [5]
> *You know I am.*

Polly was a slim girl of nineteen; she had light soft
hair and a small full mouth. Her eyes, which were
grey with a shade of green through them, had a habit
of glancing upwards when she spoke with anyone,
which made her look like a little perverse madonna.
Mrs Mooney had first sent her daughter to be a

---

1. *He was also handy with the mits* : he was a good boxer.
2. *vamped* : improvised.
3. *Polly* : Polly is another name for Molly, which in turn is
   another name for Mary. Polly Mooney is one of the several
   Marian figures with connotations of prostitution in *Dubliners*.
4. *I'm a ... naughty girl* : yet another indication of Polly's
   immorality.
5. *sham* : pretend.

typist in a corn-factor's office but, as a disreputable
sheriff's man used to come every other day to the
office, asking to be allowed to say a word to his
daughter, she had taken her daughter home again
and set her to[1] do housework. As Polly was very
lively the intention was to give her the run of the
young men. Besides, young men like to feel that
there is a young woman not very far away. Polly, of
course, flirted[2] with the young men but Mrs Mooney,
who was a shrewd[3] judge, knew that the young men
were only passing the time away: none of them
meant business. Things went on so for a long time
and Mrs Mooney began to think of sending Polly
back to typewriting when she noticed that something
was going on between Polly and one of the young
men. She watched the pair and kept her own counsel.

Polly knew that she was being watched, but still
her mother's persistent silence could not be
misunderstood. There had been no open complicity
between   mother   and   daughter,   no   open
understanding but, though people in the house began
to talk of the affair, still Mrs Mooney did not
intervene. Polly began to grow a little strange in her
manner and the young man was evidently perturbed.
At last, when she judged it to be the right moment,
Mrs Mooney intervened. She dealt with moral
problems as a cleaver deals with meat: and in this
case she had made up her mind.

It was a bright Sunday morning of early summer,
promising heat, but with a fresh breeze blowing. All

1. *set her to* : make her.
2. *flirted* [flɜːtɪd] : behaved in a superficially amorous way.
3. *shrewd* [ʃruːd] : astute, perceptive.

the windows of the boarding house were open and the lace curtains ballooned[1] gently towards the street beneath the raised sashes.[2] The belfry of George's Church sent out constant peals[3] and worshippers, singly or in groups, traversed the little circus before the church, revealing their purpose by their self-contained demeanour no less than by the little volumes in their gloved hands. Breakfast was over in the boarding house and the table of the breakfast-room was covered with plates on which lay yellow streaks[4] of eggs with morsels of bacon-fat and bacon-rind. Mrs Mooney sat in the straw arm-chair and watched the servant Mary remove the breakfast things. She made Mary collect the crusts[5] and pieces of broken bread to help to make Tuesday's bread-pudding. When the table was cleared, the broken bread collected, the sugar and butter safe under lock and key, she began to reconstruct the interview which she had had the night before with Polly. Things were as she had suspected: she had been frank[6] in her questions and Polly had been frank in her answers. Both had been somewhat awkward,[7] of course. She had been made awkward by her not wishing to receive the news in too cavalier a fashion or to seem to have connived[8] and Polly had

1. *ballooned* [bə'luːnd] : filled with air (like a balloon).
2. *sashes* : wooden frames forming part of a window.
3. *peals* [piːlz] : long loud reverberating sounds.
4. *streaks* [striːks] : long thin irregular marks.
5. *crusts* : pieces of the hard outer part of bread.
6. *frank* : candid, open and honest.
7. *awkward* ['ɔːkwəd] : embarrassed.
8. *connived* [kə'naɪvd] : been in secret complicity.

been made awkward not merely because allusions of that kind always made her awkward but also because she did not wish it to be thought that in her wise innocence she had divined the intention behind her mother's tolerance.

Mrs Mooney glanced instinctively at the little gilt clock on the mantelpiece [1] as soon as she had become aware through her revery that the bells of George's Church [2] had stopped ringing. It was seventeen minutes past eleven: she would have lots of time to have the matter out [3] with Mr Doran [4] and then catch short twelve at Marlborough Street. [5] She was sure she would win. To begin with she had all the weight of social opinion on her side: she was an outraged [6] mother. She had allowed him to live beneath her roof, assuming that he was a man of honour, and he had simply abused her hospitality. He was thirty-four or thirty-five years of age, so that youth could not be pleaded as his excuse; nor could ignorance be his excuse since he was a man who had seen something of the world. He had simply taken advantage of Polly's youth and inexperience: that

1. *mantelpiece* : ornamental structure over a fireplace.
2. *George's Church* : notice the lack of spirituality implied by the missing "Saint". Furthermore, St. George is the patron saint of England, the traditional oppressor of Ireland.
3. *have the matter out* : settle the matter (see note 4, p. 65).
4. *Doran* : "exile" or "stranger" in Irish.
5. *short twelve at Marlborough Street* : the brief religious ceremony ("Mass") at 12 o'clock. Mrs Mooney obviously doesn't mind the fact that 12 o'clock mass is very brief. Business is clearly more important to her. Also, Marlborough Street takes its name from the Duke of Marlborough, another English oppressor of the Irish.
6. *outraged* ['aʊtreɪdʒd] : angry and deeply offended.

was evident. The question was: What reparation would he make?

There must be reparation made in such cases. It is all very well for the man: he can go his ways as if nothing had happened, having had his moment of pleasure, but the girl has to bear the brunt.[1] Some mothers would be content to patch up[2] such an affair for a sum of money; she had known cases of it. But she would not do so. For her only one reparation could make up for[3] the loss of her daughter's honour: marriage.

She counted all her cards again before sending Mary up to Mr Doran's room to say that she wished to speak with him. She felt sure she would win. He was a serious young man, not rakish[4] or loud-voiced like the others. If it had been Mr Sheridan or Mr Meade or Bantam Lyons her task would have been much harder. She did not think he would face publicity. All the lodgers in the house knew something of the affair; details had been invented by some. Besides, he had been employed for thirteen years in a great Catholic wine-merchant's office and publicity would mean for him, perhaps, the loss of his sit.[5] Whereas if he agreed all might be well. She knew he had a good screw[6] for one thing and she suspected he had a bit of stuff put by.[7]

---

1. *bear the brunt* : take the consequences.
2. *patch up* : repair in a hurried way.
3. *make up for* : compensate for.
4. *rakish* : with dissolute habits.
5. *the loss of his sit* (coll.) : the loss of his job.
6. *screw* (slang) : wage.
7. *he had a bit of stuff put by* : he had saved some money.

Nearly the half-hour! She stood up and surveyed herself in the pier-glass.[1] The decisive expression of her great florid face satisfied her and she thought of some mothers she knew who could not get their daughters off their hands.[2]

Mr Doran was very anxious indeed this Sunday morning. He had made two attempts to shave but his hand had been so unsteady[3] that he had been obliged to desist. Three days' reddish beard fringed[4] his jaws and every two or three minutes a mist gathered on his glasses so that he had to take them off and polish them with his pocket-handkerchief. The recollection of his confession of the night before was a cause of acute pain to him; the priest had drawn out every ridiculous detail of the affair and in the end had so magnified his sin that he was almost thankful at being afforded a loophole[5] of reparation. The harm[6] was done. What could he do now but marry her or run away? He could not brazen it out.[7] The affair would be sure to be talked of and his employer would be certain to hear of it. Dublin is such a small city: everyone knows everyone else's business. He felt his heart leap warmly in his throat as he heard in his

1. *pier-glass* ['pɪəglaːs] : a tall dressing mirror.
2. *get ... their hands* : could not find husbands for their daughters to marry.
3. *unsteady* : not firm or secure.
4. *fringed* [frɪndʒd] : spread over, ornamented (like the threads – the "fringe" – at the edge of a carpet).
5. *loophole* ['luːphəʊl] : opening, a way of escaping serious consequences (through reparation).
6. *harm* : damage.
7. *brazen* ['breɪzn] *it out* : succeed in being impudent and without shame.

excited imagination old Mr Leonard calling out in his rasping[1] voice: *Send Mr Doran here, please*.

All his long years of service gone for nothing! All his industry and diligence thrown away! As a young man he had sown his wild oats,[2] of course; he had boasted[3] of his free-thinking and denied the existence of God to his companions in public-houses. But that was all passed and done with . . . nearly. He still bought a copy of *Reynolds's Newspaper*[4] every week but he attended to his religious duties and for nine-tenths of the year lived a regular life. He had money enough to settle down[5] on; it was not that. But the family would look down on her. First of all there was her disreputable father and then her mother's boarding house was beginning to get a certain fame. He had a notion that he was being had.[6] He could imagine his friends talking of the affair and laughing. She *was* a little vulgar; sometimes she said *I seen* and *If I had've known*. But what would grammar matter if he really loved her? He could not make up his mind whether to like her or despise her for what she had done. Of course, he had done it too. His instinct urged him to remain free, not to marry. Once you are married you are done for,[7] it said.

While he was sitting helplessly on the side of the

---

1. *rasping* : harsh, irritating and grating.
2. *had sown his wild oats* : had indulged in youthful dissipation.
3. *boasted* ['bəʊstɪd]: talked proudly.
4. *Reynold's Newspaper* : a radical Irish newspaper founded in 1850.
5. *settle down* : make a permanent home.
6. *he was being had* : he was being deceived, tricked.
7. *done for* : finished.

bed in shirt and trousers she tapped lightly at his
door and entered. She told him all, that she had
made a clean breast of it [1] to her mother and that her
mother would speak with him that morning. She
cried and threw her arms round his neck, saying:

—O, Bob! Bob! What am I to do? What am I to do
at all?

She would put an end to herself, she said.

He comforted her feebly,[2] telling her not to cry,
that it would be all right, never fear. He felt against
his shirt the agitation of her bosom.

It was not altogether his fault that it had
happened. He remembered well, with the curious
patient memory of the celibate, the first casual
caresses her dress, her breath, her fingers had given
him. Then late one night as he was undressing for
bed she had tapped at his door, timidly. She wanted
to relight her candle at his for hers had been blown
out by a gust.[3] It was her bath night. She wore a
loose open combing-jacket [4] of printed flannel. Her
white instep [5] shone in the opening of her furry
slippers and the blood glowed warmly behind her
perfumed skin. From her hands and wrists too as she
lit and steadied her candle [6] a faint perfume arose.

On nights when he came in very late it was she
who warmed up his dinner. He scarcely knew what
he was eating, feeling her beside him alone, at night,

1. *made a clean breast of it* : confessed.
2. *feebly* : weakly.
3. *gust* : sudden violent wind.
4. *combing-jacket* : dressing-gown.
5. *instep* : the prominent arched part of the human foot.
6. *steadied her candle* : put her hand in front of the candle to
    protect it from further gusts of wind.

in the sleeping house. And her thoughtfulness! If the night was anyway cold or wet or windy there was sure to be a little tumbler[1] of punch ready for him. Perhaps they could be happy together. . . .

They used to go upstairs together on tiptoe,[2] each with a candle, and on the third landing exchange reluctant good-nights. They used to kiss. He remembered well her eyes, the touch of her hand and his delirium. . . .

But delirium passes. He echoed her phrase, applying it to himself: *What am I to do?* The instinct of the celibate warned him to hold back. But the sin was there; even his sense of honour told him that reparation must be made for such a sin.

While he was sitting with her on the side of the bed Mary came to the door and said that the missus[3] wanted to see him in the parlour. He stood up to put on his coat and waistcoat, more helpless than ever. When he was dressed he went over to her to comfort her. It would be all right, never fear. He left her crying on the bed and moaning softly: *O my God!*

Going down the stairs his glasses became so dimmed with moisture[4] that he had to take them off and polish them. He longed to ascend through the roof and fly away to another country where he would never hear again of his trouble, and yet a force pushed him downstairs step by step. The implacable

---

1. *tumbler* : a flat-bottomed drinking glass.
2. *tiptoe* : see note 5, p. 12.
3. *missus* ['mɪsɪz] : an informal way of referring to the lady of the house.
4. *moisture* : condensed water vapour.

faces of his employer and of the Madam stared upon his discomfiture. On the last flight of stairs he passed Jack Mooney who was coming up from the pantry nursing two bottles of *Bass*.[1] They saluted coldly; and the lover's eyes rested for a second or two on a thick bulldog face and a pair of thick[2] short arms. When he reached the foot of the staircase he glanced up and saw Jack regarding him from the door of the return-room.[3]

Suddenly he remembered the night when one of the music-hall *artistes*, a little blond Londoner, had made a rather free allusion to Polly. The reunion had been almost broken up on account of Jack's violence. Everyone tried to quiet him. The music-hall *artiste*, a little paler than usual, kept smiling and saying that there was no harm meant: but Jack kept shouting at him that if any fellow tried that sort of a game on with *his* sister he'd bloody well put his teeth down his throat, so he would.

.   .   .   .

Polly sat for a little time on the side of the bed, crying. Then she dried her eyes and went over to the looking-glass. She dipped the end of the towel in the water-jug and refreshed her eyes with the cool water. She looked at herself in profile and readjusted a hairpin above her ear. Then she went back to the bed again and sat at the foot. She regarded the pillows for a long time and the sight of them awakened in her mind secret amiable memories. She rested the

1. *Bass* [bæs]: a strong brown beer brewed at the Bass Brewery.
2. *thick* : broad and solid (here, like a bulldog's legs).
3. *the return-room* : an extension to the house.

nape of her neck against the cool iron bed-rail and fell into a revery. There was no longer any perturbation visible on her face.

She waited on patiently, almost cheerfully, without alarm, her memories gradually giving place to hopes and visions of the future. Her hopes and visions were so intricate that she no longer saw the white pillows on which her gaze was fixed or remembered that she was waiting for anything.

At last she heard her mother calling. She started to her feet and ran to the banisters.

—Polly! Polly!

—Yes, mamma?

—Come down, dear. Mr Doran wants to speak to you.

Then she remembered what she had been waiting for.

Characters

1. The story opens with the sentence, 'Mrs Mooney was a butcher's daughter.' What does this lead us to expect of Mrs Mooney and of the story that follows?

2. 'Doran' means 'outsider' in Irish. In what ways is Mr Doran an outsider?

3. What purpose does Jack Mooney serve in the story?

4. Look at the paragraph on pp. 97-8 beginning 'Polly sat for a little time' and ending 'visible on her face'. What does it tell us about Polly's feelings and motives?

Settings

1. Boarding houses such as Mrs Mooney's were quite common at the time. They provided housing and domestic services (cooking, cleaning) for single men who could not afford a house or servants, and they provided work and income for older women no longer supported by their husbands. Given this, why do you think Mrs Mooney's boarding house was 'beginning to get a certain fame'?

2. 'It was a bright Sunday morning of early summer, promising heat, but with a fresh breeze blowing. All the windows of the boarding house were open and the lace curtains ballooned gently towards the street beneath the raised sashes.' (pp. 89-90)
    Compare and contrast this with earlier interior settings in *Dubliners*, such as Eveline's house or the priest's in "The Sisters".

Structure

Below is a list of the events of the story in the order in which they are narrated. Fill in the table with items from the list.

1. Mrs Mooney notices that Polly and Doran are intimate but says nothing.
2. She learns the truth from Polly.
3. Doran goes to confession.
4. Polly tells Doran that she has confessed to her mother.
5. Mary tells Doran that Mrs Mooney wants to see him.
6. Doran meets Jack Mooney on the stairs.
7. Doran speaks to Mrs Mooney and agrees to marry Polly.
8. Mrs Mooney calls Polly down to talk to Doran.

EVENTS THAT HAPPEN OUTSIDE THE NARRATIVE TIME	EVENTS THAT HAPPEN 'OFF-STAGE'	EVENTS THAT ARE DRAMATISED

Symbolism

1. Find the references to horse-racing in "Two Gallants" and "The Boarding House". Notice that they all have something to do with sexuality. Can you explain the connection?

2. We last see Doran descending the stairs. Is there any symbolic significance in this?

Narrator

1. An omniscient narrator (one who can tell us the thoughts of various characters) tells the story. However, at a certain point, he restricts himself to Mrs Mooney's point of view (that is, he does not tell us anything that Mrs Mooney has not thought or observed). Later he shifts to Doran's viewpoint, and finally to Polly's. When do these shifts of narrative viewpoint take place?

POINT OF VIEW	OPENING LINE FROM THAT POINT OF VIEW
Omniscient narration	
Mrs Mooney's viewpoint	
Doran's viewpoint	
Polly's viewpoint	

2. What is the narrator's attitude to:
   ◆ Mrs Mooney?
   ◆ Mr Doran?
   ◆ Polly?

Themes

1. The critic Hugh Kenner has claimed that "Two Gallants" is paired with "The Boarding House", because both are stories of 'cynical put-up jobs', that is to say deliberate acts of fraud and coercion. Compare and contrast the two stories in the light of this similarity.

2. What is the role of the Catholic Church in this story?

3. Discuss the references to prostitution in the story.

4. Look at the section of the introduction entitled 'Organisation'. Does anything seem odd about the placement of "Two Gallants" and "The Boarding House" in the category 'Stories of adolescence'?

A Little Cloud

A LITTLE CLOUD [1]

EIGHT YEARS before he had seen his friend
off at the North Wall and wished him
godspeed.[2] Gallaher had got on.[3] You could
tell that at once by his travelled air, his
well-cut tweed suit, and fearless accent.
Few fellows had talents like his and fewer still could
remain unspoiled by such success. Gallaher's heart
was in the right place and he had deserved to win. It
was something to have a friend like that.

Little Chandler's[4] thoughts ever since lunch-time
had been of his meeting with Gallaher, of Gallaher's
invitation and of the great city London where

---

1. *A Little Cloud* : in the Bible (I Kings 18:44), the little cloud
   in question puts an end a long period without rain (drought).
   Here however, the presence of Gallaher seems to form a little
   cloud over Little Chandler's life.
2. *godspeed* : a good journey (from "God speed you", an
   expression of goodwill to a departing person).
3. *got on* : made a successful career for himself.
4. *Little Chandler* : everything about him seems to be little.
   Notice the physical description of him.

Gallaher lived. He was called Little Chandler because, though he was but slightly under the average stature, he gave one the idea of being a little man. His hands were white and small, his frame was fragile, his voice was quiet and his manners were refined. He took the greatest care of his fair silken hair and moustache and used perfume discreetly on his handkerchief. The half-moons of his nails were perfect and when he smiled you caught a glimpse of[1] a row of childish white teeth.

As he sat at his desk in the King's Inns he thought what changes those eight years had brought. The friend whom he had known under a shabby[2] and necessitous guise had become a brilliant figure on the London Press. He turned often from his tiresome writing to gaze out of the office window. The glow of a late autumn sunset covered the grass plots and walks. It cast a shower of kindly golden dust on the untidy nurses and decrepit old men who drowsed[3] on the benches; it flickered[4] upon all the moving figures – on the children who ran screaming along the gravel paths[5] and on everyone who passed through the gardens. He watched the scene and thought of life; and (as always happened when he thought of life) he became sad. A gentle melancholy took possession of him. He felt how useless it was to struggle against fortune, this being the burden[6] of wisdom which the

1. *caught a glimpse of* : saw briefly.
2. *shabby* [ˈʃæbi] : poorly dressed.
3. *drowsed* [draʊzd] : were half asleep.
4. *flickered* [ˈflɪkəd] : moved backwards and forwards quickly.
5. *gravel paths* : paths made of small smooth stones.
6. *burden* : heavy weight.

Drawing of the King's Inns.

Henrietta St.

ages had bequeathed to him.

He remembered the books of poetry upon his shelves at home. He had bought them in his bachelor days and many an evening, as he sat in the little room off the hall, he had been tempted to take one down from the bookshelf and read out something to his wife. But shyness had always held him back; and so the books had remained on their shelves. At times he repeated lines to himself and this consoled him.

When his hour had struck[1] he stood up and took leave of his desk and of his fellow-clerks punctiliously. He emerged from under the feudal arch of the King's Inns, a neat[2] modest figure, and walked swiftly down Henrietta Street. The golden sunset was waning[3] and the air had grown sharp. A horde[4] of grimy children populated the street. They stood or ran in the roadway or crawled[5] up the steps before the gaping[6] doors or squatted[7] like mice upon the thresholds.[8] Little Chandler gave them no thought. He picked his way deftly[9] through all that minute vermin-like life and under the shadow of the gaunt[10] spectral mansions in which the old nobility

1. *his hour had struck* : the time for him to stop work had come.
2. *neat* : smart, elegantly dressed.
3. *waning* : becoming less bright – i.e. the sun was going down.
4. *horde* : a large group.
5. *crawled* : moved on their hands and knees.
6. *gaping* : wide open.
7. *squatted* ['skwɒtɪd] : sat with their legs drawn fully under the body and balancing their weight on the front of the feet.
8. *thresholds* ['θreʃhəʊldz] : the bottoms of the doorways.
9. *picked his way deftly* : moved skillfully through.
10. *gaunt* [gɔːnt] : excessively narrow.

of Dublin had roistered.[1] No memory of the past touched him, for his mind was full of a present joy.

He had never been in Corless's but he knew the value of the name. He knew that people went there after the theatre to eat oysters and drink liqueurs; and he had heard that the waiters there spoke French and German. Walking swiftly by at night he had seen cabs drawn up before the door and richly dressed ladies, escorted by cavaliers, alight[2] and enter quickly. They wore noisy dresses and many wraps. Their faces were powdered and they caught up[3] their dresses, when they touched earth, like alarmed Atalantas.[4] He had always passed without turning his head to look. It was his habit to walk swiftly in the street even by day and whenever he found himself in the city late at night he hurried on his way apprehensively and excitedly. Sometimes, however, he courted the causes of his fear. He chose the darkest and narrowest streets and, as he walked boldly[5] forward, the silence that was spread about his footsteps troubled him, the wandering silent figures troubled him; and at times a sound of low fugitive laughter made him tremble like a leaf.

1. *roistered* ['rɔɪstəd] : enjoyed themselves noisily.
2. *alight* [ə'laɪt] : get down from (usually a vehicle like a carriage or train).
3. *caught up* : lifted.
4. *alarmed Atalantas* : a beautiful princess and huntress in Greek mythology who refused to marry anyone who could not beat her in a running race and killed all suitors who could not run faster than her. Hippomenes distracted and frightened ("alarmed") her during a race by dropping golden apples in front of her, and in this way he won the race and married her. Atalantas is usually portrayed holding her dress up as she runs.
5. *boldly* [bəʊldli] : confidently.

He turned to the right towards Capel Street. Ignatius Gallaher on the London Press! Who would have thought it possible eight years before? Still, now that he reviewed the past, Little Chandler could remember many signs of future greatness in his friend. People used to say that Ignatius Gallaher was wild.[1] Of course, he did mix with a rakish[2] set of fellows at that time, drank freely and borrowed money on all sides. In the end he had got mixed up in some shady[3] affair, some money transaction: at least, that was one version of his flight. But nobody denied him talent. There was always a certain . . . something in Ignatius Gallaher that impressed you in spite of yourself. Even when he was out at elbows and at his wits' end[4] for money he kept up a bold face. Little Chandler remembered (and the remembrance brought a slight flush[5] of pride to his cheek) one of Ignatius Gallaher's sayings when he was in a tight corner:[6]

—Half time,[7] now, boys, he used to say light-heartedly. Where's my considering cap?[8]

That was Ignatius Gallaher all out;[9] and, damn

---

1. *wild* : unrestrained and dissolute.
2. *rakish* ['reɪkɪʃ] : fashionable and stylish but also dissolute.
3. *shady* : suspicious.
4. *out at elbows* ['elbəʊz] ... *end* : very poor and did not know what to do.
5. *flush* [flʌʃ] : a sudden emotion causing the blood to go to the face (the cheeks).
6. *in a tight corner* : in a difficult position.
7. *Half time* : the period for rest and discussion of tactics between the two halves of a football match.
8. *Where's my considering cap?* : "Let me think".
9. *That was ... all out* : That was typical of Gallaher.

it, you couldn't but admire him for it.

Little Chandler quickened his pace. For the first time in his life he felt himself superior to the people he passed. For the first time his soul revolted against the dull inelegance of Capel Street. There was no doubt about it: if you wanted to succeed you had to go away. You could do nothing in Dublin. As he crossed Grattan Bridge he looked down the river towards the lower quays[1] and pitied the poor stunted [2] houses. They seemed to him a band of tramps,[3] huddled[4] together along the river-banks, their old coats covered with dust and soot, stupefied by the panorama of sunset and waiting for the first chill of night to bid them arise, shake themselves and begone. He wondered whether he could write a poem to express his idea. Perhaps Gallaher might be able to get it into some London paper for him. Could he write something original? He was not sure what idea he wished to express but the thought that a poetic moment had touched him took life[5] within him like an infant hope. He stepped onward bravely.

Every step brought him nearer to London,[6] farther from his own sober[7] inartistic life. A light began to tremble on the horizon of his mind. He was not so

1. *quays* [kiːz] : artificial structures built into the water for loading and unloading ships.
2. *stunted* ['stʌntɪd]: low-built.
3. *tramps* : vagrants or beggars without a home.
4. *huddled* ['hʌdld] : very close together in a disorderly confused group.
5. *took life* : came to life.
6. *nearer to London* : and thus to the centre of culture and life, as opposed to the dreary provinciality of Dublin.
7. *sober* ['səʊbər]: serious, quiet and without excitement.

old – thirty-two. His temperament might be said to be just at the point of maturity. There were so many different moods and impressions that he wished to express in verse. He felt them within him. He tried to weigh his soul to see if it was a poet's soul. Melancholy was the dominant note of his temperament, he thought, but it was a melancholy tempered [1] by recurrences of faith and resignation and simple joy. If he could give expression to it in a book of poems perhaps men would listen. He would never be popular: he saw that. He could not sway [2] the crowd but he might appeal to a little circle of kindred minds. [3] The English critics, perhaps, would recognise him as one of the Celtic school [4] by reason of the melancholy tone of his poems; besides that, he would put in allusions. He began to invent sentences and phrases from the notices which his book would get. *Mr Chandler has the gift of easy and graceful verse. . . . A wistful sadness* [5] *pervades these poems. . . . The Celtic note.* It was a pity his name was not more Irish-looking. Perhaps it would be better to insert his mother's name before the surname: Thomas Malone Chandler, or better still: T. Malone Chandler. He would speak to Gallaher about it.

He pursued his revery [6] so ardently that he passed

---

1. *tempered* ['tempəd] *by* : mixed with and restrained by.
2. *sway* [sweɪ] : control or exert influence over.
3. *kindred minds* : people who thought in the same way.
4. *the Celtic* ['keltɪk] *school* : the Irish Revival of the late 19th and early 20th century. Joyce regarded this movement as provincial and refused to have anything to do with it.
5. *wistful* ['wistfl] *sadness* : sad, vague feeling of nostalgia for something which is past or unobtainable.
6. *revery* : (modern English = "reverie"). See note 4, p. 17.

his street and had to turn back. As he came near
Corless's his former agitation began to overmaster[1]
him and he halted before the door in indecision.
Finally he opened the door and entered.

The light and noise of the bar held him at the
doorway for a few moments. He looked about him,
but his sight was confused by the shining of many
red and green wine-glasses. The bar seemed to him
to be full of people and he felt that the people were
observing him curiously. He glanced quickly to right
and left (frowning[2] slightly to make his errand[3]
appear serious), but when his sight cleared a little
he saw that nobody had turned to look at him: and
there, sure enough, was Ignatius Gallaher leaning[4]
with his back against the counter and his feet
planted far apart.

—Hallo, Tommy, old hero, here you are! What is
it to be? What will you have? I'm taking whisky:
better stuff than we get across the water. Soda?
Lithia?[5] No mineral? I'm the same. Spoils the
flavour. . . . Here, *garçon*, bring us two halves of malt
whisky, like a good fellow. . . . Well, and how have
you been pulling along since I saw you last? Dear
God, how old we're getting! Do you see any signs of
aging in me – eh, what? A little grey and thin on the
top[6] – what?

---

1. *overmaster* [ˌəʊvəˈmɑːstə] : take control of.
2. *frowning* : see note 4, p. 16.
3. *errand* [ˈerənd] : short journey usually with a specific
   purpose, e.g. to carry a message, get or deliver something.
4. *leaning* [ˈliːnɪŋ]: resting the weight of his body.
5. *Lithia* : bottled mineral water.
6. *thin on the top* : with not very much hair (i.e. he was losing
   his hair).

Ignatius Gallaher took off his hat and displayed a large closely cropped head. His face was heavy, pale and clean-shaven.[1] His eyes, which were of bluish slate-colour, relieved his unhealthy pallor[2] and shone out plainly above the vivid orange tie[3] he wore. Between these rival features the lips appeared very long and shapeless and colourless. He bent his head and felt with two sympathetic fingers the thin hair at the crown. Little Chandler shook his head as a denial. Ignatius Gallaher put on his hat again.

—It pulls you down, he said, Press life. Always hurry and scurry,[4] looking for copy[5] and sometimes not finding it: and then, always to have something new in your stuff. Damn proofs[6] and printers, I say, for a few days. I'm deuced glad, I can tell you, to get back to the old country. Does a fellow good, a bit of a holiday. I feel a ton better[7] since I landed again in dear dirty Dublin. . . . Here you are, Tommy. Water? Say when.[8]

Little Chandler allowed his whisky to be very much diluted.

—You don't know what's good for you, my boy,

---

1. *clean-shaven* [ˌkliːnˈʃeɪvən]: without a beard or moustache.
2. *pallor* [ˈpælər] : unusually pale or colourless complexion.
3. *orange tie* : orange is the traditional colour of Irish Protestants, of English and Scottish descent.
4. *hurry and scurry* [ˈskʌri] : very busy.
5. *copy* [ˈkɑpi] : texts (but here, events and stories which could be written about and printed in the newspaper).
6. *proofs* [ˈpruːfs]: printed texts wihich still have to be checked for mistakes before the final version is printed.
7. *a ton better* [ˈbetə] (coll.) : much better.
8. *Say when* [wen] : "Tell me when to stop [pouring the water]" – a common colloquial phrase.

said Ignatius Gallaher. I drink mine neat.[1]

—I drink very little as a rule, said Little Chandler modestly. An odd half-one or so when I meet any of the old crowd: that's all.

—Ah, well, said Ignatius Gallaher, cheerfully, here's to us and to old times and old acquaintance.

They clinked glasses and drank the toast.

—I met some of the old gang to-day, said Ignatius Gallaher. O'Hara seems to be in a bad way. What's he doing?

—Nothing, said Little Chandler. He's gone to the dogs.[2]

—But Hogan has a good sit,[3] hasn't he?

—Yes; he's in the Land Commission.[4]

—I met him one night in London and he seemed to be very flush.[5] . . . Poor O'Hara! Boose,[6] I suppose?

—Other things, too, said Little Chandler shortly.

Ignatius Gallaher laughed.

—Tommy, he said, I see you haven't changed an atom. You're the very same serious person that used to lecture me on Sunday mornings when I had a sore head and a fur on my tongue.[7] You'd want to knock about a bit in the world.[8] Have you never been

---

1. *neat* [niːt] : undiluted, without ice or water.
2. *gone to the dogs* : deteriorated, degenerated.
3. *a good sit* : a good job.
4. *the Land Commission* : a court which managed the transfer of farm lands from landlords to tenants, with the help of British credit.
5. *be very flush* [flʌʃ] : have a lot of money.
6. *Boose* [buːz] (slang): alcoholic drink.
7. *a fur on my tongue* : an unpleasant feeling on my tongue (which implies that he had drunk too much the night before).
8. *You'd want to ... world* : "You should go and see some life in the world outside."

anywhere, even for a trip?

—I've been to the Isle of Man, said Little
Chandler.

Ignatius Gallaher laughed.

—The Isle of Man! he said. Go to London or Paris:
Paris, for choice. That'd do you good.

—Have you seen Paris?

—I should think I have! I've knocked about there
a little.

—And is it really so beautiful as they say? asked
Little Chandler.

He sipped a little of his drink while Ignatius
Gallaher finished his boldly.

—Beautiful? said Ignatius Gallaher, pausing on
the word and on the flavour of his drink. It's not so
beautiful, you know. Of course, it is beautiful. . . .
But it's the life of Paris; that's the thing. Ah, there's
no city like Paris for gaiety, movement,
excitement. . . .

Little Chandler finished his whisky and, after
some trouble, succeeded in catching the barman's
eye.[1] He ordered the same again.

—I've been to the Moulin Rouge,[2] Ignatius
Gallaher continued when the barman had removed
their glasses, and I've been to all the Bohemian
cafés.[3] Hot stuff! Not for a pious chap like you,
Tommy.

Little Chandler said nothing until the barman

---

1. *catching the barman's eye* : attracting the attention of the
barman.
2. *Moulin Rouge* [muːˌlɛ̃ 'ruːʒ] : a famous Parisian night club.
3. *Bohemian cafés* : contrast the implications of this with the
much less exciting holidays taken by Little Chandler on the
Isle of Man.

Moulin Rouge.

The pier at Douglas, in the Isle of Man.

returned with the two glasses: then he touched his friend's glass lightly and reciprocated the former toast. He was beginning to feel somewhat disillusioned. Gallaher's accent and way of expressing himself did not please him. There was something vulgar in his friend which he had not observed before. But perhaps it was only the result of living in London amid the bustle [1] and competition of the Press. The old personal charm was still there under this new gaudy [2] manner. And, after all, Gallaher had lived, he had seen the world. Little Chandler looked at his friend enviously.

—Everything in Paris is gay, said Ignatius Gallaher. They believe in enjoying life – and don't you think they're right? If you want to enjoy yourself properly you must go to Paris. And, mind you, they've a great feeling for the Irish there. When they heard I was from Ireland they were ready to eat me, man.

Little Chandler took four or five sips from his glass.

—Tell me, he said, is it true that Paris is so . . . immoral as they say?

Ignatius Gallaher made a catholic gesture with his right arm.

—Every place is immoral, he said. Of course you do find spicy bits [3] in Paris. Go to one of the students' balls, for instance. That's lively, if you like, when the *cocottes* [4] begin to let themselves loose. You know

---

1. *bustle* [bʌsl] : excited activity.
2. *gaudy* ['gɔːdi] : excessively showy.
3. *spicy bits* [bɪts] : sexually liberated women.
4. *cocottes* [kɒ'kɒts] : French slang for "prostitutes".

what they are, I suppose?

—I've heard of them, said Little Chandler.

Ignatius Gallaher drank off[1] his whisky and shook his head.

—Ah, he said, you may say what you like. There's no woman like the Parisienne – for style, for go.[2]

—Then it is an immoral city, said Little Chandler, with timid insistence – I mean, compared with London or Dublin?

—London! said Ignatius Gallaher. It's six of one and half-a-dozen of the other. You ask Hogan, my boy. I showed him a bit about London when he was over there. He'd open your eye. . . . I say, Tommy, don't make punch of that whisky: liquor up.[3]

—No, really. . . .

—O, come on, another one won't do you any harm.[4] What is it? The same again, I suppose?

—Well . . . all right.

—*François,*[5] the same again. . . . Will you smoke,[6] Tommy?

Ignatius Gallaher produced his cigar-case. The two friends lit their cigars and puffed[7] at them in silence until their drinks were served.

—I'll tell you my opinion, said Ignatius Gallaher, emerging after some time from the clouds of smoke

---

1. *drank off* : finished.
2. *for go* : for sexual adventurousness.
3. *don't make punch ... up* : don't put water in the whisky: make it strong.
4. *do you any harm* [ha:m] : will not be bad for you.
5. *François* : French for "Francis".
6. *Will you smoke ...?* : Dubliners often use "Will you ...?" where the English would use "Would you like to ...?"
7. *puffed* : see note 6, p. 4.

in which he had taken refuge, it's a rum world.[1] Talk
of immorality! I've heard of cases – what am I
saying? – I've known them: cases of ...
immorality. ...

Ignatius Gallaher puffed thoughtfully at his cigar
and then, in a calm historian's tone, he proceeded to
sketch [2] for his friend some pictures of the corruption
which was rife [3] abroad. He summarised the vices of
many capitals and seemed inclined to award the
palm to Berlin. Some things he could not vouch for [4]
(his friends had told him), but of others he had had
personal experience. He spared [5] neither rank nor
caste. He revealed many of the secrets of religious
houses on the Continent and described some of the
practices which were fashionable in high society and
ended by telling, with details, a story about an
English duchess – a story which he knew to be true.
Little Chandler was astonished.

—Ah, well, said Ignatius Gallaher, here we are in
old jog-along [6] Dublin where nothing is known of such
things.

—How dull [7] you must find it, said Little
Chandler, after all the other places you've seen!

—Well, said Ignatius Gallaher, it's a relaxation to
come over here, you know. And, after all, it's the old
country, as they say, isn't it? You can't help having

---

1. *a rum world* : a strange world.
2. *sketch* : give a simple outline.
3. *rife* [raɪf] : very common, prevailing.
4. *vouch* [vaʊtʃ] *for* : confirm the truth of.
5. *spared* [speəd] : abstain from (commenting on).
6. *jog-along* ['dʒɒɡəlɒŋ] : with the same repetitive movement.
7. *dull* [dʌl] : uninteresting, boring.

a certain feeling for it. That's human nature. . . . But
tell me something about yourself. Hogan told me you
had . . . tasted the joys of connubial bliss. Two years
ago, wasn't it?

Little Chandler blushed[1] and smiled.

—Yes, he said. I was married last May twelve
months.[2]

—I hope it's not too late in the day to offer my best
wishes, said Ignatius Gallaher. I didn't know your
address or I'd have done so at the time.

He extended his hand, which Little Chandler took.

—Well, Tommy, he said, I wish you and yours
every joy in life, old chap, and tons of money, and
may you never die till I shoot you. And that's the
wish of a sincere friend, an old friend. You know
that?

—I know that, said Little Chandler.

—Any youngsters? said Ignatius Gallaher.

Little Chandler blushed again.

—We have one child, he said.

—Son or daughter?

—A little boy.

Ignatius Gallaher slapped[3] his friend sonorously
on the back.

—Bravo, he said, I wouldn't doubt you, Tommy.

Little Chandler smiled, looked confusedly at his
glass and bit his lower lip with three childishly white
front teeth.

—I hope you'll spend an evening with us, he said,

---

1. *blushed* ['blʌʃt]: became red in the face (through sudden
   strong emotion).
2. *last May twelve months* ['mʌnθs] : i.e almost eighteen months
   ago.
3. *slapped* ['slæpt] : hit with the hand open.

before you go back. My wife will be delighted to meet
you. We can have a little music and –

—Thanks awfully,[1] old chap, said Ignatius
Gallaher, I'm sorry we didn't meet earlier. But I
must leave to-morrow night.

—To-night, perhaps . . .?

—I'm awfully sorry, old man. You see I'm over
here with another fellow, clever young chap he is too,
and we arranged to go to a little card-party. Only for
that . . .

—O, in that case. . . .

—But who knows? said Ignatius Gallaher
considerately. Next year I may take a little skip[2]
over here now that I've broken the ice. It's only a
pleasure deferred.

—Very well, said Little Chandler, the next time
you come we must have an evening together. That's
agreed now, isn't it?

—Yes, that's agreed, said Ignatius Gallaher. Next
year if I come, *parole d'honneur*.[3]

—And to clinch[4] the bargain, said Little
Chandler, we'll just have one more now.

Ignatius Gallaher took out a large gold watch and
looked at it.

—Is it to be the last? he said. Because you know,
I have an a.p.[5]

—O, yes, positively, said Little Chandler.

---

1. *Thanks awfully* ['ɔːfli] : "Many thanks".
2. *skip* : (here) a quick journey.
3. *parole d'honneur* : French for "word of honour".
4. *clinch* ['klɪntʃ]: finalise, confirm.
5. *an a.p.* : either i) an author's proof (see note 6, p. 114), or
   possibly ii) an abbreviation for "appointment" (obsolete).

—Very well, then, said Ignatius Gallaher, let us have another one as a *deoc an doruis* [1] – that's good vernacular for a small whisky, I believe.

Little Chandler ordered the drinks. The blush which had risen to his face a few moments before was establishing itself. A trifle [2] made him blush at any time: and now he felt warm and excited. Three small whiskies had gone to his head and Gallaher's strong cigar had confused his mind, for he was a delicate and abstinent person. The adventure of meeting Gallaher after eight years, of finding himself with Gallaher in Corless's surrounded by lights and noise, of listening to Gallaher's stories and of sharing for a brief space Gallaher's vagrant and triumphant life, upset the equipoise [3] of his sensitive nature. He felt acutely the contrast between his own life and his friend's, and it seemed to him unjust. Gallaher was his inferior in birth and education. He was sure that he could do something better than his friend had ever done, or could ever do, something higher than mere tawdry [4] journalism if he only got the chance. What was it that stood in his way? His unfortunate timidity! He wished to vindicate himself in some way, to assert his manhood. He saw behind Gallaher's refusal of his invitation. Gallaher was only patronising him [5] by his friendliness just as he was patronising Ireland by his visit.

The barman brought their drinks. Little Chandler

1. *deoc an doruis* : Irish for "one for the road", literally the last drink before leaving.
2. *trifle* ['traɪfl] : a cause or circumstance of small importance.
3. *equipoise* : balance.
4. *tawdry* ['tɔːdri] : showy but cheap and vulgar.
5. *patronising him* : being condescending to him.

pushed one glass towards his friend and took up the other boldly.

—Who knows? he said, as they lifted their glasses. When you come next year I may have the pleasure of wishing long life and happiness to Mr and Mrs Ignatius Gallaher.

Ignatius Gallaher in the act of drinking closed one eye expressively over the rim of his glass. When he had drunk he smacked his lips [1] decisively, set down his glass and said:

—No blooming fear [2] of that, my boy. I'm going to have my fling [3] first and see a bit of life and the world before I put my head in the sack – if I ever do.

—Some day you will, said Little Chandler calmly.

Ignatius Gallaher turned his orange tie and slate-blue eyes full upon his friend.

—You think so? he said.

—You'll put your head in the sack, repeated Little Chandler stoutly, [4] like everyone else if you can find the girl.

He had slightly emphasised his tone and he was aware that he had betrayed himself; but, though the colour had heightened in his cheek, he did not flinch [5] from his friend's gaze. Ignatius Gallaher watched him for a few moments and then said:

—If ever it occurs, you may bet your bottom dollar[6]

---

1. *smacked his lips* [lɪps]: made a sound with his lips (to express appreciation of the taste of the beer).
2. *No blooming fear* [fɪər] (coll.) : "There is absolutely no possiblility ...!".
3. *I'm going to have my fling* : I intend to enjoy myself.
4. *stoutly* ['staʊtli] : with resolve, with certainty.
5. *flinch* ['flɪntʃ] : (here) take his eyes away from.
6. *bet your bottom dollar* : be certain.

there'll be no mooning and spooning[1] about it. I
mean to marry money. She'll have a good fat account
at the bank or she won't do for me.

Little Chandler shook his head.

—Why, man alive, said Ignatius Gallaher,
vehemently, do you know what it is? I've only to say
the word and to-morrow I can have the woman and
the cash. You don't believe it? Well, I know it. There
are hundreds – what am I saying? – thousands of rich
Germans and Jews, rotten with money, that'd only
be too glad. . . . You wait a while, my boy. See if I
don't play my cards properly. When I go about[2] a
thing I mean business, I tell you. You just wait.

He tossed[3] his glass to his mouth, finished his
drink and laughed loudly. Then he looked
thoughtfully before him and said in a calmer tone:

—But I'm in no hurry. They can wait. I don't fancy
tying myself up to one woman,[4] you know.

He imitated with his mouth the act of tasting and
made a wry face.[5]

—Must get a bit stale,[6] I should think, he said.

.   .   .   .

Little Chandler sat in the room off the hall,
holding a child in his arms. To save money they kept
no servant but Annie's young sister Monica came for

1. *mooning and spooning* : wasting time on romance.
2. *go about* : start to do.
3. *tossed* : moved [his glass] quickly and lightly upwards.
4. *I don't fancy ... woman* : "I don't like the idea of being
   permanently attached to one woman."
5. *wry face* [feɪs] : an expression of disappointment or something
   unpleasant.
6. *stale* ['steɪl] : no longer fresh, insipid (usually used of food).

an hour or so in the morning and an hour or so in the evening to help. But Monica had gone home long ago. It was a quarter to nine. Little Chandler had come home late for tea and, moreover, he had forgotten to bring Annie home the parcel of coffee from Bewley's.[1] Of course she was in a bad humour and gave him short answers. She said she would do without any tea but when it came near the time at which the shop at the corner closed she decided to go out herself for a quarter of a pound of tea and two pounds of sugar. She put the sleeping child deftly[2] in his arms and said:

—Here. Don't waken him.

A little lamp with a white china shade stood upon the table and its light fell over a photograph which was enclosed in a frame of crumpled[3] horn. It was Annie's photograph. Little Chandler looked at it, pausing at the thin tight lips. She wore the pale blue summer blouse which he had brought her home as a present one Saturday. It had cost him ten and elevenpence; but what an agony of nervousness it had cost him! How he had suffered that day, waiting at the shop door until the shop was empty, standing at the counter and trying to appear at his ease while the girl piled[4] ladies' blouses before him, paying at the desk and forgetting to take up the odd penny of his change, being called back by the cashier, and, finally, striving[5] to hide his blushes as he left the

---

1. *Bewley's* : famous coffee shops in central Dublin.
2. *deftly* : with great ability.
3. *crumpled* ['krʌmpld] : not smooth, creased.
4. *piled* [paɪld] : put together in a large heap, amassed.
5. *striving* ['straɪvɪŋ] : trying very hard.

A 'little lamp' on Grattan Bridge.

Grattan Bridge.

shop by examining the parcel to see if it was securely tied. When he brought the blouse home Annie kissed him and said it was very pretty and stylish; but when she heard the price she threw the blouse on the table and said it was a regular swindle [1] to charge ten and elevenpence for that. At first she wanted to take it back but when she tried it on she was delighted with it, especially with the make [2] of the sleeves, and kissed him and said he was very good to think of her. Hm! . . .

He looked coldly into the eyes of the photograph and they answered coldly. Certainly they were pretty and the face itself was pretty. But he found something mean [3] in it. Why was it so unconscious and lady-like? The composure of the eyes irritated him. They repelled him and defied him: there was no passion in them, no rapture. [4] He thought of what Gallaher had said about rich Jewesses. Those dark Oriental eyes, he thought, how full they are of passion, of voluptuous longing! [5] . . . Why had he married the eyes in the photograph?

He caught himself up at the question [6] and glanced nervously round the room. He found something mean in the pretty furniture which he had bought for his house on the hire system. [7] Annie had chosen it herself and it reminded him of her. It too was

---

1. *a regular swindle* ['swɪndl] : a totally dishonest deception.
2. *the make* : the cut, the model.
3. *mean* : ungenerous and small-minded.
4. *rapture* ['ræptʃə]: ecstatic delight.
5. *longing* : wishing strongly for something.
6. *caught himself up at the question* : suddenly felt surprise and guilt that he was asking himself the question.
7. *on the hire system* : by paying in instalments.

prim [1] and pretty. A dull resentment against his life awoke within him. Could he not escape from his little house? Was it too late for him to try to live bravely [2] like Gallaher? Could he go to London? There was the furniture still to be paid for. If he could only write a book and get it published, that might open the way for him.

A volume of Byron's poems lay before him on the table. He opened it cautiously with his left hand lest [3] he should waken the child and began to read the first poem in the book:

> Hushed are the winds [4] and still the evening gloom,
> Not e'en a Zephyr wanders through the grove,
> Whilst I return to view my Margaret's tomb
> And scatter flowers on the dust I love.

He paused. He felt the rhythm of the verse about him in the room. How melancholy it was! Could he, too, write like that, express the melancholy of his soul in verse? There were so many things he wanted to describe: his sensation of a few hours before on Grattan Bridge, for example. If he could get back again into that mood. . . .

The child awoke and began to cry. He turned from the page and tried to hush [5] it: but it would not be hushed. He began to rock it to and fro in his arms

---

1. *prim* : formal and precise.
2. *bravely* ['breɪvli]: corageously and adventurously.
3. *lest* (archaic) : to prevent any possibility that.
4. *Hushed are the winds* : the first stanza of Byron's "On the Death of a Young Lady, Cousin of the Author and Very Dear to Him" (1802).
5. *hush* : make quiet and calm.

but its wailing cry grew keener.[1] He rocked it faster
while his eyes began to read the second stanza:

> *Within this narrow cell reclines her clay,*
> *That clay where once . . .*

It was useless. He couldn't read. He couldn't do
anything. The wailing of the child pierced the drum[2]
of his ear. It was useless, useless! He was a prisoner
for life. His arms trembled with anger and suddenly
bending to the child's face he shouted:

—Stop!

The child stopped for an instant, had a spasm of
fright and began to scream. He jumped up from his
chair and walked hastily up and down the room with
the child in his arms. It began to sob piteously, losing
its breath for four or five seconds, and then bursting
out anew.[3] The thin walls of the room echoed the
sound. He tried to soothe[4] it but it sobbed more
convulsively. He looked at the contracted and
quivering[5] face of the child and began to be
alarmed. [6] He counted seven sobs without a break
between them and caught the child to his breast in
fright. If it died! . . .

The door was burst open and a young woman ran

---

1. *its wailing* ['weɪlɪŋ] ... *keener* : its lamenting cry became
   stronger.
2. *drum* : (timpanic) membrane.
3. *bursting* ['bɜːstɪŋ] *out anew* : beginning again suddenly.
4. *soothe* [suːð] : bring to a peaceful, calm, condition.
5. *quivering* ['kwɪvərɪŋ] : shaking or trembling with a slight,
   rapid motion.
6. *alarmed* [ə'lɑːmd] : agitated with sudden fear or apprehension.

in, panting.

—What is it? What is it? she cried.

The child, hearing its mother's voice, broke out into a paroxysm of sobbing.

—It's nothing, Annie . . . it's nothing. . . . He began to cry. . . .

She flung her parcels on the floor and snatched[1] the child from him.

—What have you done to him? she cried, glaring[2] into his face.

Little Chandler sustained for one moment the gaze of her eyes and his heart closed together as he met the hatred in them. He began to stammer:

—It's nothing. . . . He . . . he began to cry. . . . I couldn't . . . I didn't do anything. . . . What?

Giving no heed to him[3] she began to walk up and down the room, clasping the child tightly in her arms and murmuring:

—My little man! My little mannie! Was 'ou frightened, love? . . . There now, love! There now! . . . Lambabaun![4] Mamma's little lamb of the world! . . . There now!

Little Chandler felt his cheeks suffused[5] with shame and he stood back out of the lamplight. He listened while the paroxysm of the child's sobbing grew less and less; and tears of remorse started to his eyes.

---

1. *snatched* : took hold of quickly.
2. *glaring* ['gleərɪŋ] : looking angrily.
3. *Giving no heed to him* : Not paying him any attention.
4. *Lambabaun* ['læmə͵bɔːn] : Irish for "lamb-child".
5. *suffused* [sə'fjuːzd]: covered, i.e. his cheeks became red.

Characters

1. Fill in the table below, placing one or more adverbs from the list opposite the character and action they describe.

angrily	shamefully	bravely	timidly	piteously
tersely	patronizingly	modestly	convulsively	tightly

CHARACTER ACTS	IN THIS MANNER (ADVERB)
Little Chandler speaks to Gallaher	
Gallaher speaks to Chandler	
Annie speaks to her husband	
Chandler thinks that Gallaher lives	
the child sobs	
Annie clasps the child	
At the end of the story, Chandler feels he has behaved	

2. Discuss the significance of Little Chandler's name in relation to the story.

3. Look at the passage on p. 118 beginning 'He was beginning to feel somewhat disillusioned' and ending 'looked at his friend enviously'. Had Gallaher's character changed over the years? If so, in what way and why?

Structure

1. The story has a three-part structure, and each part has a different setting. What are these settings?

2. How are the three parts linked together?

Narrator

1. Reread the paragraph beginning 'When his hour had struck' and ending 'a present joy' (pp. 108-9). How does the narrator establish the difference between his own perception and Little Chandler's in this paragraph?

2. '–I drink very little as a rule, said Little Chandler modestly' (p. 115): comment on the use of repetition and double meaning in this sentence.

Themes

1. 'Eight years before he had seen his friend off at the North Wall...': does this opening line remind you of anything earlier in *Dubliners*? What effect does the connection have on your reading?

2. Discuss the representation of the Celtic School of poetry, the Irish Revival, in the story.

3. What is the significance of Annie murmuring to her child 'Mamma's little lamb of the world!'?

4. What is the epiphany of this story?

CLAY

CLAY [1]

THE MATRON had given her leave [2] to go out as soon as the women's tea was over and Maria looked forward to her evening out. The kitchen was spick and span: [3] the cook said you could see yourself in the big copper boilers. The fire was nice and bright and on one of the side-tables were four very big barmbracks. [4] These barmbracks seemed uncut; but if you went closer you would see that they had been cut into long thick even slices and were ready to be handed round at tea. Maria had cut them herself.

Maria was a very, very small person indeed but

---

1. *Clay* : symbolic of death and burial.
2. *The matron had given her leave* : the woman in charge had given her permission.
3. *spick and span* : extremely clean and tidy.
4. *barmbracks* ['bɑːmbræks]: speckled buns containing currants, usually eaten at Halloween (31 October), which is when the story takes place.

she had a very long nose and a very long chin. She talked a little through her nose, always soothingly: [1] *Yes, my dear*, and *No, my dear*. She was always sent for when the women quarrelled over their tubs [2] and always succeeded in making peace. One day the matron had said to her:

—Maria, you are a veritable peace-maker! [3]

And the sub-matron and two of the Board ladies [4] had heard the compliment. And Ginger Mooney was always saying what she wouldn't do to the dummy [5] who had charge of the irons if it wasn't for Maria. Every one was so fond of Maria.

The women would have their tea at six o'clock and she would be able to get away before seven. From Ballsbridge [6] to the Pillar, [7] twenty minutes; from the Pillar to Drumcondra, twenty minutes; and twenty minutes to buy the things. She would be there before eight. She took out her purse with the silver clasps and read again the words *A Present from Belfast*. [8] She was very fond of that purse because Joe had brought it to her five years before when he and Alphy

---

1. *soothingly* ['suːðɪŋli] : in a way intended to calm.

2. *tubs* [tʌbz]: washtubs.

3. *veritable peace-maker* : from Jesus' Sermon on the Mount (Matthew, 5:9).

4. *Board ladies* : members of the Board of Governors of the institution where Maria works.

5. *dummy* ['dʌmi]: a dumb person.

6. *Ballsbridge* : roughly two miles southeast of the centre of Dublin.

7. *the Pillar* : the pillar in question is Nelson's Pillar, in honour of Admiral Horatio Lord Nelson (1758-1805). It was demolished by Irish patriots in 1966, to mark the 50th anniversary of the Easter Rebellion of 1916.

8. *A Present from Belfast* : from Protestant Northern Ireland, and therefore suspect as being pro-British.

Nelson's Pillar, Sackville Street.

Horse trams.

had gone to Belfast on a Whit-Monday[1] trip. In the purse were two half-crowns[2] and some coppers. She would have five shillings clear after paying tram fare. What a nice evening they would have, all the children singing! Only she hoped that Joe wouldn't come in drunk. He was so different when he took any drink.

Often he had wanted her to go and live with them; but she would have felt herself in the way (though Joe's wife was ever so nice with her) and she had become accustomed to the life of the laundry. Joe was a good fellow. She had nursed him and Alphy too; and Joe used often say:

—Mamma is mamma but Maria is my proper mother.

After the break-up at home the boys had got her that position in the *Dublin by Lamplight*[3] laundry, and she liked it. She used to have such a bad opinion of Protestants but now she thought they were very nice people, a little quiet and serious, but still very nice people to live with. Then she had her plants in the conservatory and she liked looking after them. She had lovely ferns and wax-plants and, whenever anyone came to visit her, she always gave the visitor one or two slips[4] from her conservatory. There was

---

1. *Whit-Monday* : a bank holiday following Whit Sunday, or Pentecost.
2. *two half-crowns* : equal to 25 new pence, and a considerable sum of money at the time.
3. *Dublin by Lamplight* : this was a Protestant institution for "fallen" women, or prostitutes. It was also known as a "Magdelene institution".
4. *slips* : small pieces cut from a plant which will grow roots if treated correctly.

one thing she didn't like and that was the tracts [1] on the walls; but the matron was such a nice person to deal with, so genteel.

When the cook told her everything was ready she went into the women's room and began to pull the big bell. In a few minutes the women began to come in by twos and threes, wiping their steaming hands [2] in their petticoats and pulling down the sleeves of their blouses over their red steaming arms. They settled down [3] before their huge mugs [4] which the cook and the dummy filled up with hot tea, already mixed with milk and sugar [5] in huge tin cans. Maria superintended the distribution of the barmbrack and saw that every woman got her four slices. There was a great deal of laughing and joking during the meal. Lizzie Fleming said Maria was sure to get the ring [6] and, though Fleming had said that for so many Hallow Eves, Maria had to laugh and say she didn't want any ring or man either; and when she laughed her grey-green eyes sparkled [7] with disappointed shyness and the tip of her nose nearly met the tip of her chin. Then Ginger Mooney lifted up her mug of

1. *tracts* : Protestant tracts, or placards with Protestant exhortations.
2. *wiping* ['waɪpɪŋ] ... *hands* : rubbing their hands, which were "steaming" from contact with hot water, to dry them.
3. *settled down* : took their places and made themselves comfortable.
4. *mugs* [mʌgz] : large cylindrical cups.
5. *hot tea, ... sugar* : a vulgar way of serving tea, typical of prisons and similar institutions.
6. *ring* : the cake traditionally eaten on All Hallows' Eve (Halloween) contains a ring. Whoever gets it is supposed to get married within a year.
7. *sparkled* ['spɑːkld] : were bright and lively.

tea and proposed Maria's health while all the other
women clattered with their mugs on the table, and
said she was sorry she hadn't a sup of porter[1] to
drink it in. And Maria laughed again till the tip of
her nose nearly met the tip of her chin and till her
minute body nearly shook itself asunder[2] because
she knew that Mooney meant well[3] though, of course,
she had the notions of a common woman.

But wasn't Maria glad when the women had
finished their tea and the cook and the dummy had
begun to clear away the tea-things! She went into
her little bedroom and, remembering that the next
morning was a mass morning,[4] changed the hand of
the alarm from seven to six. Then she took off her
working skirt and her house-boots and laid her best
skirt out on the bed and her tiny dress-boots beside
the foot of the bed. She changed her blouse too and,
as she stood before the mirror, she thought of how
she used to dress for mass on Sunday morning when
she was a young girl; and she looked with quaint[5]
affection at the diminutive body which she had so
often adorned. In spite of its years she found it a nice
tidy little body.

When she got outside the streets were shining
with rain and she was glad of her old brown
raincloak. The tram was full and she had to sit on
the little stool at the end of the car, facing all the

---

1. *sup of porter* : a drop of beer.
2. *asunder* [ə'sʌndə] : into separate parts.
3. *meant well* : had good intentions.
4. *mass morning* : All Saints' Day (1 November) is a Holy Day
   of Obligation for Catholics. The Gospel in this mass is from
   the Sermon on the Mount.
5. *quaint* [kweɪnt] : attractively strange and curious.

people, with her toes barely touching the floor. She
arranged in her mind all she was going to do and
thought how much better it was to be independent
and to have your own money in your pocket. She
hoped they would have a nice evening. She was sure
they would but she could not help thinking what a
pity it was Alphy and Joe were not speaking. They
were always falling out [1] now but when they were
boys together they used to be the best of friends: but
such was life.

She got out of her tram at the Pillar and ferreted
her way quickly among the crowds. She went into
Downes's cake-shop but the shop was so full of people
that it was a long time before she could get herself
attended to. She bought a dozen of mixed penny
cakes, and at last came out of the shop laden [2] with
a big bag. Then she thought what else would she buy:
she wanted to buy something really nice. They would
be sure to have plenty of apples and nuts. It was hard
to know what to buy and all she could think of was
cake. She decided to buy some plumcake but
Downes's plumcake had not enough almond icing on
top of it so she went over to a shop in Henry Street.
Here she was a long time in suiting herself [3] and the
stylish young lady behind the counter, who was
evidently a little annoyed by her, asked her was it
wedding-cake she wanted to buy. That made Maria
blush [4] and smile at the young lady; but the young
lady took it all very seriously and finally cut a thick

---

1. *falling out* : arguing, quarreling.
2. *laden* ['leɪdn] : loaded.
3. *suiting herself* : deciding what she wanted.
4. *blush* : see note 1, p. 121.

slice of plumcake, parcelled it up and said:

—Two-and-four,[1] please.

She thought she would have to stand in the Drumcondra tram because none of the young men seemed to notice her but an elderly gentleman made room for her. He was a stout gentleman and he wore a brown hard hat; he had a square red face and a greyish moustache. Maria thought he was a colonel-looking gentleman and she reflected how much more polite he was than the young men who simply stared straight before them. The gentleman began to chat with her about Hallow Eve and the rainy weather. He supposed the bag was full of good things for the little ones and said it was only right that the youngsters should enjoy themselves while they were young. Maria agreed with him and favoured him with demure nods and hems.[2] He was very nice with her, and when she was getting out at the Canal Bridge she thanked him and bowed, and he bowed to her and raised his hat and smiled agreeably; and while she was going up along the terrace, bending her tiny head under the rain, she thought how easy it was to know a gentleman even when he has a drop taken.[3]

Everybody said: *O, here's Maria!* when she came to Joe's house. Joe was there, having come home from business, and all the children had their Sunday dresses on. There were two big girls in from next door and games were going on. Maria gave the bag

1. *two-and-four* : two shillings and four pence (roughly 12 new pence).
2. *demure nods and hems* : acknowledging and agreeing with what is said in a quiet and serious manner.
3. *when he has a drop taken* : when he has drunk a bit too much.

of cakes to the eldest boy, Alphy, to divide and Mrs Donnelly said it was too good of her to bring such a big bag of cakes and made all the children say:

—Thanks, Maria.

But Maria said she had brought something special for papa and mamma, something they would be sure to like, and she began to look for her plumcake. She tried in Downes's bag and then in the pockets of her raincloak and then on the hall-stand but nowhere could she find it. Then she asked all the children had any of them eaten it – by mistake, of course – but the children all said no and looked as if they did not like to eat cakes if they were to be accused of stealing. Everybody had a solution for the mystery and Mrs Donnelly said it was plain that Maria had left it behind her in the tram. Maria, remembering how confused the gentleman with the greyish moustache had made her, coloured with shame and vexation and disappointment. At the thought of the failure of her little surprise and of the two and fourpence she had thrown away for nothing she nearly cried outright.[1]

But Joe said it didn't matter and made her sit down by the fire. He was very nice with her. He told her all that went on in his office, repeating for her a smart answer[2] which he had made to the manager. Maria did not understand why Joe laughed so much over the answer he had made but she said that the manager must have been a very overbearing[3] person to deal with. Joe said he wasn't so bad when you

---

1. *outright* [aʊtˈraɪt] : openly.
2. *smart answer* : clever, ingenious, or witty reply.
3. *overbearing* [ˌəʊvəˈbeərɪŋ]: strong and dominating.

knew how to take him, that he was a decent sort so long as you didn't rub him the wrong way.[1] Mrs Donnelly played the piano for the children and they danced and sang. Then the two next-door girls handed round the nuts. Nobody could find the nutcrackers and Joe was nearly getting cross[2] over it and asked how did they expect Maria to crack nuts without a nutcracker. But Maria said she didn't like nuts and that they weren't to bother about[3] her. Then Joe asked would she take a bottle of stout[4] and Mrs Donnelly said there was port wine too in the house if she would prefer that. Maria said she would rather they didn't ask her to take anything: but Joe insisted.

So Maria let him have his way[5] and they sat by the fire talking over old times and Maria thought she would put in a good word for Alphy. But Joe cried that God might strike him stone dead if ever he spoke a word to his brother again and Maria said she was sorry she had mentioned the matter. Mrs Donnelly told her husband it was a great shame for him to speak that way of his own flesh and blood but Joe said that Alphy was no brother of his and there was nearly being a row on the head of it.[6] But

---

1. *so long as ... way* : as long as you knew how to treat him so that he did not become angry or irritable.
2. *getting cross* : becoming angry.
3. *bother about* [ə'baʊt] : trouble or worry about.
4. *stout* [staʊt] : strong brown beer.
5. *have his way* : do what he wanted.
6. *there was nearly ... head of it* : a heated argument ("a row") almost started because of what had been said.

Joe said he would not lose his temper on account of
the night it was[1] and asked his wife to open some
more stout. The two next-door girls had arranged
some Hallow Eve games and soon everything was
merry again. Maria was delighted to see the children
so merry and Joe and his wife in such good spirits.
The next-door girls put some saucers on the table
and then led the children up to the table, blindfold.[2]
One got the prayer-book and the other three got the
water; and when one of the next-door girls got the
ring Mrs Donnelly shook her finger at the blushing
girl as much as to say: *O, I know all about it!* They
insisted then on blindfolding Maria and leading her
up to the table to see what she would get; and, while
they were putting on the bandage, Maria laughed
and laughed again till the tip of her nose nearly met
the tip of her chin.

They led her up to the table amid laughing and
joking and she put her hand out in the air as she was
told to do. She moved her hand about here and there
in the air and descended on one of the saucers. She
felt a soft wet substance[3] with her fingers and was
surprised that nobody spoke or took off her bandage.
There was a pause for a few seconds; and then a
great deal of scuffling and whispering.[4] Somebody
said something about the garden, and at last

1. *on account of the night it was* : because it was the night before
   All Saints' Day (1 November) (see note 4, p. 142).

2. *saucers* ['sɔːsəz] ... *blindfold* ['blaɪndfəʊld] : The children
   must choose a saucer with their eyes covered ("blindfold") and
   the saucers contain objects which are thought to suggest a
   person's fate.

3. *a soft wet substance* : the clay in question.

4. *scuffling* ['skʌflɪŋ] *and whispering* ['wɪspərɪŋ] : confused
   sounds of movement and talking in a very low voice.

Mrs Donnelly said something very cross to one of the next-door girls and told her to throw it out at once: that was no play.[1] Maria understood that it was wrong that time and so she had to do it over again: and this time she got the prayer-book.

After that Mrs Donnelly played Miss McCloud's Reel[2] for the children and Joe made Maria take a glass of wine. Soon they were all quite merry again and Mrs Donnelly said Maria would enter a convent before the year was out because she had got the prayer-book. Maria had never seen Joe so nice to her as he was that night, so full of pleasant talk and reminiscences. She said they were all very good to her.

At last the children grew tired and sleepy and Joe asked Maria would she not sing some little song before she went, one of the old songs. Mrs Donnelly said *Do, please, Maria!* and so Maria had to get up and stand beside the piano. Mrs Donnelly bade[3] the children be quiet and listen to Maria's song. Then she played the prelude and said *Now, Maria!* and Maria, blushing very much, began to sing in a tiny quavering[4] voice. She sang *I Dreamt that I Dwelt*,[5] and when she came to the second verse she sang again:

> *I dreamt that I dwelt in marble halls*
> *With vassals and serfs at my side*

---

1. *that was no play* : that was not fair.
2. *Miss McCloud's Reel* : a traditional Irish fiddle tune.
3. *bade* [bæd] (bid, bade, bidden) : ordered, told.
4. *quavering* ['kweɪvərɪŋ] : shaking, trembling.
5. *I Dreamt that I Dwelt* : a tune from Balfe's "The Bohemian Girl". (see "Eveline" p. 51.)

And of all who assembled within those walls
That I was the hope and the pride.

I had riches too great to count, could boast [1]
Of a high ancestral name,
But I also dreamt, which pleased me most,
That you loved me still the same.

But no one tried to show her her mistake;[2] and when she had ended her song Joe was very much moved. He said that there was no time like the long ago and no music for him like poor old Balfe, whatever other people might say; and his eyes filled up so much with tears that he could not find what he was looking for and in the end he had to ask his wife to tell him where the corkscrew was.

1. *boast* [bəʊst] : speak of with great pride.
2. *her mistake* : Maria mistakenly repeats the first verse instead of the second.

Characters

1. 'Maria was a very, very small person indeed but she had a very long nose and a very long chin' (pp. 137-8). How does the language with which Maria is described affect the reader's impression of her physical appearance?

2. Maria's particular facial formation, with the nose and chin almost touching, is known colloquially as 'nutcrackers'. Reread the paragraph on pp. 145-6 beginning 'But Joe said' and ending 'but Joe insisted' in the light of this information. What does it tell us about Joe? What does it tell us about Maria? the narrator?

3. What social class is Maria from, and how does it affect the quality of her life as a single woman?

4. Describe Joe's character.

Settings

1. Fill in the table below.

PAGES	SCENES	SETTINGS
	the women's tea	
	Maria buys plumcake	
	Maria chats with the gentleman	
	the party	

2. Discuss the settings of "Clay" (both the physical settings and the temporal setting of Halloween).

Structure

Do you notice any links between this story and other stories in *Dubliners*?

Symbolism

1. Discuss the meaning and the symbolism of the title.

2. Does Maria's name have any symbolic significance?

Narrator

1. Reread the opening of the story, up to 'Everyone was so fond of Maria', then glance back at the openings of earlier stories. What is different about this narrative voice?

2. One important narrative technique used in the story is flashback. Find examples of flashback in the story. How do they add to our understanding of Maria's situation?

3. Compare the use of flashback in "Clay" and "Eveline".

Themes

1. What themes can you find in "Clay"?

2. Do any of these themes link the story to other stories in *Dubliners*?

3. Is there an epiphany in this story? And if so, what is revealed and to whom?

A PAINFUL CASE

A PAINFUL CASE [1]

MR JAMES DUFFY [2] lived in Chapelizod [3] because he wished to live as far as possible from the city of which he was a citizen and because he found all the other suburbs of Dublin mean, [4] modern and pretentious. He lived in an old sombre [5] house and from his windows he could look into the disused distillery or upwards along the shallow river on which Dublin is built. The lofty [6] walls of his uncarpeted room were free from pictures. He had himself bought every article of furniture in the room: a black iron bedstead, an iron washstand, four cane chairs,

1. *A Painful Case* : the painful case in question could be either the sad story of Mrs Sinico, or the sterile existence of Mr Duffy himself.
2. *DUFFY* : the Irish root of this surname ("duff") suggests darkness, dusk.
3. *Chapelizod* [ˌtʃæpl'ɪzəd] : a village three miles west of Dublin.
4. *mean* [miːn] : inferior; low in the social hierarchy.
5. *sombre* ['sɒmbər] : depressingly dark.
6. *lofty* ['lɒfti] : very high.

a clothes-rack, a coal-scuttle, a fender and irons[1] and a square table on which lay a double desk. A bookcase had been made in an alcove [2] by means of shelves of white wood. The bed was clothed with white bed-clothes and a black and scarlet rug covered the foot. A little hand-mirror hung above the washstand and during the day a white-shaded lamp stood as the sole ornament of the mantelpiece.[3] The books on the white wooden shelves were arranged from below upwards according to bulk.[4] A complete Wordsworth [5] stood at one end of the lowest shelf and a copy of the *Maynooth Catechism*,[6] sewn into the cloth cover of a notebook, stood at one end of the top shelf. Writing materials were always on the desk. In the desk lay a manuscript translation of Hauptmann's [7]

1. *a coal-scuttle,* ['skʌtl] *a fender* ['fendər] *and irons* : equipment necessary in houses where there is a coal fire: coal-scuttle – a bucket kept next to the fire and containing coal; fender – a low metal frame at the front of the fireplace to stop hot coals from falling off the fire into the room; irons – instruments (poker, tongs and shovel) used when looking after a fire.

2. *alcove* ['ælkəʊv] : recess in a wall.

3. *mantelpiece* ['mæntlpiːs] : an ornamental structure of wood, marble etc. above a fireplace.

4. *bulk* [bʌlk]: size.

5. *A complete Wordsworth* : at the beginning of the twentieth century, Wordsworth was generally regarded as a "safe" poet conforming to the authority of Church and State.

6. *Maynooth Catechism* : Maynooth is a few miles from Chapelizod and is the site of St. Patrick's College, the chief seminary in Ireland. The catechism in question was approved for use throughout Ireland.

7. *Hauptmann* : Gerhart Hauptmann (1862-1946), a German dramatist, novelist and poet.

Michael Kramer,[1] the stage directions of which were written in purple ink, and a little sheaf of papers held together by a brass pin. In these sheets a sentence was inscribed from time to time and, in an ironical moment, the headline of an advertisement for *Bile Beans*[2] had been pasted on to the first sheet. On lifting the lid of the desk a faint fragrance escaped – the fragrance of new cedarwood pencils or of a bottle of gum[3] or of an over-ripe apple[4] which might have been left there and forgotten.

Mr Duffy abhorred anything which betokened[5] physical or mental disorder. A mediæval doctor would have called him saturnine.[6] His face, which carried the entire tale of his years, was of the brown tint of Dublin streets.[7] On his long and rather large head grew dry black hair and a tawny[8] moustache did not quite cover an unamiable mouth. His cheekbones also gave his face a harsh[9] character; but there was no harshness in the eyes which, looking at the world from under their tawny eyebrows, gave the impression of a man ever alert to greet a redeeming instinct[10] in others but often disappointed. He lived

---

1. *Michael Kramer* : a play by Hauptmann, published in 1900. Kramer is a hermit who is incapable of communication.
2. *Bile Beans* : a patent medicine for bilious conditions.
3. *gum* [gʌm] : glue.
4. *over-ripe* [ˈəʊvəraɪp] *apple* : an apple which is too mature and is beginning to decay.
5. *betokened* [bɪˈtəʊkənd] : signified.
6. *saturnine* : heavy, grave, gloomy.
7. *brown tint of Dublin streets* : again one of the colours of paralysis.
8. *tawny* [ˈtɔːni] : yellow-brown.
9. *harsh* : severe, rigorous, unfeeling.
10. *redeeming instinct* [ˈɪnstɪŋkt] : part of the personality which would save people or compensate for their faults.

at a little distance from his body, regarding his own acts with doubtful side-glances. He had an odd autobiographical habit which led him to compose in his mind from time to time a short sentence about himself containing a subject in the third person and a predicate in the past tense.[1] He never gave alms [2] to beggars and walked firmly, carrying a stout hazel.[3]

He had been for many years cashier of a private bank in Baggot Street. Every morning he came in from Chapelizod by tram. At midday he went to Dan Burke's and took his lunch – a bottle of lager beer [4] and a small trayful of arrowroot biscuits.[5] At four o'clock he was set free. He dined in an eating-house in George's Street where he felt himself safe from the society of Dublin's gilded youth [6] and where there was a certain plain honesty in the bill of fare.[7] His evenings were spent either before his landlady's piano or roaming about [8] the outskirts [9] of the city. His liking for Mozart's music brought him sometimes to an opera or a concert: these were the only dissipations of his life.

1. *He had an odd autobiographical habit ... past tense* : compare this trait of Mr Duffy's with Little Chandler ("A Little Cloud").
2. *alms* [ɑːmz] : gifts of money.
3. *stout hazel* ['heɪzl] : a walking stick made from hazel wood.
4. *lager beer* ['lɑːgə 'bɪər] : a light beer.
5. *arrowroot biscuits* : oat biscuits.
6. *gilded youth* [juːθ] : young people who seemed lively, bright and attractive (like gold).
7. *bill of fare* [feə] : the menu.
8. *roaming* ['rəumɪŋ] *about* : moving without any fixed purpose.
9. *outskirts* ['autskɜːts] : periphery, the part furthest from the centre.

He had neither companions nor friends, church nor creed. He lived his spiritual life without any communion with others, visiting his relatives at Christmas and escorting them to the cemetery when they died. He performed these two social duties for old dignity's sake[1] but conceded nothing further to the conventions which regulate the civic life. He allowed himself to think that in certain circumstances he would rob his bank but, as these circumstances never arose, his life rolled out evenly[2] – an adventureless tale.

One evening he found himself sitting beside two ladies in the Rotunda. The house, thinly peopled and silent, gave distressing prophecy of failure. The lady who sat next him looked round at the deserted house once or twice and then said:

—What a pity there is such a poor house to-night! It's so hard on people[3] to have to sing to empty benches.

He took the remark as an invitation to talk. He was surprised that she seemed so little awkward.[4] While they talked he tried to fix her permanently in his memory. When he learned that the young girl beside her was her daughter he judged her to be a year or so younger than himself. Her face, which must have been handsome, had remained intelligent. It was an oval face with strongly marked features.

---

1. *for old dignity's sake* [seɪk] : out of consideration for respect and tradition.
2. *rolled out evenly* [ˈiːvnli] : was uniform, without incident.
3. *hard on people* [ˈpiːpl] : difficult to endure.
4. *so little awkward* [ˈɔːkwəd] : i.e she did not seem at all awkward, but rather relaxed and unembarrassed.

A railway station.

The Rotunda.

The eyes were very dark blue and steady.[1] Their gaze began with a defiant[2] note but was confused by what seemed a deliberate swoon[3] of the pupil into the iris, revealing for an instant a temperament of great sensibility. The pupil reasserted[4] itself quickly, this half-disclosed nature fell again under the reign of prudence, and her astrakhan jacket, moulding[5] a bosom of a certain fulness, struck the note of defiance more definitely.

He met her again a few weeks afterwards at a concert in Earlsfort Terrace and seized the moments when her daughter's attention was diverted[6] to become intimate. She alluded once or twice to her husband but her tone was not such as to make the allusion a warning. Her name was Mrs Sinico. Her husband's great-great-grandfather had come from Leghorn.[7] Her husband was captain of a mercantile boat plying[8] between Dublin and Holland; and they had one child.

Meeting her a third time by accident he found courage to make an appointment. She came. This was the first of many meetings; they met always in the evening and chose the most quiet quarters for their walks together. Mr Duffy, however, had a distaste for underhand[9] ways and, finding that they

1. *steady* ['stedi] : constant, resolute.
2. *defiant* [dɪ'faɪənt] : challenging, openly resisting.
3. *swoon* [swuːn] : condition of rapture or ecstasy.
4. *reasserted* [ˌriːə'sɜːtɪd] : affirmed again.
5. *moulding* ['məʊldɪŋ] : taking the form of.
6. *diverted* [daɪ'vɜːtɪd] : distracted, directed somewhere else.
7. *Leghorn* ['leghɔːn] : the Italian town of Livorno.
8. *plying* [plaɪɪŋ] : travelling to and from.
9. *underhand* : secret, clandestine.

were compelled to meet stealthily,[1] he forced [2] her to ask him to her house. Captain Sinico encouraged his visits, thinking that his daughter's hand was in question. He had dismissed his wife so sincerely from his gallery of pleasures that he did not suspect that anyone else would take an interest in her. As the husband was often away and the daughter out giving music lessons Mr Duffy had many opportunities of enjoying the lady's society. Neither he nor she had had any such adventure before and neither was conscious of any incongruity. Little by little he entangled[3] his thoughts with hers. He lent her books, provided her with ideas, shared his intellectual life with her. She listened to all.

Sometimes in return for his theories she gave out some fact of her own life. With almost maternal solicitude she urged him to let his nature open to the full; she became his confessor. He told her that for some time he had assisted at the meetings of an Irish Socialist Party where he had felt himself a unique figure amidst a score of sober workmen in a garret [4] lit by an inefficient oil-lamp. When the party had divided into three sections, each under its own leader and in its own garret, he had discontinued his attendances. The workmen's discussions, he said, were too timorous; the interest they took in the

---

1. *stealthily* ['stelθɪli] : secretly, so as not to be observed.
2. *forced* : obliged.
3. *entangled* [en'tæŋgld] : interlaced, closely involved in such a way that separation is difficult.
4. *garret* ['gærət] : an appartment at the top of a house, usually inhabited by poor people.

question of wages was inordinate.[1] He felt that they were hard-featured realists and that they resented an exactitude[2] which was the product of a leisure not within their reach. No social revolution, he told her, would be likely to[3] strike Dublin for some centuries.

She asked him why did he not write out his thoughts. For what, he asked her, with careful scorn.[4] To compete with phrasemongers,[5] incapable of thinking consecutively for sixty seconds? To submit himself to the criticisms of an obtuse middle class which entrusted its morality to policemen and its fine arts to impresarios?

He went often to her little cottage outside Dublin; often they spent their evenings alone. Little by little, as their thoughts entangled, they spoke of subjects less remote. Her companionship was like a warm soil about an exotic.[6] Many times she allowed the dark to fall upon them, refraining from[7] lighting the lamp. The dark discreet room, their isolation, the music that still vibrated in their ears united them. This union exalted him, wore away the rough edges[8] of his character, emotionalised his mental life.

1. *the interest ... inordinate* [ɪnˈɔːdɪnət] : they took an excessive interest in the question of pay.
2. *exactitude* [ɪgˈzæktɪtjuːd] : attention to small details.
3. *No ... would be likely to* : It was highly improbable that ... .
4. *scorn* [skɔːn] : derision, mockery.
5. *phrasemongers* [ˈfreɪzˌmʌŋgəz] : sellers of words (a derisive term for cheap journalism).
6. *an exotic* : an exotic plant.
7. *refraining* [rɪˈfreɪnɪŋ] *from* : abstaining from.
8. *wore* (wear, wore, worn) *away the rough edges* [edʒɪz] : i.e. made smoother (making his character less harsh).

Sometimes he caught himself[1] listening to the sound of his own voice. He thought that in her eyes he would ascend to an angelical stature; and, as he attached the fervent nature of his companion more and more closely to him, he heard the strange impersonal voice which he recognised as his own, insisting on the soul's incurable loneliness. We cannot give ourselves, it said: we are our own. The end of these discourses was that one night during which she had shown every sign of unusual excitement, Mrs Sinico caught up his hand[2] passionately and pressed it to her cheek.

Mr Duffy was very much surprised. Her interpretation of his words disillusioned him. He did not visit her for a week; then he wrote to her asking her to meet him. As he did not wish their last interview to be troubled by the influence of their ruined confessional they met in a little cakeshop near the Parkgate. It was cold autumn weather but in spite of the cold they wandered[3] up and down the roads of the Park for nearly three hours. They agreed to break off their intercourse: every bond,[4] he said, is a bond to sorrow. When they came out of the Park they walked in silence towards the tram; but here she began to tremble so violently that, fearing another collapse on her part, he bade her good-bye quickly and left her. A few days later he received a parcel containing his books and music.

1. *caught* [kɔːt] (catch, caught, caught) *himself* : he found himself.
2. *caught up his hand* : took his hand in her own.
3. *wandered* [ˈwɒndəd] : moved without purpose.
4. *bond* [bɒnd] : strong tie or link (here, between people).

Four years passed. Mr Duffy returned to his even way of life.[1] His room still bore witness[2] of the orderliness of his mind. Some new pieces of music encumbered[3] the music-stand in the lower room and on his shelves stood two volumes by Nietzsche: *Thus Spake Zarathustra* and *The Gay Science*. He wrote seldom in the sheaf of papers which lay in his desk. One of his sentences, written two months after his last interview with Mrs Sinico, read: Love between man and man is impossible because there must not be sexual intercourse and friendship between man and woman is impossible because there must be sexual intercourse. He kept away from concerts lest[4] he should meet her. His father died; the junior partner of the bank retired. And still every morning he went into the city by tram and every evening walked home from the city after having dined moderately in George's Street and read the evening paper for dessert.

One evening as he was about to put a morsel[5] of corned beef[6] and cabbage into his mouth his hand stopped. His eyes fixed themselves on a paragraph in the evening paper which he had propped against the water-carafe. He replaced the morsel of food on his plate and read the paragraph attentively. Then he drank a glass of water, pushed his plate to one side, doubled the paper down before him between his

---

1. *even way of life* : uniform, smooth, without incident or fluctuation.
2. *bore* (bear, bore, borne) *witness* : testified to.
3. *encumbered* [ɪnˈkʌmbəd] : filled, weighed upon.
4. *lest* [lest] : see note 3, p. 129.
5. *a morsel* [ˈmɔːsl] : a small quantity (usually referring to food).
6. *corned beef* : beef preserved in salt and often tinned.

elbows and read the paragraph over and over again. The cabbage began to deposit a cold white grease on his plate. The girl came over to him to ask was his dinner not properly cooked. He said it was very good and ate a few mouthfuls of it with difficulty. Then he paid his bill and went out.

He walked along quickly through the November twilight,[1] his stout hazel stick striking the ground regularly, the fringe of the buff *Mail*[2] peeping out of a side-pocket of his tight reefer overcoat.[3] On the lonely road which leads from the Parkgate to Chapelizod he slackened his pace.[4] His stick struck the ground less emphatically and his breath, issuing irregularly, almost with a sighing sound, condensed in the wintry air. When he reached his house he went up at once to his bedroom and, taking the paper from his pocket, read the paragraph again by the failing light[5] of the window. He read it not aloud, but moving his lips as a priest does when he reads the prayers *Secreto*.[6] This was the paragraph:

DEATH OF A LADY AT SYDNEY PARADE

A Painful Case

To-day at the City of Dublin Hospital the Deputy Coroner (in the absence of Mr Leverett) held an

---

1. *twilight* ['twaɪlaɪt] : the time between daylight and darkness when the sun is below the horizon.
2. *the buff Mail* : a right-wing, pro-English newspaper.
3. *reefer overcoat* : a double-breasted jacket of thick cloth.
4. *slackened his pace* [peɪs] : walked more slowly.
5. *failing* ['feɪlɪŋ] *light* : light which was becoming less and less.
6. *Secreto* : in a low voice (Latin: "set apart").

inquest on the body of Mrs Emily Sinico, aged forty-three years, who was killed at Sydney Parade Station yesterday evening. The evidence showed that the deceased lady, while attempting to cross the line, was knocked down by the engine of the ten o'clock slow train from Kingstown,[1] thereby sustaining injuries of the head and right side which led to her death.

James Lennon, driver of the engine, stated that he had been in the employment of the railway company for fifteen years. On hearing the guard's whistle he set the train in motion and a second or two afterwards brought it to rest in response to loud cries. The train was going slowly.

P. Dunne, railway porter, stated that as the train was about to start he observed a woman attempting to cross the lines. He ran towards her and shouted but, before he could reach her, she was caught by the buffer[2] of the engine and fell to the ground.

A juror – You saw the lady fall?

Witness – Yes.

Police Sergeant Croly deposed that when he arrived he found the deceased lying on the platform apparently dead. He had the body taken to the waiting-room pending[3] the arrival of the ambulance.

Constable 57E corroborated.

Dr Halpin, assistant house surgeon of the City of Dublin Hospital, stated that the deceased had two

1. *Kingstown* : now Dun Laoghaire.
2. *buffer* ['bʌfər] : apparatus for absorbing shock or impact at the front and back of a train.
3. *pending* : while waiting for.

lower ribs fractured and had sustained severe contusions of the right shoulder. The right side of the head had been injured in the fall. The injuries were not sufficient to have caused death in a normal person. Death, in his opinion, had been probably due to shock and sudden failure of the heart's action.

Mr H. B. Patterson Finlay, on behalf of[1] the railway company, expressed his deep regret at the accident. The company had always taken every precaution to prevent people crossing the lines except by the bridges, both by placing notices in every station and by the use of patent spring gates [2] at level crossings. The deceased had been in the habit of crossing the lines late at night from platform to platform and, in view of certain other circumstances of the case, he did not think the railway officials were to blame.[3]

Captain Sinico, of Leoville, Sydney Parade, husband of the deceased, also gave evidence. He stated that the deceased was his wife. He was not in Dublin at the time of the accident as he had arrived only that morning from Rotterdam. They had been married for twenty-two years and had lived happily until about two years ago when his wife began to be rather intemperate[4] in her habits.

Miss Mary Sinico said that of late her mother had been in the habit of going out at night to buy spirits. She, witness, had often tried to reason with her

1. *on behalf of* : speaking for.
2. *patent spring gates* : gates made to a special design and functioning by means of a spring mechanism.
3. *to blame* : guilty, responsible.
4. *intemperate in her habits* : i.e. she began to drink a lot.

mother and had induced her to join a league.[1] She was not at home until an hour after the accident.

The jury returned a verdict in accordance with the medical evidence and exonerated Lennon from all blame.

The Deputy Coroner said it was a most painful case, and expressed great sympathy with Captain Sinico and his daughter. He urged on[2] the railway company to take strong measures to prevent the possibility of similar accidents in the future. No blame attached to anyone.

Mr Duffy raised his eyes from the paper and gazed out of his window on the cheerless[3] evening landscape. The river lay quiet beside the empty distillery and from time to time a light appeared in some house on the Lucan road. What an end! The whole narrative of her death revolted him and it revolted him to think that he had ever spoken to her of what he held sacred. The threadbare[4] phrases, the inane[5] expressions of sympathy, the cautious words of a reporter won over[6] to conceal the details of a commonplace vulgar death attacked his stomach. Not merely had she degraded herself; she had degraded him. He saw the squalid tract[7] of her vice, miserable and malodorous. His soul's companion! He

1. *league* : a temperance league, or society for ex-drinkers.
2. *urged on* [ɜːdʒd] : pressed.
3. *cheerless* [ˈtʃɪələs] : without comfort, dispiriting, gloomy.
4. *threadbare* [ˈθredbeə] : overused and no longer new.
5. *inane* [ɪˈneɪn] : empty, senseless and silly.
6. *won over* : who had been persuaded.
7. *tract* : course, duration.

thought of the hobbling wretches [1] whom he had seen
carrying cans and bottles to be filled by the barman.
Just God, what an end! Evidently she had been unfit
to live, without any strength of purpose, an easy prey
to habits, one of the wrecks on which civilisation has
been reared.[2] But that she could have sunk so low!
Was it possible he had deceived himself so utterly
about her? He remembered her outburst [3] of that
night and interpreted it in a harsher sense than he
had ever done. He had no difficulty now in approving
of the course he had taken.

As the light failed and his memory began to
wander he thought her hand touched his. The shock
which had first attacked his stomach was now
attacking his nerves. He put on his overcoat and hat
quickly and went out. The cold air met him on the
threshold;[4] it crept into the sleeves of his coat. When
he came to the public-house at Chapelizod Bridge he
went in and ordered a hot punch.

The proprietor served him obsequiously but did
not venture to talk. There were five or six
working-men in the shop discussing the value of a
gentleman's estate in County Kildare. They drank at
intervals from their huge pint tumblers [5] and
smoked, spitting often on the floor and sometimes
dragging the sawdust over their spits with their
heavy boots. Mr Duffy sat on his stool and gazed at

---

1. *hobbling wretches* ['retʃɪs]: poor unfortunate people who walk
    with an uneven movement.
2. *reared* [rɪəd] : created.
3. *outburst* ['aʊtbɜːst] : violent display of emotion.
4. *threshold* ['θreʃhəʊld]: the entrance to the house.
5. *pint tumblers* ['tʌmbləz]: large glasses holding a pint of beer.

them, without seeing or hearing them. After a while
they went out and he called for another punch. He
sat a long time over it.[1] The shop was very quiet. The
proprietor sprawled[2] on the counter reading the
Herald and yawning. Now and again a tram was
heard swishing along the lonely road outside.

As he sat there, living over his life with her and
evoking alternately the two images in which he now
conceived her, he realised that she was dead, that
she had ceased to exist, that she had become a
memory. He began to feel ill at ease. He asked
himself what else could he have done. He could not
have carried on a comedy of deception with her; he
could not have lived with her openly. He had done
what seemed to him best. How was he to blame? Now
that she was gone he understood how lonely her life
must have been, sitting night after night alone in
that room. His life would be lonely too until he, too,
died, ceased to exist, became a memory – if anyone
remembered him.

It was after nine o'clock when he left the shop. The
night was cold and gloomy. He entered the park by
the first gate and walked along under the gaunt[3]
trees. He walked through the bleak alleys[4] where
they had walked four years before. She seemed to be
near him in the darkness. At moments he seemed to
feel her voice touch his ear, her hand touch his. He

---

1. *He sat a long time over it* : It took him a long time to drink
   it.
2. *sprawled* ['sprɔːld]: with his limbs stretched out widely in a
   relaxed way.
3. *gaunt* [gɔːnt] : tall, thin and angular.
4. *bleak alleys* ['ælɪz] : desolate little streets.

stood still to listen. Why had he withheld[1] life from her? Why had he sentenced her to death? He felt his moral nature falling to pieces.

When he gained the crest[2] of the Magazine Hill he halted and looked along the river towards Dublin, the lights of which burned redly and hospitably in the cold night. He looked down the slope and, at the base, in the shadow of the wall of the park, he saw some human figures lying. Those venal and furtive loves filled him with despair. He gnawed the rectitude of his life;[3] he felt that he had been outcast[4] from life's feast. One human being had seemed to love him and he had denied her life and happiness: he had sentenced her to ignominy, a death of shame. He knew that the prostrate creatures down by the wall were watching him and wished him gone. No one wanted him; he was outcast from life's feast. He turned his eyes to the grey gleaming river, winding[5] along towards Dublin. Beyond the river he saw a goods train winding out of Kingsbridge Station, like a worm with a fiery head winding through the darkness, obstinately and laboriously. It passed slowly out of sight; but still he heard in his ears the laborious drone[6] of the engine reiterating the syllables of her name.

He turned back the way he had come, the rhythm

---

1. *withheld* [wɪð'held] : denied, not allowed.
2. *gained the crest* : arrived at the top.
3. *He gnawed ... life* : He tormented himself with the rigidity of his life.
4. *outcast* ['aʊtkɑːst] : a person exiled or rejected.
5. *winding* ['waɪndɪŋ] : moving one way and then the other with a curving motion.
6. *drone* [drəʊn] : continuous deep humming sound.

of the engine pounding[1] in his ears. He began to doubt the reality of what memory told him. He halted under a tree and allowed the rhythm to die away. He could not feel her near him in the darkness nor her voice touch his ear. He waited for some minutes listening. He could hear nothing: the night was perfectly silent. He listened again: perfectly silent. He felt that he was alone.

1. *pounding* ['paʊndɪŋ] : beating heavily.

Characters

1. Which of the following nouns can be seen as referring to aspects of Mrs Sinico's character? (Find evidence in the text for each of your choices.)

stupidity	severity	intelligence	egotism	passion	torpor
defiance	cheerfulness	sensibility	rigidity	attentiveness	

2. Look at the description of Mr Duffy's home (the first paragraph of the story). What does it tell us about Mr Duffy's character?

Symbolism

1. Among the contents of Duffy's desk is 'an over-ripe apple' (p. 157). Critics have seen this as a symbol of the temptation to which Mr Duffy does not succumb. What are the religious implications of the uneaten apple?

2. How does Mrs Sinico's first remark – 'What a pity there is such a poor house tonight! It is so hard on people to have to sing to empty benches' (p. 159) – prepare the reader for her story?

3. 'Death, in his opinion, had been probably due to shock and sudden failure of the heart's action' (p. 168). What are the symbolic implications of this?

Narrator

'He felt his moral nature falling to pieces' (p. 172).
What does the narrator mean by this? And how does the 'moral
nature' of the narrator differ from that of Mr Duffy up to this
point in the story?

Themes

1. Describe the epiphany in the story.

2. Compare and contrast "Eveline" and "A Painful Case" in
   terms of their common theme of temptation.

3. 'No social revolution, he told her, would be likely to strike
   Dublin for some centuries' (p. 163): there is an irony in this
   remark of which Duffy is completely unaware. What is it?

A MOTHER

A Mother

M R HOLOHAN, assistant secretary of the *Eire Abu* Society,[1] had been walking up and down Dublin for nearly a month, with his hands and pockets full of dirty pieces of paper, arranging about the series of concerts. He had a game leg[2] and for this his friends called him Hoppy Holohan. He walked up and down constantly, stood by the hour at street corners arguing the point and made notes; but in the end it was Mrs Kearney who arranged everything.

Miss Devlin had become Mrs Kearney out of spite.[3] She had been educated in a high-class convent where she had learned French and music. As she was naturally pale and unbending[4] in manner she made

---

1. *Eire Abu Society* : a patriotic and cultural society, whose Gaelic motto meant "Ireland for Victory".
2. *game leg* : he is unable to walk well (i.e. he walks with a limp).
3. *out of spite* [spaɪt] : from a sense of injury or insult.
4. *unbending* [ˌʌnˈbendɪŋ] : severe, rigid.

few friends at school. When she came to the age of marriage she was sent out to many houses where her playing and ivory [1] manners were much admired. She sat amid the chilly circle of her accomplishments, waiting for some suitor to brave it [2] and offer her a brilliant life. But the young men whom she met were ordinary and she gave them no encouragement, trying to console her romantic desires by eating a great deal of Turkish Delight in secret. However, when she drew near the limit and her friends began to loosen their tongues about her she silenced them by marrying Mr Kearney, who was a bootmaker on Ormond Quay.

He was much older than she. His conversation, which was serious, took place at intervals in his great brown beard. After the first year of married life Mrs Kearney perceived that such a man would wear better [3] than a romantic person but she never put her own romantic ideas away. He was sober, thrifty [4] and pious; he went to the altar every first Friday,[5] sometimes with her, oftener by himself. But she never weakened in her religion and was a good wife to him. At some party in a strange house when she lifted her eyebrow ever so slightly he stood up to take his leave and, when his cough troubled him, she put

1. *ivory* ['aɪvəri]: polished but cold.
2. *brave it* : have enough courage.
3. *wear better* : last longer.
4. *thrifty* [θrɪfti] : economical, careful with expenditure.
5. *every first Friday* : Christ is supposed to have promised to Blessed Margaret Mary Alacoque (see "Eveline", p. 49) that anyone who received communion on nine consecutive Fridays would not die without the sacraments.

the eider-down quilt [1] over his feet and made a strong rum punch. For his part he was a model father. By paying a small sum every week into a society [2] he ensured for both his daughters a dowry [3] of one hundred pounds each when they came to the age of twenty-four. He sent the elder daughter, Kathleen, to a good convent, where she learned French and music and afterwards paid her fees at the Academy. [4] Every year in the month of July Mrs Kearney found occasion to say to some friend:

—My good man is packing us off [5] to Skerries for a few weeks.

If it was not Skerries it was Howth or Greystones. [6]

When the Irish Revival [7] began to be appreciable Mrs Kearney determined to take advantage of her daughter's name [8] and brought an Irish teacher to the house. Kathleen and her sister sent Irish picture postcards to their friends and these friends sent back other Irish picture postcards. On special Sundays when Mr Kearney went with his family to the

---

1. *eider-down quilt* [kwɪlt]: a warm cover filled with feathers from the Eider Duck.
2. *a society* : one of the many insurance societies offering policies for weddings, funerals etc.
3. *dowry* ['dauəri] : property or money brought by a bride to her husband.
4. *the Academy* : the Royal Academy of Music.
5. *packing us off* : sending us away.
6. *Skerries, Howth, Greystones* : fashionable seaside resorts.
7. *the Irish Revival* : see "A Little Cloud", p. 112.
8. *her daughter's name* : Kathleen is a typical Irish name. Kathleen ni Houlihan is a traditional symbol of Ireland (see Yeats' play, 'Cathleen Ni Houlihan'). Notice also that the organiser of the concerts is called Holohan.

pro-cathedral[1] a little crowd of people would assemble after mass at the corner of Cathedral Street. They were all friends of the Kearneys – musical friends or Nationalist friends; and, when they had played every little counter of[2] gossip, they shook hands with one another all together laughing at the crossing of so many hands and said good-bye to one another in Irish. Soon the name of Miss Kathleen Kearney began to be heard often on people's lips. People said that she was very clever at music and a very nice girl and, moreover, that she was a believer in the language movement. Mrs Kearney was well content at this. Therefore she was not surprised when one day Mr Holohan came to her and proposed that her daughter should be the accompanist at a series of four grand concerts which his Society was going to give in the Antient Concert Rooms. She brought him into the drawing-room, made him sit down and brought out the decanter and the silver biscuit-barrel.[3] She entered heart and soul into the details of the enterprise, advised and dissuaded; and finally a contract was drawn up by which Kathleen was to receive eight guineas for her services as accompanist at the four grand concerts.

As Mr Holohan was a novice in such delicate matters as the wording of bills and the disposing of

---

1. *pro-cathedral* : the two cathedrals in Dublin, St Patrick's and Christ Church, were taken over by the Irish (Protestant) Church. Consequently, Irish Catholics have to make do with a pro-cathedral, the Church of the Conception in Marlborough Street (see "The Boarding House", p. 91).

2. *when they had played ... counter of* : when they had exhausted all the possibilities of enjoyment to be had from.

3. *decanter ... biscuit-barrel* : glass bottle usually containing wine; a rounded container for biscuits.

'Marlborough Street', the pro-cathedral.

The way to the Antient Concert Rooms.

items for a programme Mrs Kearney helped him. She
had tact. She knew what *artistes*[1] should go into
capitals and what *artistes* should go into small type.
She knew that the first tenor would not like to come
on after Mr Meade's comic turn. To keep the
audience continually diverted she slipped the
doubtful items[2] in between the old favourites.
Mr Holohan called to see her every day to have her
advice on some point. She was invariably friendly
and advising – homely, in fact. She pushed the
decanter towards him, saying:

—Now, help yourself, Mr Holohan!

And while he was helping himself she said:

—Don't be afraid! Don't be afraid of it!

Everything went on smoothly. Mrs Kearney
bought some lovely blush-pink charmeuse[3] in Brown
Thomas's[4] to let into the front of Kathleen's dress.
It cost a pretty penny;[5] but there are occasions when
a little expense is justifiable. She took a dozen of
two-shilling tickets for the final concert and sent
them to those friends who could not be trusted to
come otherwise. She forgot nothing and, thanks to
her, everything that was to be done was done.

The concerts were to be on Wednesday, Thursday,
Friday and Saturday. When Mrs Kearney arrived
with her daughter at the Antient Concert Rooms on
Wednesday night she did not like the look of things.

---

1. *artistes* [ɑːˈtiːstz]: (see "The Boarding House", note 3, p. 86)
2. *doubtful items* : acts which she thought might not be liked by
    the public.
3. *charmeuse* [ˌʃɑːrˈmɜːz] : satin.
4. *Brown Thomas's* : an exclusive lace and linen shop.
5. *a pretty penny* : a lot of money.

A few young men, wearing bright blue badges in their coats, stood idle[1] in the vestibule; none of them wore evening dress. She passed by with her daughter and a quick glance through the open door of the hall showed her the cause of the stewards' idleness. At first she wondered had she mistaken the hour. No, it was twenty minutes to eight.

In the dressing-room behind the stage she was introduced to the secretary of the Society, Mr Fitzpatrick. She smiled and shook his hand. He was a little man with a white vacant face. She noticed that he wore his soft brown hat carelessly on the side of his head and that his accent was flat.[2] He held a programme in his hand and, while he was talking to her, he chewed one end of it into a moist pulp. He seemed to bear disappointments lightly.[3] Mr Holohan came into the dressing-room every few minutes with reports from the box-office.[4] The *artistes* talked among themselves nervously, glanced from time to time at the mirror and rolled and unrolled their music. When it was nearly half-past eight the few people in the hall began to express their desire to be entertained. Mr Fitzpatrick came in, smiled vacantly at the room, and said:

—Well now, ladies and gentlemen, I suppose we'd better open the ball.

Mrs Kearney rewarded his very flat final syllable with a quick stare[5] of contempt and then said to her

1. *idle* : without working (they were the stewards).
2. *his accent was flat* : this observation indicates Mrs Kearney's snobbery.
3. *bear ... lightly* : remain unaffected by disappointments.
4. *box-office* : the ticket office.
5. *stare* [steər] : penetrating glance.

daughter encouragingly:

—Are you ready, dear?

When she had an opportunity she called Mr Holohan aside and asked him to tell her what it meant. Mr Holohan did not know what it meant. He said that the committee had made a mistake in arranging for four concerts: four was too many.

—And the *artistes!* said Mrs Kearney. Of course they are doing their best, but really they are not good.

Mr Holohan admitted that the *artistes* were no good but the committee, he said, had decided to let the first three concerts go as they pleased[1] and reserve all the talent for Saturday night. Mrs Kearney said nothing but, as the mediocre items followed one another on the platform and the few people in the hall grew fewer and fewer, she began to regret that she had put herself to any expense for such a concert. There was something she didn't like in the look of things[2] and Mr Fitzpatrick's vacant smile irritated her very much. However, she said nothing and waited to see how it would end. The concert expired shortly before ten and every one went home quickly.

The concert on Thursday night was better attended but Mrs Kearney saw at once that the house was filled with paper.[3] The audience behaved indecorously as if the concert were an informal dress

---

1. *let ... go as they pleased* [pliːzd] : not worry about what might happen in the first three concerts.

2. *the look of things* : the way the situation appeared.

3. *the house was filled with paper* : i.e. people who had been given complimentary tickets.

rehearsal. Mr Fitzpatrick seemed to enjoy himself; he was quite unconscious that Mrs Kearney was taking angry note of his conduct. He stood at the edge of the screen, from time to time jutting out[1] his head and exchanging a laugh with two friends in the corner of the balcony. In the course of the evening Mrs Kearney learned that the Friday concert was to be abandoned and that the committee was going to move heaven and earth[2] to secure a bumper house[3] on Saturday night. When she heard this she sought out[4] Mr Holohan. She buttonholed him[5] as he was limping out quickly with a glass of lemonade for a young lady and asked him was it true. Yes, it was true.

—But, of course, that doesn't alter the contract, she said. The contract was for four concerts.

Mr Holohan seemed to be in a hurry; he advised her to speak to Mr Fitzpatrick. Mrs Kearney was now beginning to be alarmed. She called Mr Fitzpatrick away from his screen and told him that her daughter had signed for four concerts and that, of course, according to the terms of the contract, she should receive the sum originally stipulated for whether the society gave the four concerts or not. Mr Fitzpatrick, who did not catch the point at issue very quickly, seemed unable to resolve the difficulty and said that he would bring the matter before the committee. Mrs Kearney's anger began to flutter in her cheek

---

1. *jutting* [ˈdʒʌtɪŋ] *out* : suddenly pushing out.
2. *move heaven and earth* : do everything possible.
3. *a bumper house* : a very large audience.
4. *sought* [sɔːt] *out* (seek, sought, sought) : searched for and found.
5. *she buttonholed him* : detained him by talking.

and she had all she could do to keep from asking: [1]

—And who is the *Cometty*,[2] pray?

But she knew that it would not be ladylike to do that: so she was silent.

Little boys were sent out into the principal streets of Dublin early on Friday morning with bundles of handbills.[3] Special puffs [4] appeared in all the evening papers reminding the music-loving public of the treat which was in store [5] for it on the following evening. Mrs Kearney was somewhat reassured but she thought well to tell her husband part of her suspicions. He listened carefully and said that perhaps it would be better if he went with her on Saturday night. She agreed. She respected her husband in the same way as she respected the General Post Office, as something large, secure and fixed; and though she knew the small number of his talents she appreciated his abstract value as a male. She was glad that he had suggested coming with her. She thought her plans over.

The night of the grand concert came. Mrs Kearney, with her husband and daughter, arrived at the Antient Concert Rooms three-quarters of an hour before the time at which the concert was to begin. By ill luck it was a rainy evening.

---

1. *Mrs Kearney's anger ... keep from asking* : i.e she felt the blood pulsing in her face in anger and she only just succeeded in restraining herself from asking.

2. *Cometty* : Mrs Kearney is making fun of his accent.

3. *bundles of handbills* ['hændbɪlz] : a lot of publicity leaflets.

4. *puffs* : small advertisements reminding people of the event.

5. *the treat ... in store* : the special occasion which was prepared for them.

Mrs Kearney placed her daughter's clothes and
music in charge of her husband and went all over the
building looking for Mr Holohan or Mr Fitzpatrick.
She could find neither. She asked the stewards was
any member of the committee in the hall and, after
a great deal of trouble, a steward brought out a little
woman named Miss Beirne to whom Mrs Kearney
explained that she wanted to see one of the
secretaries. Miss Beirne expected them any minute
and asked could she do anything. Mrs Kearney
looked searchingly at the oldish face which was
screwed[1] into an expression of trustfulness and
enthusiasm and answered:

—No, thank you!

The little woman hoped they would have a good
house. She looked out at the rain until the
melancholy of the wet street effaced[2] all the
trustfulness and enthusiasm from her twisted
features. Then she gave a little sigh and said:

—Ah, well! We did our best, the dear knows.[3]

Mrs Kearney had to go back to the dressing-room.

The *artistes* were arriving. The bass and the
second tenor had already come. The bass,
Mr Duggan, was a slender young man with a
scattered[4] black moustache. He was the son of a hall
porter in an office in the city and, as a boy, he had
sung prolonged bass notes in the resounding hall.
From this humble state he had raised himself until
he had become a first-rate *artiste*. He had appeared

1. *screwed* [skruːd] : contorted.
2. *effaced* [ɪˈfeɪsd]: cancelled, deleted.
3. *the dear knows* : a mild Irish oath.
4. *scattered* : disordered.

in grand opera. One night, when an operatic *artiste* had fallen ill, he had undertaken the part of the king in the opera of *Maritana* at the Queen's Theatre. He sang his music with great feeling and volume and was warmly welcomed by the gallery; but, unfortunately, he marred[1] the good impression by wiping his nose in his gloved hand once or twice out of thoughtlessness. He was unassuming[2] and spoke little. He said *yous*[3] so softly that it passed unnoticed and he never drank anything stronger than milk for his voice's sake.[4] Mr Bell, the second tenor, was a fair-haired little man who competed every year for prizes at the Feis Ceoil.[5] On his fourth trial he had been awarded a bronze medal. He was extremely nervous and extremely jealous of other tenors and he covered his nervous jealousy with an ebullient[6] friendliness. It was his humour to have people know what an ordeal a concert was to him. Therefore when he saw Mr Duggan he went over to him and asked:

—Are you in it too?

—Yes, said Mr Duggan.

Mr Bell laughed at his fellow-sufferer, held out his hand and said:

—Shake!

Mrs Kearney passed by these two young men and

---

1. *marred* : damaged, ruined.
2. *unassuming* [ˌʌnəˈsjuːmɪŋ] : modest, not arrogant.
3. *yous* : this form of "you", common in several regional varieties (not only Irish), tends to be associated with lack of education.
4. *for his voice's sake* [seɪk] : so as to preserve his voice.
5. *Feis Ceoil* [ˌfɪs ˈkeɪl]: an annual music festival dating back to 1897.
6. *ebullient* [ɪˈbʌlɪənt] : excited and enthusiastic.

went to the edge of the screen to view the house.[1] The
seats were being filled up rapidly and a pleasant
noise circulated in the auditorium. She came back
and spoke to her husband privately. Their
conversation was evidently about Kathleen for they
both glanced at her often as she stood chatting to one
of her Nationalist friends, Miss Healy, the contralto.
An unknown solitary woman with a pale face walked
through the room. The women followed with keen[2]
eyes the faded blue dress which was stretched upon
a meagre body. Some one said that she was Madame
Glynn, the soprano.

—I wonder where did they dig her up,[3] said
Kathleen to Miss Healy. I'm sure I never heard of
her.

Miss Healy had to smile. Mr Holohan limped[4] into
the dressing-room at that moment and the two young
ladies asked him who was the unknown woman.
Mr Holohan said that she was Madam Glynn from
London. Madam Glynn took her stand[5] in a corner of
the room, holding a roll of music stiffly[6] before her
and from time to time changing the direction of her
startled gaze.[7] The shadow took her faded dress into
shelter but fell revengefully into the little cup behind

1. *the house* : the audience.
2. *keen* : observant, attentive.
3. *dig her up* : find her (literally "exhume from under the
   ground", implying that she looks dead).
4. *limped* [lɪmpt] : walked with difficulty placing more weight
   on one leg than on the other.
5. *took her stand* [stænd] : moved into her position.
6. *stiffly* : in a formal, unrelaxed way.
7. *her startled gaze* [geɪz] : her look of astonishment or shock.

her collar-bone.[1] The noise of the hall became more
audible. The first tenor and the baritone arrived
together. They were both well dressed, stout[2] and
complacent and they brought a breath of opulence
among the company.

Mrs Kearney brought her daughter over to them,
and talked to them amiably. She wanted to be on
good terms with them but, while she strove[3] to be
polite, her eyes followed Mr Holohan in his limping
and devious courses. As soon as she could she
excused herself and went out after him.

—Mr Holohan, I want to speak to you for a
moment, she said.

They went down to a discreet part of the corridor.
Mrs Kearney asked him when was her daughter
going to be paid. Mr Holohan said that
Mr Fitzpatrick had charge of that. Mrs Kearney said
that she didn't know anything about Mr Fitzpatrick.
Her daughter had signed a contract for eight guineas
and she would have to be paid. Mr Holohan said that
it wasn't his business.[4]

—Why isn't it your business? asked Mrs Kearney.
Didn't you yourself bring her the contract? Anyway,
if it's not your business it's my business and I mean
to see to it.[5]

—You'd better speak to Mr Fitzpatrick, said
Mr Holohan distantly.

---

1. *little cup ... bone* : clavicle.
2. *stout* : fat, corpulent.
3. *strove* [strəʊv] (strive, strove, striven) : tried hard.
4. *business* : notice Mrs Kearney's preoccupation with business.
   Compare her to Mrs Mooney in "The Boarding House".
5. *I mean to see to it* : "I intend to do something about it.

—I don't know anything about Mr Fitzpatrick, repeated Mrs Kearney. I have my contract, and I intend to see that it is carried out.

When she came back to the dressing-room her cheeks were slightly suffused.[1] The room was lively. Two men in outdoor dress had taken possession of the fireplace and were chatting familiarly with Miss Healy and the baritone. They were the *Freeman* man [2] and Mr O'Madden Burke. The *Freeman* man had come in to say that he could not wait for the concert as he had to report the lecture which an American priest was giving in the Mansion House.[3] He said they were to leave the report for him at the *Freeman* office and he would see that it went in. He was a grey-haired man, with a plausible voice and careful manners. He held an extinguished cigar in his hand and the aroma of cigar smoke floated near him. He had not intended to stay a moment because concerts and *artistes* bored him considerably but he remained leaning against [4] the mantelpiece. Miss Healy stood in front of him, talking and laughing. He was old enough to suspect one reason for her politeness but young enough in spirit to turn the moment to account.[5] The warmth, fragrance and colour of her body appealed to his senses. He was pleasantly conscious that the bosom which he saw rise and fall slowly beneath him rose and fell at that moment for him, that the laughter and fragrance and

1. *suffused* [sə'fjuːzd] : coloured (from the blood in her cheeks).
2. *the Freeman man* : the journalist for the *Freeman's Journal*.
3. *Mansion House* : official residence of the Lord Mayor of Dublin.
4. *leaning against* : see note 4, p. 113.
5. *turn ... to account* [ə'kaʊnt] : gain some advantage from.

wilful [1] glances were his tribute. When he could stay no longer he took leave of her regretfully.

—O'Madden Burke will write the notice, he explained to Mr Holohan, and I'll see it in.[2]

—Thank you very much, Mr Hendrick, said Mr Holohan. You'll see it in, I know. Now, won't you have a little something before you go?

—I don't mind, said Mr Hendrick.

The two men went along some tortuous passages and up a dark staircase and came to a secluded room where one of the stewards was uncorking bottles for a few gentlemen. One of these gentlemen was Mr O'Madden Burke, who had found out the room by instinct. He was a suave elderly man who balanced his imposing body, when at rest, upon a large silk umbrella. His magniloquent western name was the moral umbrella upon which he balanced the fine problem of his finances. He was widely respected.

While Mr Holohan was entertaining the *Freeman* man Mrs Kearney was speaking so animatedly to her husband that he had to ask her to lower her voice. The conversation of the others in the dressing-room had become strained.[3] Mr Bell, the first item, stood ready with his music but the accompanist made no sign. Evidently something was wrong. Mr Kearney looked straight before him, stroking[4] his beard, while Mrs Kearney spoke into Kathleen's ear with subdued emphasis. From the hall came sounds of encouragement, clapping and stamping of feet. The

1. *wilful* : resolute, determined.
2. *I'll see it in* : "I'll make sure it is included [in the newspaper]".
3. *strained* : difficult to maintain.
4. *stroking* ['strəʊkɪŋ]: passing his hand over the surface of.

first tenor and the baritone and Miss Healy stood together, waiting tranquilly, but Mr Bell's nerves were greatly agitated because he was afraid the audience would think that he had come late.

Mr Holohan and Mr O'Madden Burke came into the room. In a moment Mr Holohan perceived the hush.[1] He went over to Mrs Kearney and spoke with her earnestly. While they were speaking the noise in the hall grew louder. Mr Holohan became very red and excited. He spoke volubly, but Mrs Kearney said curtly[2] at intervals:

—She won't go on. She must get her eight guineas.

Mr Holohan pointed desperately towards the hall where the audience was clapping and stamping. He appealed to Mr Kearney and to Kathleen. But Mr Kearney continued to stroke his beard and Kathleen looked down, moving the point of her new shoe: it was not her fault. Mrs Kearney repeated:

—She won't go on without her money.

After a swift struggle of tongues Mr Holohan hobbled out in haste.[3] The room was silent. When the strain of the silence had become somewhat painful Miss Healy said to the baritone:

—Have you seen Mrs Pat Campbell[4] this week?

The baritone had not seen her but he had been told that she was very fine. The conversation went no further. The first tenor bent his head and began to count the links of the gold chain which was

---

1. *hush* : silence.
2. *curtly* ['kɜːtli] : briefly and discourteously.
3. *hobbled* ['hɒbld] *out in haste* : went out with an uneven walk as quickly as possible (see note 1, p. 170).
4. *Mrs Pat Campbell* : a famous English actress.

extended across his waist, smiling and humming[1] random notes to observe the effect on the frontal sinus. From time to time every one glanced at Mrs Kearney.

The noise in the auditorium had risen to a clamour when Mr Fitzpatrick burst into[2] the room, followed by Mr Holohan, who was panting.[3] The clapping and stamping in the hall was punctuated by whistling. Mr Fitzpatrick held a few bank-notes in his hand. He counted out four into Mrs Kearney's hand and said she would get the other half at the interval. Mrs Kearney said:

—This is four shillings short.[4]

But Kathleen gathered in her skirt and said: *Now, Mr Bell*, to the first item, who was shaking like an aspen.[5] The singer and the accompanist went out together. The noise in the hall died away. There was a pause of a few seconds: and then the piano was heard.

The first part of the concert was very successful except for Madam Glynn's item. The poor lady sang *Killarney*[6] in a bodiless gasping voice,[7] with all the old-fashioned mannerisms of intonation and pronunciation which she believed lent elegance to her singing. She looked as if she had been

---

1. *humming* : singing to himself in a very low voice.
2. *burst* [bɜːst] *into* : came in very suddenly.
3. *panting* [ˈpæntɪŋ]: breathing heavily in quick, short breaths.
4. *four shillings short* [ʃɔːt]: four shillings less than the agreed sum.
5. *shaking like an aspen* : shaking like a leaf.
6. *Killarney* : a sentimental song by the Irish composer Michael W. Balfe (1808-70).
7. *a bodiless gasping voice* : a weak voice with incorrect breathing.

resurrected from an old stage-wardrobe and the cheaper parts of the hall made fun of her high wailing notes.[1] The first tenor and the contralto, however, brought down the house.[2] Kathleen played a selection of Irish airs which was generously applauded. The first part closed with a stirring patriotic recitation delivered by a young lady who arranged amateur theatricals.[3] It was deservedly applauded; and, when it was ended, the men went out for the interval, content.

All this time the dressing-room was a hive of excitement.[4] In one corner were Mr Holohan, Mr Fitzpatrick, Miss Beirne, two of the stewards, the baritone, the bass, and Mr O'Madden Burke. Mr O'Madden Burke said it was the most scandalous exhibition he had ever witnessed. Miss Kathleen Kearney's musical career was ended in Dublin after that, he said. The baritone was asked what did he think of Mrs Kearney's conduct. He did not like to say anything. He had been paid his money and wished to be at peace with men. However, he said that Mrs Kearney might have taken the *artistes* into consideration. The stewards and the secretaries debated hotly as to what should be done when the interval came.

—I agree with Miss Beirne, said Mr O'Madden Burke. Pay her nothing.

---

1. *wailing* ['weɪlɪŋ] *notes* : long, lamenting, sad sounding notes.
2. *brought down the house* : was applauded very enthusiastically by the audience ("the house").
3. *amateur theatricals* : performances of plays by non-professional actors.
4. *a hive of excitement* : full of excitement.

In another corner of the room were Mrs Kearney
and her husband, Mr Bell, Miss Healy and the young
lady who had to recite the patriotic piece.
Mrs Kearney said that the committee had treated
her scandalously. She had spared neither trouble nor
expense and this was how she was repaid.

They thought they had only a girl to deal with and
that, therefore, they could ride roughshod over [1] her.
But she would show them their mistake. They
wouldn't have dared to have treated her like that if
she had been a man. But she would see that her
daughter got her rights: she wouldn't be fooled. If
they didn't pay her to the last farthing she would
make Dublin ring. Of course she was sorry for the
sake of the *artistes*. But what else could she do? She
appealed to the second tenor who said he thought she
had not been well treated. Then she appealed to Miss
Healy. Miss Healy wanted to join the other group but
she did not like to do so because she was a great
friend of Kathleen's and the Kearneys had often
invited her to their house.

As soon as the first part was ended Mr Fitzpatrick
and Mr Holohan went over to Mrs Kearney and told
her that the other four guineas would be paid after
the committee meeting on the following Tuesday and
that, in case her daughter did not play for the second
part, the committee would consider the contract
broken and would pay nothing.

—I haven't seen any committee, said Mrs Kearney
angrily. My daughter has her contract. She will get
four pounds eight into her hand or a foot she won't

1.   *ride roughshod* ['rʌfʃɒd] *over* : disregard, treat badly.

put on that platform.[1]

—I'm surprised at you, Mrs Kearney, said Mr Holohan. I never thought you would treat us this way.

—And what way did you treat me? asked Mrs Kearney.

Her face was inundated with an angry colour and she looked as if she would attack some one with her hands.

—I'm asking for my rights, she said.

—You might have some sense of decency, said Mr Holohan.

—Might I, indeed? . . . And when I ask when my daughter is going to be paid I can't get a civil answer.

She tossed her head[2] and assumed a haughty[3] voice:

—You must speak to the secretary. It's not my business. I'm a great fellow fol-the-diddle-I-do.[4]

—I thought you were a lady, said Mr Holohan, walking away from her abruptly.

After that Mrs Kearney's conduct was condemned on all hands:[5] everyone approved of what the committee had done. She stood at the door, haggard[6] with rage, arguing with her husband and daughter, gesticulating with them. She waited until it was time for the second part to begin in the hope that the

---

1. *a foot she won't put on that platform* : standard English would prefer "she won't put a foot on that platform."
2. *tossed her head* : threw back her head in a disdainful gesture.
3. *haughty* ['hɔːti] : disdainful and superior.
4. *fol-the-diddle-I-do* : implies that Mrs Kearney thinks Mr Holohan is not being honest.
5. *on all hands* : unanimously.
6. *haggard* ['hægəd] : wild-looking and fatigued.

secretaries would approach her. But Miss Healy had kindly consented to play one or two accompaniments. Mrs Kearney had to stand aside to allow the baritone and his accompanist to pass up to the platform. She stood still for an instant like an angry stone image and, when the first notes of the song struck her ear, she caught up her daughter's cloak and said to her husband:

—Get a cab!

He went out at once. Mrs Kearney wrapped the cloak round her daughter and followed him. As she passed through the doorway she stopped and glared into Mr Holohan's face.

—I'm not done with you yet,[1] she said.

—But I'm done with you, said Mr Holohan.

Kathleen followed her mother meekly.[2] Mr Holohan began to pace up and down the room, in order to cool himself for he felt his skin on fire.

—That's a nice lady! he said. O, she's a nice lady!

—You did the proper[3] thing, Holohan, said Mr O'Madden Burke, poised upon[4] his umbrella in approval.

---

1. *I'm not done with you yet* [jet] : "I have not finished with you yet".
2. *meekly* : submissively.
3. *proper* : correct.
4. *poised* [pɔɪzd] *upon* : balanced upon.

Characters

1. Describe Mrs Kearney's character, using brief quotations from the text to support your view.

2. We are told a great deal about Mrs Kearney but very little about Kathleen. Where do we get the clearest indication of Kathleen's character?

3. What purpose does Mr O'Madden Burke serve in the story?

Structure

The story traces a series of almost military manoeuvres of alliance and opposition. Fill in the chart below with names from the list. (If none of the names applies, put "no one".

SCENES	MRS KEARNEY IS ALLIED WITH	AND OPPOSED BY
Before the concerts begin		
Before the interval in the Saturday concert		
At the end of the story		

Mr Holohan	Kathleen	Mr O'Madden Burke	Mr Bell
Miss Healy	Mr Fitzpatrick	the bass	Mr Kearney
the baritone	Miss Beirne	the young lady (who recites patriotic poetry)	

Symbolism

We are told that when Mrs Kearney was single, she used to eat a lot of Turkish Delight in secret (p. 180). This is one of many references to the East in *Dubliners.* Find examples from other stories and comment upon their symbolic significance in *Dubliners* as a whole.

Narrator

1. Complete the following sentences by marking the most appropriate of the endings provided in the right hand column:

	☐ an omniscient narrator
	☐ several narrators
The story is narrated by	☐ James Joyce
	☐ a first-person narrator

	☐ ironic
	☐ unreliable
The narrator is	☐ objective
	☐ naive

2. Complete the following sentence using one or more verbs from the list provided (or other verbs of your own). Support your choice with examples from the text.

    The narrator _____ most of the characters in the story.

loves	hates	cherishes	ignores
despises	criticizes	pities	envies

Themes

1.   There are frequent references to friends in "A Mother".
      Taken together, what do these references suggest about
      friendship in the particular stratum of Dublin society depicted
      in the story?

2.   Find all the references to the Irish Revival in the story.
      Compare and contrast the representation of the Irish Revival
      with that of the Celtic School in "A Little Cloud".

THE DEAD

THE DEAD

LILY,[1] the caretaker's daughter, was literally run off her feet. Hardly had she brought one gentleman into the little pantry[2] behind the office on the ground floor and helped him off with his overcoat than the wheezy[3] hall-door bell clanged[4] again and she had to scamper[5] along the bare hallway to let in another guest. It was well for her[6] she had not to attend to the ladies also. But Miss Kate and Miss Julia had thought of that and had converted the bathroom upstairs into a ladies' dressing-room. Miss Kate and Miss Julia were there,

---

1. *Lily* : the lily is a symbol of death and rebirth at funerals, and also of the Resurrection at Easter.
2. *pantry* : a small room in which provisions (crockery, cutlery, table linen etc.) are usually kept.
3. *wheezy* [wi:zi] : making an unpleasant whistling noise.
4. *clanged* [klæŋd] : made a loud metallic sound.
5. *scamper* ['skæmpər] : run quickly.
6. *It was well for her* : it was fortunate for her (but the expression carries overtones of envy or bitterness).

gossiping and laughing, and fussing,[1] walking after each other to the head of the stairs, peering down over the banisters and calling down to Lily to ask her who had come.

It was always a great affair, the Misses Morkan's annual dance. Everybody who knew them came to it, members of the family, old friends of the family, the members of Julia's choir, any of Kate's pupils that were grown up enough and even some of Mary Jane's pupils too. Never once had it fallen flat.[2] For years and years it had gone off in splendid style as long as anyone could remember; ever since Kate and Julia, after the death of their brother Pat, had left the house in Stoney Batter[3] and taken Mary Jane, their only niece, to live with them in the dark gaunt[4] house on Usher's Island,[5] the upper part of which they had rented from Mr Fulham, the corn-factor[6] on the ground floor. That was a good thirty years ago if it was a day.[7] Mary Jane, who was then a little girl in short clothes, was now the main prop[8] of the household for she had the organ in Haddington Road. She had been through the Academy and gave a pupils' concert every year in the upper room of the Antient Concert Rooms. Many of her pupils belonged

1. *fussing* : displaying excessive concern over small matters.
2. *fallen flat* : been received without enthusiasm.
3. *Stoney Batter* : a northern suburb of Dublin.
4. *gaunt* [gɔːnt] : tall and thin.
5. *Usher's* [ˈʌʃəz] *Island* : a quay on the Liffey.
6. *corn-factor* : a dealer in corn.
7. *if it was a day* : colloquial expression meaning "at least": thus, the event referred to happened at least thirty years ago.
8. *main prop* : the person who provided most economic support.

to the better-class families on the Kingstown and Dalkey line. Old as they were, her aunts also did their share. Julia, though she was quite grey, was still the leading soprano in Adam and Eve's,[1] and Kate, being too feeble[2] to go about much, gave music lessons to beginners on the old square piano in the back room. Lily, the caretaker's daughter, did house-maid's work for them. Though their life was modest they believed in eating well; the best of everything: diamond-bone sirloins,[3] three-shilling tea and the best bottled stout. But Lily seldom made a mistake in the orders so that she got on well with her three mistresses. They were fussy,[4] that was all. But the only thing they would not stand was back answers.

Of course they had good reason to be fussy on such a night. And then it was long after ten o'clock and yet there was no sign of Gabriel[5] and his wife. Besides they were dreadfully afraid that Freddy Malins might turn up screwed.[6] They would not wish for worlds that any of Mary Jane's pupils should see him under the influence;[7] and when he was like that it was sometimes very hard to manage him. Freddy Malins always came late but they wondered what

---

1. *Adam and Eve's* : a popular name for the Church of St. Francis of Assisi on Merchant's Quay.

2. *feeble* : weak.

3. *diamond-bone sirloins* ['sɜːlɔɪnz] : an expensive cut of meat.

4. *fussy* : see note 1, page 208.

5. *Gabriel* ['geɪbrɪəl] : the archangel Gabriel announced the birth of Jesus to Mary (Luke I: 26-38). Interestingly, Gabriel is often represented holding a lily signifying surrender to the will of God.

6. *screwed* : drunk.

7. *under the influence* : when he had had too much to drink.

could be keeping[1] Gabriel: and that was what brought them every two minutes to the banisters[2] to ask Lily had Gabriel or Freddy come.

—O, Mr Conroy, said Lily to Gabriel when she opened the door for him, Miss Kate and Miss Julia thought you were never coming. Good-night, Mrs Conroy.

—I'll engage they did,[3] said Gabriel, but they forget that my wife here takes three mortal hours to dress herself.

He stood on the mat, scraping the snow from his goloshes,[4] while Lily led his wife to the foot of the stairs and called out:

—Miss Kate, here's Mrs Conroy.

Kate and Julia came toddling[5] down the dark stairs at once. Both of them kissed Gabriel's wife, said she must be perished alive[6] and asked was Gabriel with her.

—Here I am as right as the mail,[7] Aunt Kate! Go on up, I'll follow, called out Gabriel from the dark.

He continued scraping his feet vigorously while the three women went upstairs, laughing, to the ladies' dressing-room. A light fringe[8] of snow lay like

---

1. *keeping* [ˈkiːpɪŋ] : detaining.
2. *banisters* [ˈbænɪstəz] : the upright structure (posts and handrail) on the outer side of the stairs.
3. *I'll engage they did* : I'll bet they did.
4. *goloshes* [gəˈlɒʃɪz] : rubber overshoes.
5. *toddling* [ˈtɒdlɪŋ] : walking with short, unsteady steps (like a small child, a "toddler").
6. *perished alive* : freezing to death, extremely cold.
7. *right as the mail* : perfectly all right. "Right as rain" would be more usual.
8. *fringe* : line edge (also see note 4, p. 93).

a cape on the shoulders of his overcoat and like toecaps on the toes of his goloshes; and, as the buttons of his overcoat slipped with a squeaking noise through the snow-stiffened frieze, a cold fragrant air from out-of-doors escaped from crevices [1] and folds.

—Is it snowing again, Mr Conroy? asked Lily.

She had preceded him into the pantry to help him off with his overcoat. Gabriel smiled at the three syllables she had given his surname and glanced at her. She was a slim, growing girl, pale in complexion and with hay-coloured hair. The gas [2] in the pantry made her look still paler. Gabriel had known her when she was a child and used to sit on the lowest step nursing a rag doll. [3]

—Yes, Lily, he answered, and I think we're in for a night of it. [4]

He looked up at the pantry ceiling, which was shaking with the stamping and shuffling [5] of feet on the floor above, listened for a moment to the piano and then glanced at the girl, who was folding his overcoat carefully at the end of a shelf.

—Tell me, Lily, he said in a friendly tone, do you still go to school?

—O no, sir, she answered. I'm done schooling this year and more.

—O, then, said Gabriel gaily, I suppose we'll be

1. *crevices* : thin narrow spaces (in his clothes).
2. *The gas* : The light from the gas lamp.
3. *nursing a rag doll* : holding a doll, made from old material (rags), as if it were a baby.
4. *we're in for a night of it* : a colloquial phrase meaning "the weather is going to be bad tonight".
5. *shuffling* : walking without lifting the feet off the ground.

going to your wedding one of these fine days with
your young man, eh?

The girl glanced back at him over her shoulder
and said with great bitterness:

—The men that is now is only all palaver [1] and
what they can get out of you.

Gabriel coloured as if he felt he had made a
mistake and, without looking at her, kicked off his
goloshes and flicked [2] actively with his muffler at his
patent-leather shoes.

He was a stout tallish young man. The high colour
of his cheeks pushed upwards even to his forehead
where it scattered itself in a few formless patches of
pale red; and on his hairless face there scintillated
restlessly the polished lenses and the bright gilt rims [3]
of the glasses which screened his delicate and
restless [4] eyes. His glossy black hair was parted in
the middle and brushed in a long curve behind his
ears where it curled slightly beneath the groove [5] left
by his hat.

When he had flicked lustre into his shoes he stood
up and pulled his waistcoat down more tightly on his
plump body. Then he took a coin rapidly from his
pocket.

—O Lily, he said, thrusting [6] it into her hands, it's
Christmas-time, isn't it? Just . . . here's a little . . .

---

1. *The men that is now ... palaver* [pə'lɑːvər]: "men nowadays
   are only full of troublesome, nonsensical talk" (Lily's speech
   is grammatically incorrect here).
2. *flicked* : gave a light stroke.
3. *gilt rims* : gold or silver coloured edges.
4. *restless* ['restləs] : continuously moving.
5. *the groove* [gruːv] : small longitudinal space, channel.
6. *thrusting* [θrʌstɪŋ] : pushing forcefully.

He walked rapidly towards the door.

—O no, sir! cried the girl, following him. Really, sir, I wouldn't take it.

—Christmas-time! Christmas-time! said Gabriel, almost trotting to the stairs and waving his hand to her in deprecation.[1]

The girl, seeing that he had gained the stairs,[2] called out after him:

—Well, thank you, sir.

He waited outside the drawing-room door until the waltz should finish, listening to the skirts that swept against it and to the shuffling of feet. He was still discomposed by the girl's bitter and sudden retort. It had cast a gloom[3] over him which he tried to dispel by arranging his cuffs and the bows of his tie. He then took from his waistcoat pocket a little paper and glanced at the headings he had made for his speech. He was undecided about the lines from Robert Browning for he feared they would be above the heads[4] of his hearers. Some quotation that they would recognise from Shakespeare or from the Melodies[5] would be better. The indelicate clacking[6] of the men's heels and the shuffling of their soles reminded him that their grade of culture differed from his. He would only make himself ridiculous by

1. *waving ... deprecation* [deprɪˈkeɪʃn] : indicating with a gesture that the act of giving her money was of no importance.
2. *gained the stairs* : arrived at the stairs.
3. *cast a gloom* [gluːm] : made him feel disconsolate.
4. *Browning ... above the heads* : Browning's poetry is considered difficult.
5. *the Melodies* : Irish Melodies (1807-34) by Thomas Moore. A much more accessible kind of poetry.
6. *clacking* [ˈklækɪŋ]: sharp wooden sound.

quoting poetry to them which they could not understand. They would think that he was airing[1] his superior education. He would fail with them just as he had failed with the girl in the pantry. He had taken up a wrong tone. His whole speech was a mistake from first to last, an utter failure.

Just then his aunts and his wife came out of the ladies' dressing-room. His aunts were two small plainly dressed old women. Aunt Julia was an inch or so the taller. Her hair, drawn low over the tops of her ears, was grey; and grey also, with darker shadows, was her large flaccid face. Though she was stout in build and stood erect her slow eyes and parted lips gave her the appearance of a woman who did not know where she was or where she was going. Aunt Kate was more vivacious. Her face, healthier than her sister's, was all puckers and creases,[2] like a shrivelled red apple, and her hair, braided[3] in the same old-fashioned way, had not lost its ripe nut colour.

They both kissed Gabriel frankly. He was their favourite nephew, the son of their dead elder sister, Ellen, who had married T.J. Conroy of the Port and Docks.

—Gretta tells me you're not going to take a cab back to Monkstown to-night, Gabriel, said Aunt Kate.

—No, said Gabriel, turning to his wife, we had quite enough of that last year, hadn't we? Don't you

1. *airing* : displaying, showing off.
2. *puckers and creases* : small folds and lines in the skin.
3. *braided* ['breɪdɪd]: arranged by passing three lengths of hair over and under each other to form a single long length.

remember, Aunt Kate, what a cold Gretta got out of it? Cab windows rattling[1] all the way, and the east wind blowing in after we passed Merrion. Very jolly it was. Gretta caught a dreadful cold.

Aunt Kate frowned severely and nodded her head at every word.

—Quite right, Gabriel, quite right, she said. You can't be too careful.

—But as for Gretta there, said Gabriel, she'd walk home in the snow if she were let.[2]

Mrs Conroy laughed.

—Don't mind him, Aunt Kate, she said. He's really an awful bother,[3] what with green shades for Tom's eyes at night and making him do the dumb-bells,[4] and forcing Eva to eat the stirabout.[5] The poor child! And she simply hates the sight of it! . . . O, but you'll never guess what he makes me wear now!

She broke out into a peal of laughter[6] and glanced at her husband, whose admiring and happy eyes had been wandering from her dress to her face and hair. The two aunts laughed heartily too, for Gabriel's solicitude was a standing joke[7] with them.

—Goloshes![8] said Mrs Conroy. That's the latest. Whenever it's wet underfoot I must put on my

1. *rattling* ['rætlɪŋ]: making a sound caused by rapid shaking.
2. *if she were let* : if she were allowed to.
3. *He's really an awful bother* ['bɒðə]: "He causes a lot of trouble."
4. *do the dumb-bells* ['dʌmbelz] : do weightlifting.
5. *stirabout* : porridge.
6. *peal of laughter* ['lɑːftər] : a loud melodious laugh.
7. *a standing joke* [dʒəʊk] : something which is seen as irremediably ridiculous.
8. *Goloshes* : rubber overshoes for protection.

goloshes. To-night even he wanted me to put them on, but I wouldn't. The next thing he'll buy me will be a diving suit.

Gabriel laughed nervously and patted[1] his tie reassuringly while Aunt Kate nearly doubled herself,[2] so heartily[3] did she enjoy the joke. The smile soon faded from Aunt Julia's face and her mirthless[4] eyes were directed towards her nephew's face. After a pause she asked:

—And what are goloshes, Gabriel?

—Goloshes, Julia! exclaimed her sister. Goodness me, don't you know what goloshes are? You wear them over your . . . over your boots, Gretta, isn't it?

—Yes, said Mrs Conroy. Guttapercha[5] things. We both have a pair now. Gabriel says everyone wears them on the continent.

—O, on the continent, murmured Aunt Julia, nodding her head slowly.

Gabriel knitted his brows[6] and said, as if he were slightly angered:

—It's nothing very wonderful but Gretta thinks it very funny because she says the word reminds her of Christy Minstrels.[7]

—But tell me, Gabriel, said Aunt Kate, with

---

1. *patted* : struck lightly with his hand.
2. *nearly doubled herself* : bent her body forward so much (with laughing) that her head nearly touched the floor.
3. *heartily* : vigorously and with genuine emotion.
4. *mirthless* ['mɜːθləs]: joyless, sad.
5. *Guttapercha* [ˌɡʌtəˈpɜːtʃə] : India rubber.
6. *knitted his brows* : frowned (see note 4, p. 16).
7. *Christy Minstrels* ['mɪnstrəlz] : Edwin T. Christy's minstrel shows, famous for their blackface imitation of southern Negro dialect and song.

brisk [1] tact. Of course, you've seen about the room.
Gretta was saying . . .

—O, the room is all right, replied Gabriel. I've
taken one in the Gresham.[2]

—To be sure,[3] said Aunt Kate, by far the best
thing to do. And the children, Gretta, you're not
anxious about them?

—O, for one night, said Mrs Conroy. Besides,
Bessie will look after them.

—To be sure, said Aunt Kate again. What a
comfort it is to have a girl like that, one you can
depend on! There's that Lily, I'm sure I don't know
what has come over her lately. She's not the girl she
was at all.

Gabriel was about to ask his aunt some questions
on this point but she broke off suddenly to gaze after
her sister who had wandered down the stairs and
was craning[4] her neck over the banisters.

—Now, I ask you, she said, almost testily,[5] where
is Julia going? Julia! Julia! Where are you going?

Julia, who had gone halfway down one flight,[6]
came back and announced blandly:

—Here's Freddy.

At the same moment a clapping of hands[7] and a
final flourish of the pianist told that the waltz had

1. *brisk* : quick and efficient.
2. *the Gresham* ['greʃəm] : a fashionable hotel. The Conroys are
   evidently quite well off financially.
3. *To be sure* : Certainly.
4. *craning* ['kreɪnɪŋ] : stretching.
5. *testily* ['testɪli] : irrascibly.
6. *flight* : a series of stairs between two floors or landings.
7. *a clapping of hands* : applause.

ended. The drawing-room door was opened from
within and some couples came out. Aunt Kate drew
Gabriel aside [1] hurriedly and whispered into his ear:

—Slip down, [2] Gabriel, like a good fellow and see
if he's all right, and don't let him up if he's screwed.
I'm sure he's screwed. I'm sure he is.

Gabriel went to the stairs and listened over the
banisters. He could hear two persons talking in the
pantry. Then he recognised Freddy Malins' laugh. He
went down the stairs noisily.

—It's such a relief, said Aunt Kate to Mrs Conroy,
that Gabriel is here. I always feel easier in my mind [3]
when he's here. . . . Julia, there's Miss Daly and Miss
Power will take some refreshment. Thanks for your
beautiful waltz, Miss Daly. It made lovely time.

A tall wizen-faced [4] man, with a stiff grizzled
moustache and swarthy skin, [5] who was passing out
with his partner said:

—And may we have some refreshment, too, Miss
Morkan?

—Julia, said Aunt Kate summarily, and here's
Mr Browne and Miss Furlong. Take them in, Julia,
with Miss Daly and Miss Power.

—I'm the man for the ladies, said Mr Browne,

1. *drew Gabriel aside* [ə'saɪd] : led Gabriel away from the
   others.
2. *Slip down* : Go downstairs quickly and quietly without being
   noticed.
3. *easier in my mind* : happier, more reassured.
4. *wizen-faced* ['wɪzn-feɪsd] : dried up face, full of puckers and
   creases (see note 2, p. 214).
5. *grizzled* ['grɪzld] *moustache and swarthy* ['swɔːðɪ] *skin* : a
   moustache with some grey hairs in it and dark skin.

pursing[1] his lips until his moustache bristled[2] and smiling in all his wrinkles. You know, Miss Morkan, the reason they are so fond of me is –

He did not finish his sentence, but, seeing that Aunt Kate was out of earshot,[3] at once led the three young ladies into the back room. The middle of the room was occupied by two square tables placed end to end, and on these Aunt Julia and the caretaker were straightening and smoothing[4] a large cloth. On the sideboard were arrayed dishes and plates, and glasses and bundles of knives and forks and spoons. The top of the closed square piano served also as a sideboard for viands[5] and sweets. At a smaller sideboard in one corner two young men were standing, drinking hop-bitters.[6]

Mr Browne led his charges thither[7] and invited them all, in jest, to some ladies' punch, hot, strong and sweet. As they said they never took anything strong he opened three bottles of lemonade for them. Then he asked one of the young men to move aside, and, taking hold of the decanter, filled out for himself a goodly measure of whisky. The young men eyed him respectfully while he took a trial sip.[8]

---

1. *pursing* [pə'sjuːɪŋ] : contracting.
2. *bristled* ['brɪstld] : stood up, became erect and prickly.
3. *out of earshot* ['ɪəʃɒt] : too far away to be able to hear.
4. *smoothing* : removing the folds and puckers.
5. *viands* : food.
6. *hop-bitters* : a drink like ginger-beer, flavoured with hops.
7. *thither* ['ðɪðər] (archaic) : there.
8. *a trial sip* : a small quantity to see what it tasted like.

—God help me, he said, smiling, it's the doctor's orders.[1]

His wizened face broke into a broader smile, and the three young ladies laughed in musical echo to his pleasantry, swaying[2] their bodies to and fro, with nervous jerks of their shoulders. The boldest[3] said:

—O, now, Mr Browne, I'm sure the doctor never ordered anything of the kind.

Mr Browne took another sip of his whisky and said, with sidling[4] mimicry:

—Well, you see, I'm like the famous Mrs Cassidy, who is reported to have said: *Now, Mary Grimes, if I don't take it, make me take it, for I feel I want it.*

His hot face had leaned forward a little too confidentially and he had assumed a very low Dublin accent so that the young ladies, with one instinct, received his speech in silence. Miss Furlong, who was one of Mary Jane's pupils, asked Miss Daly what was the name of the pretty waltz she had played; and Mr Browne, seeing that he was ignored, turned promptly to the two young men who were more appreciative.

A red-faced young woman, dressed in pansy,[5] came into the room, excitedly clapping her hands and crying:

—Quadrilles![6] Quadrilles!

Close on her heels[7] came Aunt Kate, crying:

---

1. *it's the doctor's orders* : a colloquial expression meaning "it's very good!"
2. *swaying* [sweɪɪŋ]: moving rhythmically.
3. *boldest* [bəʊldɪst] : the most corageous, most daring.
4. *sidling* ['saɪdlɪŋ] : furtive, timid.
5. *pansy* ['pænzi] : blue or purple (the colour of the pansy flower [genus Viola]).
6. *Quadrilles* [kwə'drɪlz] : a square dance of French origin.
7. *Close on her heels* : close behind her.

—Two gentlemen and three ladies, Mary Jane!

—O, here's Mr Bergin and Mr Kerrigan, said Mary Jane. Mr Kerrigan, will you take Miss Power? Miss Furlong, may I get you a partner, Mr Bergin. O, that'll just do now.

—Three ladies, Mary Jane, said Aunt Kate.

The two young gentlemen asked the ladies if they might have the pleasure, and Mary Jane turned to Miss Daly.

—O, Miss Daly, you're really awfully good,[1] after playing for the last two dances, but really we're so short of ladies to-night.

—I don't mind in the least, Miss Morkan.

—But I've a nice partner for you, Mr Bartell D'Arcy, the tenor. I'll get him to sing later on. All Dublin is raving about[2] him.

—Lovely voice, lovely voice! said Aunt Kate.

As the piano had twice begun the prelude to the first figure Mary Jane led her recruits quickly from the room. They had hardly gone when Aunt Julia wandered slowly into the room, looking behind her at something.

—What is the matter, Julia? asked Aunt Kate anxiously. Who is it?

Julia, who was carrying in a column of table-napkins, turned to her sister and said, simply, as if the question had surprised her:

—It's only Freddy, Kate, and Gabriel with him.

In fact right behind her Gabriel could be seen piloting[3]

---

1. *awfully good* (coll.) : very good.
2. *raving* ['reɪvɪŋ] *about* : expressing great enthusiasm about and admiration for.
3. *piloting* ['paɪlətɪŋ] : guiding.

Freddy Malins across the landing. The latter, a young man of about forty, was of Gabriel's size and build, with very round shoulders. His face was fleshy and pallid, touched with colour only at the thick hanging lobes of his ears and at the wide wings of his nose. He had coarse [1] features, a blunt [2] nose, a convex and receding brow,[3] tumid and protruded lips. His heavy-lidded eyes and the disorder of his scanty hair made him look sleepy. He was laughing heartily in a high key at a story which he had been telling Gabriel on the stairs and at the same time rubbing the knuckles of his left fist backwards and forwards into his left eye.

—Good evening, Freddy, said Aunt Julia.

Freddy Malins bade the Misses Morkan good-evening in what seemed an offhand fashion [4] by reason of the habitual catch in his voice and then, seeing that Mr Browne was grinning [5] at him from the sideboard, crossed the room on rather shaky [6] legs and began to repeat in an undertone [7] the story he had just told to Gabriel.

—He's not so bad, is he? said Aunt Kate to Gabriel.

Gabriel's brows were dark but he raised them quickly and answered:

—O no, hardly noticeable.

1. *coarse* : unrefined, vulgar.
2. *blunt* : not sharp or pointed.
3. *receding* [rɪ'siːdɪŋ] *brow* : the hair at the front of his head was becoming thin.
4. *an offhand fashion* : a casual and dismissive way.
5. *grinning* : smiling broadly showing his teeth.
6. *shaky* ['ʃeɪki] : unstable.
7. *undertone* : a very low voice.

—Now, isn't he a terrible fellow! she said. And his poor mother made him take the pledge [1] on New Year's Eve. But come on, Gabriel, into the drawing-room.

Before leaving the room with Gabriel she signalled to Mr Browne by frowning and shaking her forefinger in warning to and fro. Mr Browne nodded in answer and, when she had gone, said to Freddy Malins:

—Now, then, Teddy, I'm going to fill you out a good glass of lemonade just to buck you up. [2]

Freddy Malins, who was nearing the climax of his story, waved the offer aside [3] impatiently but Mr Browne, having first called Freddy Malins' attention to a disarray in his dress, filled out and handed him a full glass of lemonade. Freddy Malins' left hand accepted the glass mechanically, his right hand being engaged in the mechanical readjustment of his dress. Mr Browne, whose face was once more wrinkling with mirth, poured out for himself a glass of whisky while Freddy Malins exploded, before he had well reached the climax of his story, in a kink [4] of high-pitched bronchitic laughter and, setting down his untasted and overflowing glass, began to rub the knuckles of his left fist backwards and forwards into his left eye, repeating words of his last phrase as well as his fit of laughter would allow him.

.   .   .   .

Gabriel could not listen while Mary Jane was

1. *the pledge* : see note 4, p. 85.
2. *buck you up* : make you feel better.
3. *waved ... aside* : dismissed.
4. *kink* : sudden explosion.

playing her Academy piece, full of runs and difficult passages, to the hushed drawing-room. He liked music but the piece she was playing had no melody for him and he doubted whether it had any melody for the other listeners, though they had begged Mary Jane to play something. Four young men, who had come from the refreshment-room to stand in the doorway at the sound of the piano, had gone away quietly in couples after a few minutes. The only persons who seemed to follow the music were Mary Jane herself, her hands racing along the key-board or lifted from it at the pauses like those of a priestess in momentary imprecation, and Aunt Kate standing at her elbow to turn the page.

Gabriel's eyes, irritated by the floor, which glittered with beeswax under the heavy chandelier, wandered to the wall above the piano. A picture of the balcony scene[1] in *Romeo and Juliet* hung there and beside it was a picture of the two murdered princes in the Tower[2] which Aunt Julia had worked in red, blue and brown wools when she was a girl. Probably in the school they had gone to as girls that kind of work had been taught for one year his mother had worked for him as a birthday present a waistcoat of purple tabinet,[3] with little foxes' heads upon it, lined with brown satin and having round mulberry[4]

---

1. *the balcony scene* : Act II, Scene 2 of Shakespeare's *Romeo and Juliet*.
2. *the two murdered princes in the Tower* : an allusion to the two young sons of Edward IV who were murdered in the Tower of London, possibly by Richard III.
3. *tabinet* ['tæbɪnət] : an Irish fabric made of silk and wool.
4. *mulberry* ['mʌlbəri]: a dark purple colour, like the fruit of the same name.

buttons. It was strange that his mother had had no musical talent though Aunt Kate used to call her the brains carrier of the Morkan family. Both she and Julia had always seemed a little proud of their serious and matronly sister. Her photograph stood before the pier-glass.[1] She had an open book on her knees and was pointing out something in it to Constantine who, dressed in a man-o'-war suit, lay at her feet. It was she who had chosen the names for her sons for she was very sensible of the dignity of family life. Thanks to her, Constantine was now senior curate in Balbriggan and, thanks to her, Gabriel himself had taken his degree in the Royal University.[2] A shadow passed over his face as he remembered her sullen[3] opposition to his marriage. Some slighting[4] phrases she had used still rankled[5] in his memory; she had once spoken of Gretta as being country cute[6] and that was not true of Gretta at all. It was Gretta who had nursed her during all her last long illness in their house at Monkstown.

He knew that Mary Jane must be near the end of her piece for she was playing again the opening melody with runs of scales after every bar and while

---

1. *pier-glass* [pɪə-glɑːs] : a tall dressing mirror.
2. *the Royal University* : established in 1882, the forerunner of the National University. It reflected English (and therefore Protestant) academic standards.
3. *sullen* : morose, resentful.
4. *slighting* [slaɪtɪŋ] : disrespectful.
5. *rankled* ['ræŋkld] : continued to cause bitter feelings.
6. *country cute* [kjuːt] : unintelligent (like a person from the country): "cute" is a pejorative abbreviation of "acute", and the expression is part of a saying "country cute and city clever" meaning that city people are more intelligent than country people.

he waited for the end the resentment died down in his heart. The piece ended with a trill of octaves in the treble and a final deep octave in the bass. Great applause greeted Mary Jane as, blushing and rolling up her music nervously, she escaped from the room. The most vigorous clapping came from the four young men in the doorway who had gone away to the refreshment-room at the beginning of the piece but had come back when the piano had stopped.

Lancers[1] were arranged. Gabriel found himself partnered with Miss Ivors. She was a frank-mannered talkative young lady, with a freckled face[2] and prominent brown eyes. She did not wear a low-cut bodice and the large brooch[3] which was fixed in the front of her collar bore on it an Irish device.

When they had taken their places she said abruptly:

—I have a crow to pluck[4] with you.

—With me? said Gabriel.

She nodded her head gravely.

—What is it? asked Gabriel, smiling at her solemn manner.

—Who is G.C.? answered Miss Ivors, turning her eyes upon him.

Gabriel coloured and was about to knit his brows, as if he did not understand, when she said bluntly:

1. *Lancers* ['lɑːnsərz]: a type of quadrille (see note 6, p. 220).
2. *freckled* ['frekld] *face*: with many small light brown marks on the face.
3. *large brooch*: Celtic brooches and other artefacts were common during the "Irish Revival".
4. *crow to pluck*: Irish for a "bone to pick", which means "to have a problem to resolve or discuss with someone".

—O, innocent Amy![1] I have found out that you write for *The Daily Express*.[2] Now, aren't you ashamed of yourself?

—Why should I be ashamed of myself? asked Gabriel, blinking his eyes and trying to smile.

—Well, I'm ashamed of you, said Miss Ivors frankly. To say you'd write for a rag[3] like that. I didn't think you were a West Briton.[4]

A look of perplexity appeared on Gabriel's face. It was true that he wrote a literary column every Wednesday in *The Daily Express*, for which he was paid fifteen shillings. But that did not make him a West Briton surely. The books he received for review were almost more welcome than the paltry[5] cheque. He loved to feel the covers and turn over the pages of newly printed books. Nearly every day when his teaching in the college was ended he used to wander down the quays to the second-hand booksellers, to Hickey's on Bachelor's Walk, to Webb's or Massey's on Aston's Quay, or to O'Clohissey's in the by-street. He did not know how to meet her charge.[6] He wanted to say that literature was above politics. But they were friends of many years' standing and their careers had been parallel, first at the University and then as teachers: he could not risk a grandiose

---

1. *innocent Amy* ['eɪmi] : don't pretend to be innocent.
2. *The Daily Express* : an Irish newspaper published in Dublin (1851-1921), but essentially pro-British.
3. *rag* : a popular low-quality newspaper.
4. *West Briton* : an Irishman who accepts that Ireland should be governed from London, and sees Ireland as merely a western province of Britain.
5. *paltry* ['pɔːltri] : insignificant (i.e. a very small amount).
6. *charge* : accusation.

phrase with her. He continued blinking[1] his eyes and trying to smile and murmured lamely[2] that he saw nothing political in writing reviews of books.

When their turn to cross had come he was still perplexed and inattentive. Miss Ivors promptly took his hand in a warm grasp and said in a soft friendly tone:

—Of course, I was only joking. Come, we cross now.

When they were together again she spoke of the University question[3] and Gabriel felt more at ease. A friend of hers had shown her his review of Browning's poems. That was how she had found out the secret: but she liked the review immensely. Then she said suddenly:

—O, Mr Conroy, will you come for an excursion to the Aran Isles[4] this summer? We're going to stay there a whole month. It will be splendid out in the Atlantic. You ought to come. Mr Clancy is coming, and Mr Kilkelly and Kathleen Kearney.[5] It would be splendid for Gretta too if she'd come. She's from Connacht,[6] isn't she?

1. *blinking* ['blɪŋkɪŋ] : involuntarily opening and shutting.
2. *lamely* [leɪmli] : weakly, without conviction.
3. *the University question* : the problem of how to provide Irish Catholics with a university education comparable to that offered by the great Protestant university of Trinity College, Dublin. Eventually, after the establishment of the Royal University (see note 2, p. 225), Catholic University was reorganized as University College, Dublin.
4. *the Aran Isles* : three islands off the west coast of Ireland. People who were interested in the Irish revival went there on a kind of pilgrimage.
5. *Kathleen Kearney* : see note 8, p. 181.
6. *Connacht* ['kɒnɔːt]: or "Connaught", the western province of Ireland from which Joyce's wife, Nora, also came.

—Her people are, said Gabriel shortly.

—But you will come, won't you? said Miss Ivors, laying her warm hand eagerly on his arm.

—The fact is, said Gabriel, I have already arranged to go –

—Go where? asked Miss Ivors.

—Well, you know, every year I go for a cycling tour with some fellows and so –

—But where? asked Miss Ivors.

—Well, we usually go to France or Belgium or perhaps Germany, said Gabriel awkwardly.

—And why do you go to France and Belgium, said Miss Ivors, instead of visiting your own land?

—Well, said Gabriel, it's partly to keep in touch with [1] the languages and partly for a change.

—And haven't you your own language to keep in touch with – Irish? asked Miss Ivors.

—Well, said Gabriel, if it comes to that,[2] you know, Irish is not my language.

Their neighbours had turned to listen to the cross-examination. Gabriel glanced right and left nervously and tried to keep his good humour under the ordeal [3] which was making a blush invade his forehead.

—And haven't you your own land to visit, continued Miss Ivors, that you know nothing of, your own people, and your own country?

—O, to tell you the truth, retorted [4] Gabriel suddenly, I'm sick of my own country, sick of it!

1. *keep in touch with* : help remember, practise.
2. *if it comes to that* : an expression meaning "as a matter of fact" or "the truth is".
3. *ordeal* [ɔːˈdiːl] : severe test.
4. *retorted* [rɪˈtɔːtɪd] : replied angrily.

—Why? asked Miss Ivors.

Gabriel did not answer for his retort had heated him.

—Why? repeated Miss Ivors.

They had to go visiting together and, as he had not answered her, Miss Ivors said warmly:

—Of course, you've no answer.

Gabriel tried to cover his agitation by taking part in the dance with great energy. He avoided her eyes for he had seen a sour[1] expression on her face. But when they met in the long chain he was surprised to feel his hand firmly pressed. She looked at him from under her brows for a moment quizzically[2] until he smiled. Then, just as the chain was about to start again, she stood on tiptoe and whispered into his ear:

—West Briton!

When the lancers were over Gabriel went away to a remote corner of the room where Freddy Malins' mother was sitting. She was a stout feeble old woman with white hair. Her voice had a catch[3] in it like her son's and she stuttered[4] slightly. She had been told that Freddy had come and that he was nearly all right. Gabriel asked her whether she had had a good crossing. She lived with her married daughter in Glasgow and came to Dublin on a visit once a year. She answered placidly that she had had a beautiful crossing and that the captain had been most attentive to her. She spoke also of the beautiful

---

1. *sour* ['sauər] : sullen, unfriendly.
2. *quizzically* ['kwɪzɪkli] : in a mildly puzzled way.
3. *catch* [kætʃ] : a slight impediment.
4. *stuttered* ['stʌtəd] : talked with involuntary repetition of sounds or syllables.

house her daughter kept in Glasgow, and of all the nice friends they had there. While her tongue rambled on[1] Gabriel tried to banish from his mind all memory of the unpleasant incident with Miss Ivors. Of course the girl or woman, or whatever she was, was an enthusiast but there was a time for all things. Perhaps he ought not to have answered her like that. But she had no right to call him a West Briton before people, even in joke. She had tried to make him ridiculous before people, heckling[2] him and staring at him with her rabbit's eyes.

He saw his wife making her way towards him through the waltzing couples. When she reached him she said into his ear:

—Gabriel, Aunt Kate wants to know won't you carve the goose as usual.[3] Miss Daly will carve the ham and I'll do the pudding.

—All right, said Gabriel.

—She's sending in the younger ones first as soon as this waltz is over so that we'll have the table to ourselves.

—Were you dancing? asked Gabriel.

—Of course I was. Didn't you see me? What words had you[4] with Molly Ivors?

—No words. Why? Did she say so?

—Something like that. I'm trying to get that Mr D'Arcy to sing. He's full of conceit, I think.

—There were no words, said Gabriel moodily, only

1. *rambled* ['ræmbld] *on* : talked inconsequentially.
2. *heckling* : interrupting aggressively.
3. *wants to know ... as usual* : "wants to know if you will carve the goose as usual".
4. *What words had you* : "What was your argument about?"

she wanted me to go for a trip to the west of Ireland and I said I wouldn't.

His wife clasped her hands excitedly and gave a little jump.

—O, do go, Gabriel, she cried. I'd love to see Galway again.

—You can go if you like, said Gabriel coldly.

She looked at him for a moment, then turned to Mrs Malins and said:

—There's a nice husband for you, Mrs Malins.

While she was threading her way back across the room Mrs Malins, without adverting to[1] the interruption, went on to tell Gabriel what beautiful places there were in Scotland and beautiful scenery. Her son-in-law brought them every year to the lakes and they used to go fishing. Her son-in-law was a splendid fisher. One day he caught a fish, a beautiful big big fish, and the man in the hotel boiled it for their dinner.

Gabriel hardly heard what she said. Now that supper was coming near he began to think again about his speech and about the quotation. When he saw Freddy Malins coming across the room to visit his mother Gabriel left the chair free for him and retired into the embrasure of the window. The room had already cleared and from the back room came the clatter of plates and knives. Those who still remained in the drawing-room seemed tired of dancing and were conversing quietly in little groups. Gabriel's warm trembling fingers tapped the cold pane of the window. How cool it must be outside! How pleasant it would be to walk out alone, first

---

1. *adverting* [æd'vɜːtɪŋ] *to* : referring to, remarking on.

along by the river and then through the park! The snow would be lying on the branches of the trees and forming a bright cap on the top of the Wellington Monument.[1] How much more pleasant it would be there than at the supper-table!

He ran over the headings of his speech: Irish hospitality, sad memories, the Three Graces, Paris, the quotation from Browning. He repeated to himself a phrase he had written in his review: *One feels that one is listening to a thought-tormented music.* Miss Ivors had praised the review. Was she sincere? Had she really any life of her own behind all her propagandism? There had never been any ill-feeling between them until that night. It unnerved [2] him to think that she would be at the supper-table, looking up at him while he spoke with her critical quizzing eyes. Perhaps she would not be sorry to see him fail in his speech. An idea came into his mind and gave him courage. He would say, alluding to Aunt Kate and Aunt Julia: *Ladies and Gentlemen, the generation which is now on the wane [3] among us may have had its faults but for my part I think it had certain qualities of hospitality, of humour, of humanity, which the new and very serious and hypereducated generation that is growing up around us seems to me to lack.* Very good: that was one for Miss Ivors. What did he care that his aunts were only two ignorant old women?

---

1. *the Wellington Monument* : in Phoenix Park. The Duke of Wellington (1769-1852) was born in Ireland but refused to think of himself as Irish.
2. *unnerved* [ˌʌnˈnɜːvd] : deprived of courage.
3. *on the wane* [weɪn] : becoming smaller, gradually disappearing.

A murmur in the room attracted his attention. Mr Browne was advancing from the door, gallantly escorting Aunt Julia, who leaned upon his arm, smiling and hanging[1] her head. An irregular musketry of applause escorted her also as far as the piano and then, as Mary Jane seated herself on the stool, and Aunt Julia, no longer smiling, half turned so as to pitch her voice fairly[2] into the room, gradually ceased. Gabriel recognised the prelude. It was that of an old song of Aunt Julia's – *Arrayed for the Bridal.*[3] Her voice, strong and clear in tone, attacked with great spirit the runs which embellish the air and though she sang very rapidly she did not miss even the smallest of the grace notes. To follow the voice, without looking at the singer's face, was to feel and share the excitement of swift and secure flight. Gabriel applauded loudly with all the others at the close of the song and loud applause was borne in from the invisible supper-table. It sounded so genuine that a little colour struggled[4] into Aunt Julia's face as she bent to replace in the music-stand the old leather-bound song-book that had her initials on the cover. Freddy Malins, who had listened with his head perched[5] sideways to hear her better, was still applauding when every one else had ceased and talking animatedly to his mother who nodded her head gravely and slowly in acquiescence. At last,

1. *hanging* : holding [her head] low.
2. *pitch her voice fairly* : establish the tonality of her voice well.
3. *Arrayed for the Bridal* : an aria from Bellini's "I Puritani" (1835).
4. *struggled* [ʃrʌgd] : pushed its way gradually.
5. *perched* : held in un unnatural position.

when he could clap no more he stood up suddenly and hurried across the room to Aunt Julia whose hand he seized and held in both his hands, shaking it when words failed him or the catch in his voice proved too much for him.

—I was just telling my mother, he said, I never heard you sing so well, never. No, I never heard your voice so good as it is to-night. Now! Would you believe that now? That's the truth. Upon my word and honour that's the truth. I never heard your voice sound so fresh and so . . . so clear and fresh, never.

Aunt Julia smiled broadly and murmured something about compliments as she released her hand from his grasp. Mr Browne extended his open hand towards her and said to those who were near him in the manner of a showman introducing a prodigy to an audience:

—Miss Julia Morkan, my latest discovery!

He was laughing very heartily at this himself when Freddy Malins turned to him and said:

—Well, Browne, if you're serious you might make a worse discovery. All I can say is I never heard her sing half so well as long as I am coming here.[1] And that's the honest truth.

—Neither did I, said Mr Browne. I think her voice has greatly improved.

Aunt Julia shrugged her shoulders[2] and said with meek pride:

—Thirty years ago I hadn't a bad voice as voices go.

---

1. *as long as I am coming here* : "as long as I have been coming here".

2. *shrugged* [ʃrʌgd] *her shoulders* : raised and contracted her shoulders momentarily (an expression of [apparent] lack of interest).

—I often told Julia, said Aunt Kate emphatically, that she was simply thrown away in that choir. But she never would be said[1] by me.

She turned as if to appeal to the good sense of the others against a refractory[2] child while Aunt Julia gazed in front of her, a vague smile of reminiscence playing on her face.

—No, continued Aunt Kate, she wouldn't be said or led by anyone, slaving[3] there in that choir night and day, night and day. Six o'clock on Christmas morning! And all for what?

—Well, isn't it for the honour of God, Aunt Kate? asked Mary Jane, twisting round[4] on the piano-stool and smiling.

Aunt Kate turned fiercely[5] on her niece and said:

—I know all about the honour of God, Mary Jane, but I think it's not at all honourable for the pope to turn out the women out of the choirs[6] that have slaved there all their lives and put little whipper-snappers[7] of boys over their heads. I suppose it is for the good of the Church if the pope does it. But it's not just, Mary Jane, and it's not right.

She had worked herself into a passion and would have continued in defence of her sister for

1. *never would be said* : obsolete usage for "never would be told".
2. *refractory* [rɪ'fræktəri] : obstinate, rebellious.
3. *slaving* : working hard (like a slave).
4. *twisting round* : turning the top part of her body to look behind her.
5. *fiercely* [fɪəsli] : angrily.
6. *women out of the choirs* : in his "Motu Proprio" of 1903, Pope Pius X forbade both the use of instruments other than the organ and the presence of women in choirs.
7. *whipper-snappers* ['wɪpə‚snæpəz] : young, insignificant but pretentious people.

it was a sore subject[1] with her but Mary Jane, seeing that all the dancers had come back, intervened pacifically:

—Now, Aunt Kate, you're giving scandal to Mr Browne who is of the other persuasion.[2]

Aunt Kate turned to Mr Browne, who was grinning at this allusion to his religion, and said hastily:

—O, I don't question the pope's being right. I'm only a stupid old woman and I wouldn't presume to do such a thing. But there's such a thing as common everyday politeness and gratitude. And if I were in Julia's place I'd tell that Father Healy[3] straight up to his face . . .

—And besides, Aunt Kate, said Mary Jane, we really are all hungry and when we are hungry we are all very quarrelsome.[4]

—And when we are thirsty we are also quarrelsome, added Mr Browne.

—So that we had better go to supper, said Mary Jane, and finish the discussion afterwards.

On the landing outside the drawing-room Gabriel found his wife and Mary Jane trying to persuade Miss Ivors to stay for supper. But Miss Ivors, who had put on her hat and was buttoning her cloak, would not stay. She did not feel in the least hungry and she had already overstayed her time.

---

1. *a sore subject* : a subject causing distress or annoyance.
2. *the other persuasion* : i.e. Protestant.
3. *Father Healy* : in 1891, Joyce wrote a poem entitled "Et Tu Healy". Its subject matter was the betrayal of Charles Stewart Parnell by Timothy M. Healy. Remember, too, that the pianist who takes Kathleen Kearney's place in "A Mother" is also called Miss Healy.
4. *quarrelsome* [ˈkwɒrəlsəm] : inclined to quarrel (= argue).

—But only for ten minutes, Molly, said Mrs Conroy. That won't delay you.

—To take a pick itself,[1] said Mary Jane, after all your dancing.

—I really couldn't, said Miss Ivors.

—I am afraid you didn't enjoy yourself at all, said Mary Jane hopelessly.

—Ever so much, I assure you, said Miss Ivors, but you really must let me run off now.

—But how can you get home? asked Mrs Conroy.

—O, it's only two steps up the quay.

Gabriel hesitated a moment and said:

—If you will allow me, Miss Ivors, I'll see you home if you really are obliged to go.

But Miss Ivors broke away from them.

—I won't hear of it, she cried. For goodness sake go in to your suppers and don't mind me. I'm quite well able to take care of myself.

—Well, you're the comical girl, Molly, said Mrs Conroy frankly.

—*Beannacht libh*,[2] cried Miss Ivors, with a laugh, as she ran down the staircase.

Mary Jane gazed after her, a moody puzzled expression on her face, while Mrs Conroy leaned over the banisters to listen for the hall-door. Gabriel asked himself was he the cause of her abrupt departure. But she did not seem to be in ill humour: she had gone away laughing. He stared blankly down the staircase.

At that moment Aunt Kate came toddling out of

---

1. *To take a pick itself* : "Just have a bite to eat".
2. *Beannacht libh* [bə‚nɑːkt ‚liːb] : a farewell salutation in Irish.

the supper-room, almost wringing her hands[1] in despair.

—Where is Gabriel? she cried. Where on earth is Gabriel? There's everyone waiting in there, stage to let,[2] and nobody to carve the goose!

—Here I am, Aunt Kate! cried Gabriel, with sudden animation, ready to carve a flock[3] of geese, if necessary.

A fat brown goose lay at one end of the table and at the other end, on a bed of creased paper strewn[4] with sprigs of parsley, lay a great ham, stripped of its outer skin and peppered over with crust crumbs,[5] a neat paper frill[6] round its shin and beside this was a round of spiced beef. Between these rival ends ran parallel lines of side-dishes: two little minsters of jelly,[7] red and yellow; a shallow[8] dish full of blocks of blancmange and red jam, a large green leaf-shaped dish with a stalk-shaped handle, on which lay bunches of purple raisins and peeled almonds, a companion dish on which lay a solid rectangle of Smyrna figs, a dish of custard topped with grated nutmeg, a small bowl full of chocolates and sweets wrapped in gold and silver papers and a glass vase in which stood some tall celery stalks. In the centre

1. *wringing* ['rɪŋɪŋ] *her hands* : twisting her hands together as a sign of distress.
2. *stage to let* : "the stage is empty".
3. *flock* (collective noun) : a great number.
4. *strewn* [struːn] : spread loosely around.
5. *crust crumbs* : small fragments of the hard part of bread.
6. *paper frill* : decoration made from a length of paper.
7. *minsters of jelly* : jelly shaped in the form of a church.
8. *shallow* ['ʃæləʊ] : not deep.

of the table there stood, as sentries [1] to a fruit-stand which upheld a pyramid of oranges and American apples, two squat [2] old-fashioned decanters of cut glass, one containing port and the other dark sherry. On the closed square piano a pudding in a huge yellow dish lay in waiting and behind it were three squads [3] of bottles of stout and ale and minerals, drawn up according to the colours of their uniforms, the first two black, with brown and red labels, the third and smallest squad white, with transverse green sashes.

Gabriel took his seat boldly at the head of the table and, having looked to the edge of the carver, plunged [4] his fork firmly into the goose. He felt quite at ease now for he was an expert carver and liked nothing better than to find himself at the head of a well-laden [5] table.

—Miss Furlong, what shall I send you? he asked. A wing or a slice of the breast?

—Just a small slice of the breast.

—Miss Higgins, what for you?

—O, anything at all, Mr Conroy.

While Gabriel and Miss Daly exchanged plates of goose and plates of ham and spiced beef Lily went from guest to guest with a dish of hot floury potatoes wrapped in a white napkin. This was Mary Jane's

---

1. *sentries* ['sentrɪz] : guards (usually military).

2. *squat* [skwɒt] : short and wide at the bottom.

3. *squads* [skwɒdz] : a small number of soldiers assembled together for some purpose. Joyce continues the metaphor: the bottles are "drawn up (= ordered) according to the colour of their uniforms".

4. *plunged* ['plʌndʒd] : pushed quickly and deeply.

5. *well-laden* [ˌwel'leɪdən] : "laden" (= loaded) with a lot of food.

idea and she had also suggested apple sauce for the
goose but Aunt Kate had said that plain roast goose
without apple sauce had always been good enough
for her and she hoped she might never eat worse.
Mary Jane waited on [1] her pupils and saw that they
got the best slices and Aunt Kate and Aunt Julia
opened and carried across from the piano bottles of
stout and ale for the gentlemen and bottles of
minerals for the ladies. There was a great deal of
confusion and laughter and noise, the noise of orders
and counter-orders, of knives and forks, of corks and
glass-stoppers. Gabriel began to carve second
helpings as soon as he had finished the first round
without serving himself. Every one protested loudly
so that he compromised by taking a long draught of
stout for he had found the carving hot work. Mary
Jane settled down quietly to her supper but Aunt
Kate and Aunt Julia were still toddling round the
table, walking on each other's heels, getting in each
other's way and giving each other unheeded [2] orders.
Mr Browne begged of them to sit down and eat their
suppers and so did Gabriel but they said there was
time enough so that, at last Freddy Malins stood up
and, capturing Aunt Kate, plumped her down on her
chair [3] amid general laughter.

When everyone had been well served Gabriel said,
smiling:

—Now, if anyone wants a little more of what
vulgar people call stuffing [4] let him or her speak.

1. *waited on* : attended, gave assistance to.
2. *unheeded* [ˌʌnˈhiːdɪd] : not listened to.
3. *plumped her down on her chair* : sat her down heavily.
4. *stuffing* : savoury ingredients put into meat, poultry etc., in
cooking.

A chorus of voices invited him to begin his own supper and Lily came forward with three potatoes which she had reserved for him.

—Very well, said Gabriel amiably, as he took another preparatory draught, kindly forget my existence, ladies and gentlemen, for a few minutes.

He set to[1] his supper and took no part in the conversation with which the table covered Lily's removal of the plates. The subject of talk was the opera company which was then at the Theatre Royal. Mr Bartell D'Arcy, the tenor, a dark-complexioned young man with a smart moustache, praised very highly the leading contralto of the company but Miss Furlong thought she had a rather vulgar style of production. Freddy Malins said there was a negro chieftain singing in the second part of the Gaiety pantomime who had one of the finest tenor voices he had ever heard.

—Have you heard him? he asked Mr Bartell D'Arcy across the table.

—No, answered Mr Bartell D'Arcy carelessly.

—Because, Freddy Malins explained, now I'd be curious to hear your opinion of him. I think he has a grand voice.

—It takes Teddy[2] to find out the really good things, said Mr Browne familiarly to the table.

—And why couldn't he have a voice too? asked Freddy Malins sharply. Is it because he's only a black?

Nobody answered this question and Mary Jane led

---

1. *set to* : began in a serious manner.
2. *It takes Teddy* : "Teddy has the ability" or "You need a person like Teddy".

the table back to the legitimate [1] opera. One of her
pupils had given her a pass for *Mignon*. Of course it
was very fine, she said, but it made her think of poor
Georgina Burns. Mr Browne could go back farther
still, to the old Italian companies that used to come
to Dublin-Tietjens, Ilma de Murzka, Campanini, the
great Trebelli, Giuglini, Ravelli, Aramburo. Those
were the days, he said, when there was something
like singing to be heard in Dublin. He told too of how
the top gallery of the old Royal used to be packed [2]
night after night, of how one night an Italian tenor
had sung five encores to *Let me Like a Soldier Fall*,
introducing a high C every time, and of how the
gallery boys would sometimes in their enthusiasm
unyoke [3] the horses from the carriage of some great
prima donna and pull her themselves through the
streets to her hotel. Why did they never play the
grand old operas now, he asked, *Dinorah, Lucrezia
Borgia*? Because they could not get the voices to sing
them: that was why.

—O, well, said Mr Bartell D'Arcy, I presume there
are as good singers to-day as there were then.

—Where are they? asked Mr Browne defiantly.

—In London, Paris, Milan, said Mr Bartell D'Arcy
warmly. I suppose Caruso, for example, is quite as
good, if not better than any of the men you have
mentioned.

—Maybe so, said Mr Browne. But I may tell you
I doubt it strongly.

—O, I'd give anything to hear Caruso sing, said

1. *legitimate* : serious, or "grand" opera.
2. *packed* : very full.
3. *unyoke* [ʌnˈjəʊk] : untie, detach.

Mary Jane.

—For me, said Aunt Kate, who had been picking a bone, there was only one tenor. To please me, I mean. But I suppose none of you ever heard of him.

—Who was he, Miss Morkan? asked Mr Bartell D'Arcy politely.

—His name, said Aunt Kate, was Parkinson. I heard him when he was in his prime and I think he had then the purest tenor voice that was ever put into a man's throat.

—Strange, said Mr Bartell D'Arcy. I never even heard of him.

—Yes, yes, Miss Morkan is right, said Mr Browne. I remember hearing of old Parkinson, but he's too far back for me.

—A beautiful pure sweet mellow[1] English tenor, said Aunt Kate with enthusiasm.

Gabriel having finished, the huge pudding was transferred to the table. The clatter of forks and spoons began again. Gabriel's wife served out spoonfuls of the pudding and passed the plates down the table. Midway down they were held up by Mary Jane, who replenished them with raspberry or orange jelly or with blancmange and jam. The pudding was of Aunt Julia's making and she received praises for it from all quarters.[2] She herself said that it was not quite brown enough.

—Well, I hope, Miss Morkan, said Mr Browne, that I'm brown enough for you because, you know, I'm all brown.[3]

---

1. *mellow* ['meləʊ]: gentle but full and mature.
2. *from all quarters* : from all sides.
3. *I'm all brown* : again, brown indicates paralysis (see also note 4, p. 25).

All the gentlemen, except Gabriel, ate some of the
pudding out of compliment to Aunt Julia. As Gabriel
never ate sweets the celery had been left for him.
Freddy Malins also took a stalk of celery and ate it
with his pudding. He had been told that celery was
a capital thing[1] for the blood and he was just then
under doctor's care. Mrs Malins, who had been silent
all through the supper, said that her son was going
down to Mount Melleray[2] in a week or so. The table
then spoke of Mount Melleray, how bracing[3] the air
was down there, how hospitable the monks were and
how they never asked for a penny-piece from their
guests.

—And do you mean to say, asked Mr Browne
incredulously, that a chap can go down there and put
up[4] there as if it were a hotel and live on the fat of
the land[5] and then come away without paying a
farthing?[6]

—O, most people give some donation to the
monastery when they leave, said Mary Jane.

—I wish we had an institution like that in our
Church, said Mr Browne candidly.

He was astonished to hear that the monks never
spoke, got up at two in the morning and slept in their

---

1. *a capital thing* : "an excellent thing".
2. *Mount Melleray* : in County Waterford in southeastern
   Ireland, the site of a Cistercian abbey. The abbey guest house
   often received convalescent alcoholics, in theory free of charge,
   though it was usual to make a donation to the abbey.
3. *bracing* ['breɪsɪŋ]: invigorating.
4. *put up* : lodge, board (see "The Boarding House").
5. *live on the fat of the land* : live on what is provided (i.e. in
   comfort with plenty to eat).
6. *farthing* ['faːðɪŋ] : a quarter of an old penny.

coffins.[1] He asked what they did it for.

—That's the rule of the order, said Aunt Kate firmly.

—Yes, but why? asked Mr Browne.

Aunt Kate repeated that it was the rule, that was all. Mr Browne still seemed not to understand. Freddy Malins explained to him, as best he could, that the monks were trying to make up for[2] the sins committed by all the sinners in the outside world. The explanation was not very clear for Mr Browne grinned and said:

—I like that idea very much but wouldn't a comfortable spring bed do them as well[3] as a coffin?

—The coffin, said Mary Jane, is to remind them of the last end.

As the subject had grown lugubrious[4] it was buried in a silence of the table during which Mrs Malins could be heard saying to her neighbour in an indistinct undertone:

—They are very good men, the monks, very pious men.

The raisins and almonds and figs and apples and oranges and chocolates and sweets were now passed about the table and Aunt Julia invited all the guests to have either port or sherry. At first Mr Bartell D'Arcy refused to take either but one of his neighbours nudged[5] him and whispered something to him upon which he allowed his glass to be filled.

---

1. *coffins* : these monks do not in fact sleep in their coffins.
2. *make up for* : compensate for.
3. *do ... as well* : "serve ... as well", "be just as good as".
4. *lugubrious* [lə'guːbrɪəs]: dismal, mournful.
5. *nudged* [nʌdʒd] : pushed lightly with the elbow to attract attention.

Gradually as the last glasses were being filled the conversation ceased. A pause followed, broken only by the noise of the wine and by unsettlings [1] of chairs. The Misses Morkan, all three, looked down at the tablecloth. Some one coughed once or twice and then a few gentlemen patted [2] the table gently as a signal for silence. The silence came and Gabriel pushed back his chair and stood up.

The patting at once grew louder in encouragement and then ceased altogether. Gabriel leaned his ten trembling fingers on the tablecloth and smiled nervously at the company. Meeting a row of upturned faces he raised his eyes to the chandelier. The piano was playing a waltz tune and he could hear the skirts sweeping against the drawing-room door. People, perhaps, were standing in the snow on the quay outside, gazing up at the lighted windows and listening to the waltz music. The air was pure there. In the distance lay the park where the trees were weighted [3] with snow. The Wellington Monument wore a gleaming cap of snow that flashed westward over the white field of Fifteen Acres. [4]

He began:

—Ladies and Gentlemen.

—It has fallen to my lot [5] this evening, as in years past, to perform a very pleasing task but a task for which I am afraid my poor powers as a speaker are all too inadequate.

---

1. *unsettlings* : disturbance, movement.
2. *patted* : see note 1, p. 216.
3. *weighted* : weighed down.
4. *Fifteen Acres* : part of Phoenix Park.
5. *It has fallen to my lot* : I have been chosen.

—No, no! said Mr Browne.

—But, however that may be, I can only ask you to-night to take the will for the deed[1] and to lend me your attention for a few moments while I endeavour to express to you in words what my feelings are on this occasion.

—Ladies and Gentlemen. It is not the first time that we have gathered together under this hospitable roof, around this hospitable board.[2] It is not the first time that we have been the recipients – or perhaps, I had better say, the victims – of the hospitality of certain good ladies.

He made a circle in the air with his arm and paused. Every one laughed or smiled at Aunt Kate and Aunt Julia and Mary Jane who all turned crimson with pleasure. Gabriel went on more boldly:

—I feel more strongly with every recurring year that our country has no tradition which does it so much honour and which it should guard so jealously as that of its hospitality. It is a tradition that is unique as far as my experience goes (and I have visited not a few places abroad) among the modern nations. Some would say, perhaps, that with us it is rather a failing than anything to be boasted of.[3] But granted even that,[4] it is, to my mind, a princely failing, and one that I trust will long be cultivated among us. Of one thing, at least, I am sure. As long as this one roof shelters the good ladies aforesaid –

---

1. *take the will for the deed* : excuse my inadequacy (in oratory skills).
2. *board* : table.
3. *boasted* ['bɔʊstɪd] *of* : speak of with pride.
4. *But granted even that* : even if we accept that.

and I wish from my heart it may do so for many and
many a long year to come – the tradition of genuine
warm-hearted courteous Irish hospitality, which our
forefathers have handed down to us and which we in
turn must hand down to our descendants, is still
alive among us.

A hearty[1] murmur of assent ran round the table.
It shot through Gabriel's mind that Miss Ivors was
not there and that she had gone away discourteously:
and he said with confidence in himself:

—Ladies and Gentlemen.

—A new generation is growing up in our midst, a
generation actuated by new ideas and new
principles. It is serious and enthusiastic for these
new ideas and its enthusiasm, even when it is
misdirected, is, I believe, in the main sincere. But we
are living in a sceptical and, if I may use the phrase,
a thought-tormented age: and sometimes I fear that
this new generation, educated or hypereducated as
it is, will lack those qualities of humanity, of
hospitality, of kindly humour which belonged to an
older day. Listening to-night to the names of all
those great singers of the past it seemed to me, I
must confess, that we were living in a less spacious
age. Those days might, without exaggeration, be
called spacious days: and if they are gone beyond
recall let us hope, at least, that in gatherings such
as this we shall still speak of them with pride and
affection, still cherish[2] in our hearts the memory of
those dead and gone great ones whose fame the world
will not willingly let die.

1. *hearty* : enthusiastic.
2. *cherish* : value, hold dear.

—Hear, hear! said Mr Browne loudly.

—But yet, continued Gabriel, his voice falling into a softer inflection, there are always in gatherings such as this sadder thoughts that will recur to our minds: thoughts of the past, of youth, of changes, of absent faces that we miss here tonight. Our path through life is strewn[1] with many such sad memories: and were we to brood upon[2] them always we could not find the heart[3] to go on bravely with our work among the living. We have all of us living duties and living affections which claim, and rightly claim, our strenuous endeavours.

—Therefore, I will not linger[4] on the past. I will not let any gloomy moralising intrude upon us here to-night. Here we are gathered together for a brief moment from the bustle[5] and rush of our everyday routine. We arc met here as friends, in the spirit of good-fellowship, as colleagues, also to a certain extent, in the true spirit of *camaraderie*, and as the guest of – what shall I call them? – the Three Graces of the Dublin musical world.

The table burst into applause and laughter at this sally.[6] Aunt Julia vainly asked each of her neighbours in turn to tell her what Gabriel had said.

—He says we are the Three Graces, Aunt Julia, said Mary Jane.

Aunt Julia did not understand but she looked up,

---

1. *strewn* : (here) full [of], covered.
2. *brood upon* : contemplate.
3. *we could not find the heart* : make ourselves, bring ourselves.
4. *linger* : (here) continue talking about.
5. *bustle* [bʌsl] : excited activity.
6. *sally* : (here) an utterance spoken suddenly.

smiling, at Gabriel, who continued in the same vein:

—Ladies and Gentlemen.

—I will not attempt to play to-night the part that Paris played on another occasion. I will not attempt to choose between them. The task would be an invidious one and one beyond my poor powers. For when I view them in turn, whether it be our chief hostess herself, whose good heart, whose too good heart, has become a byword [1] with all who know her, or her sister, who seems to be gifted with perennial youth and whose singing must have been a surprise and a revelation to us all to-night, or, last but not least, when I consider our youngest hostess, talented, cheerful, hard-working and the best of nieces, I confess, Ladies and Gentlemen, that I do not know to which of them I should award the prize.

Gabriel glanced down at his aunts and, seeing the large smile on Aunt Julia's face and the tears which had risen to Aunt Kate's eyes, hastened to his close. He raised his glass of port gallantly, while every member of the company fingered a glass expectantly, and said loudly:

—Let us toast [2] them all three together. Let us drink to their health, wealth, long life, happiness and prosperity and may they long continue to hold the proud and self-won position which they hold in their profession and the position of honour and affection which they hold in our hearts.

All the guests stood up, glass in hand, and, turning towards the three seated ladies, sang in

1. *has become a byword* ['baɪwɜːd] : is widely recognised.
2. *toast* : drink to.

unison, with Mr Browne as leader:

> *For they are jolly gay fellows,*
> *For they are jolly gay fellows,*
> *For they are jolly gay fellows,*
> *Which nobody can deny.* [1]

Aunt Kate was making frank use of[2] her handkerchief and even Aunt Julia seemed moved.[3] Freddy Malins beat time[4] with his pudding-fork and the singers turned towards one another, as if in melodious conference, while they sang with emphasis:

> *Unless he tells a lie,*[5]
> *Unless he tells a lie.*

Then, turning once more towards their hostesses, they sang:

> *For they are jolly gay fellows,*
> *For they are jolly gay fellows,*
> *For they are jolly gay fellows,*
> *Which nobody can deny.*

The acclamation which followed was taken up[6] beyond the door of the supper-room by many of the

---

1. *For they are ... deny*: The first three lines of this popular drinking song are usually "For he's a jolly good fellow".
2. *making frank use of*: openly using.
3. *moved*: affected by emotion.
4. *beat time*: marked or followed the music.
5. *Unless he tells a lie*: these two lines are usually "And so say all of us".
6. *taken up*: begun again (following those in the room).

other guests and renewed time after time, Freddy Malins acting as officer with his fork on high.

. . . .

The piercing morning air came into the hall where they were standing so that Aunt Kate said:

—Close the door, somebody. Mrs Malins will get her death of cold.

—Browne is out there, Aunt Kate, said Mary Jane.

—Browne is everywhere, said Aunt Kate, lowering her voice.

Mary Jane laughed at her tone.

—Really, she said archly,[1] he is very attentive.

—He has been laid on here like the gas,[2] said Aunt Kate in the same tone, all during the Christmas.

She laughed herself this time good-humouredly and then added quickly:

—But tell him to come in, Mary Jane, and close the door. I hope to goodness[3] he didn't hear me.

At that moment the hall-door was opened and Mr Browne came in from the doorstep, laughing as if his heart would break. He was dressed in a long green overcoat with mock[4] astrakhan cuffs and collar and wore on his head an oval fur cap. He pointed down the snow-covered quay from where the sound of shrill prolonged whistling was borne in.

—Teddy will have all the cabs in Dublin out, he said.

1. *archly* ['ɑːtʃli]: in an affectedly playful manner.
2. *He has been laid on here like the gas* : implies that Mr Browne is there all the time.
3. *I hope to goodness* : "I really hope".
4. *mock* : imitation.

Gabriel advanced from the little pantry behind the office, struggling into[1] his overcoat and, looking round the hall, said:

—Gretta not down yet?

—She's getting on her things, Gabriel, said Aunt Kate.

—Who's playing up there? asked Gabriel.

—Nobody. They're all gone.

—O no, Aunt Kate, said Mary Jane. Bartell D'Arcy and Miss O'Callaghan aren't gone yet.

—Someone is strumming[2] at the piano, anyhow, said Gabriel.

Mary Jane glanced at Gabriel and Mr Browne and said with a shiver:[3]

—It makes me feel cold to look at you two gentlemen muffled up[4] like that. I wouldn't like to face your journey home at this hour.

—I'd like nothing better this minute, said Mr Browne stoutly,[5] than a rattling fine[6] walk in the country or a fast drive with a good spanking goer between the shafts.[7]

—We used to have a very good horse and trap[8] at home, said Aunt Julia sadly.

—The never-to-be-forgotten Johnny, said Mary

---

1. *struggling* ['strʌɡlɪŋ] *into* : putting on with difficulty.
2. *strumming* : playing without ability or care.
3. *shiver* : a momentary trembling (from the cold).
4. *muffled* ['mʌfld] *up* : covered to provide protection against the weather.
5. *stoutly* ['staʊtli]: energetically.
6. *rattling fine* : a quick and enjoyable.
7. *spanking goer between the shafts* : a quick energetic horse pulling the trap (see note 8 below).
8. *trap* : a horse-drawn vehicle.

Jane, laughing.

Aunt Kate and Gabriel laughed too.

—Why, what was wonderful about Johnny? asked Mr Browne.

—The late lamented[1] Patrick Morkan, our grandfather, that is, explained Gabriel, commonly known in his later years as the old gentleman, was a glue-boiler.

—O, now, Gabriel, said Aunt Kate, laughing, he had a starch mill.

—Well, glue or starch, said Gabriel, the old gentleman had a horse by the name of Johnny. And Johnny used to work in the old gentleman's mill, walking round and round in order to drive the mill. That was all very well; but now comes the tragic part about Johnny. One fine day the old gentleman thought he'd like to drive out with the quality[2] to a military review in the park.

—The Lord have mercy on his soul, said Aunt Kate compassionately.

—Amen, said Gabriel. So the old gentleman, as I said, harnessed[3] Johnny and put on his very best tall hat and his very best stock collar[4] and drove out in grand style from his ancestral mansion somewhere near Back Lane, I think.

Every one laughed, even Mrs Malins, at Gabriel's manner and Aunt Kate said:

—O now, Gabriel, he didn't live in Back Lane, really. Only the mill was there.

---

1. *The late lamented* : deceased, dead (a euphemism).
2. *the quality* : the upper classes.
3. *harnessed* ['hɑːnɪst]: attached to.
4. *stock collar* : an old-fashioned type of formal collar.

—Out from the mansion of his forefathers,[1] continued Gabriel, he drove with Johnny. And everything went on beautifully until Johnny came in sight of King Billy's[2] statue: and whether he fell in love with the horse King Billy sits on or whether he thought he was back again in the mill, anyhow he began to walk round the statue.

Gabriel paced[3] in a circle round the hall in his goloshes amid the laughter of the others.

—Round and round he went, said Gabriel, and the old gentleman, who was a very pompous old gentleman, was highly indignant. *Go on, sir! What do you mean, sir? Johnny! Johnny! Most extraordinary conduct! Can't understand the horse!*

The peals[4] of laughter which followed Gabriel's imitation of the incident were interrupted by a resounding[5] knock at the hall-door. Mary Jane ran to open it and let in Freddy Malins. Freddy Malins, with his hat well back on his head and his shoulders humped[6] with cold, was puffing and steaming[8] after his exertions.

—I could only get one cab, he said.

—O, we'll find another along the quay, said Gabriel.

---

1. *forefathers* ['fɔːˌfɑːðəz] : ancestors.
2. *King Billy* : William of Orange, King William III of England (reigned from 1689-1702). After the Battle of the Boyne in 1690 he was always remembered as a great oppressor by the Irish.
3. *paced* [peɪst] : walked slowly with regular steps.
4. *peals* [piːlz] : long loud reverberating sounds.
5. *resounding* : loud and reverberating.
6. *humped* : raised and contracted.
7. *puffing and steaming* : breathing heavily and noisily.

—Yes, said Aunt Kate. Better not keep Mrs Malins standing in the draught.[1]

Mrs Malins was helped down the front steps by her son and Mr Browne and, after many manoeuvres, hoisted[2] into the cab. Freddy Malins clambered[3] in after her and spent a long time settling her on the seat, Mr Browne helping him with advice. At last she was settled comfortably and Freddy Malins invited Mr Browne into the cab. There was a good deal of confused talk, and then Mr Browne got into the cab. The cabman settled his rug over his knees, and bent down for the address. The confusion grew greater and the cabman was directed differently by Freddy Malins and Mr Browne, each of whom had his head out through a window of the cab. The difficulty was to know where to drop[4] Mr Browne along the route and Aunt Kate, Aunt Julia and Mary Jane helped the discussion from the doorstep with cross-directions and contradictions and abundance of laughter. As for Freddy Malins he was speechless with laughter. He popped his head in and out[5] of the window every moment, to the great danger of his hat, and told his mother how the discussion was progressing, till at last Mr Browne shouted to the bewildered[6] cabman above the din[7] of everybody's laughter:

—Do you know Trinity College?

1. *draught* ['drɑːft] : current of cold air.
2. *hoisted* : lifted with some difficulty.
3. *clambered* ['klæmbəd]: climbed in with difficulty and effort.
4. *drop* : set down, let [Mr Browne] get out.
5. *popped ... in and out* : moved ... in and out rapidly.
6. *bewildered* [bɪ'wɪldəd] : confused, perplexed.
7. *din* : loud confused sounds.

—Yes, sir, said the cabman.

—Well, drive bang up against[1] Trinity College gates, said Mr Browne, and then we'll tell you where to go. You understand now?

—Yes, sir, said the cabman.

—Make like a bird for Trinity College.

—Right, sir, cried the cabman.

The horse was whipped up[2] and the cab rattled off along the quay amid a chorus of laughter and adieus.

Gabriel had not gone to the door with the others. He was in a dark part of the hall gazing up the staircase. A woman was standing near the top of the first flight, in the shadow also. He could not see her face but he could see the terracotta and salmonpink panels of her skirt which the shadow made appear black and white. It was his wife. She was leaning on the banisters, listening to something. Gabriel was surprised at her stillness and strained his ear[3] to listen also. But he could hear little save[4] the noise of laughter and dispute on the front steps, a few chords struck on the piano and a few notes of a man's voice singing.

He stood still in the gloom[5] of the hall, trying to catch the air[6] that the voice was singing and gazing[7] up at his wife. There was grace and mystery in her attitude as if she were a symbol of something. He

1. *bang up against* : just in front of.
2. *whipped* [wɪpt] *up* : made to move (by using a whip).
3. *strained* [streɪnd] *his ear* : listened very carefully.
4   *save* : apart from.
5. *gloom* : partial darkness.
6. *catch the air* : recognise the words and melody and identify the song.
7. *gazing* [ˈgeɪzɪŋ] : looking steadily and intently.

Sackville Street monuments to O'Connell and Nelson.

Grafton Street looking towards Trinity College.

asked himself what is a woman standing on the stairs in the shadow, listening to distant music, a symbol of. If he were a painter he would paint her in that attitude. Her blue felt[1] hat would show off[2] the bronze of her hair against the darkness and the dark panels of her skirt would show off the light ones. *Distant Music* he would call the picture if he were a painter.

The hall-door was closed; and Aunt Kate, Aunt Julia and Mary Jane came down the hall, still laughing.

—Well, isn't Freddy terrible? said Mary Jane. He's really terrible.

Gabriel said nothing but pointed up the stairs towards where his wife was standing. Now that the hall-door was closed the voice and the piano could be heard more clearly. Gabriel held up his hand for them to be silent. The song seemed to be in the old Irish tonality and the singer seemed uncertain both of his words and of his voice. The voice, made plaintive[3] by distance and by the singer's hoarseness,[4] faintly illuminated the cadence of the air with words expressing grief:

> *O, the rain falls on my heavy locks*[5]
> *And the dew*[6] *wets my skin,*
> *My babe lies cold . . .*

---

1. *felt* : strong fibrous material made from wool.
2. *show off* : display to great effect.
3. *plaintive* : sad and sorrowful.
4. *hoarseness* : raucous and unpleasant quality to the voice (because Bartell D'Arcy has a cold).
5. *locks* : small pieces of hair (of the head).
6. *dew* [djuː] : drops of water which form on cold surfaces during the night.

—O, exclaimed Mary Jane. It's Bartell D'Arcy singing, and he wouldn't sing all the night. O, I'll get him to sing a song before he goes.

—O, do, Mary Jane, said Aunt Kate.

Mary Jane brushed past[1] the others and ran to the staircase but before she reached it the singing stopped and the piano was closed abruptly.

—O, what a pity! she cried. Is he coming down, Gretta?

Gabriel heard his wife answer yes and saw her come down towards them. A few steps behind her were Mr Bartell D'Arcy and Miss O'Callaghan.

—O, Mr D'Arcy, cried Mary Jane, it's downright mean[2] of you to break off like that when we were all in raptures listening to you.

—I have been at him all the evening, said Miss O'Callaghan, and Mrs Conroy too and he told us he had a dreadful cold and couldn't sing.

—O, Mr D'Arcy, said Aunt Kate, now that was a great fib[3] to tell.

—Can't you see that I'm as hoarse as a crow? said Mr D'Arcy roughly.

He went into the pantry hastily and put on his overcoat. The others, taken aback[4] by his rude[5] speech, could find nothing to say. Aunt Kate wrinkled[6] her brows and made signs to the others to

1. *brushed past* : lightly touched [the others] while moving past.
2. *downright mean* : positively unkind.
3. *fib* : (not very serious) lie.
4. *taken aback* [ə'bæk] : disconcerted.
5. *rude* : impolite, discourteous.
6. *wrinkled* ['rɪŋkld] : contracted so that lines appeared.

drop the subject. Mr D'Arcy stood swathing[1] his neck carefully and frowning.

—It's the weather, said Aunt Julia, after a pause.

—Yes, everybody has colds, said Aunt Kate readily, everybody.

—They say, said Mary Jane, we haven't had snow like it for thirty years; and I read this morning in the newspapers that the snow is general all over Ireland.

—I love the look of snow, said Aunt Julia sadly.

—So do I, said Miss O'Callaghan. I think Christmas is never really Christmas unless we have the snow on the ground.

—But poor Mr D'Arcy doesn't like the snow, said Aunt Kate, smiling.

Mr D'Arcy came from the pantry, fully swathed and buttoned, and in a repentant tone told them the history of his cold. Every one gave him advice and said it was a great pity and urged him to be very careful of his throat in the night air. Gabriel watched his wife who did not join in the conversation. She was standing right under the dusty fanlight and the flame of the gas lit up the rich bronze of her hair which he had seen her drying at the fire a few days before. She was in the same attitude and seemed unaware of the talk about her. At last she turned towards them and Gabriel saw that there was colour on her cheeks and that her eyes were shining. A sudden tide[2] of joy went leaping out of his heart.

—Mr D'Arcy, she said, what is the name of that song you were singing?

1. *swathing* ['sweɪðɪŋ] : covering.
2. *tide* : strong waves.

—It's called *The Lass of Aughrim*, said Mr D'Arcy, but I couldn't remember it properly.[1] Why? Do you know it?

—*The Lass of Aughrim*, she repeated. I couldn't think of the name.

—It's a very nice air, said Mary Jane. I'm sorry you were not in voice to-night.

—Now, Mary Jane, said Aunt Kate, don't annoy Mr D'Arcy. I won't have him annoyed.

Seeing that all were ready to start she shepherded [2] them to the door where good-night was said:

—Well, good-night, Aunt Kate, and thanks for the pleasant evening.

—Good-night, Gabriel. Good-night, Gretta!

—Good-night, Aunt Kate, and thanks ever so much. Good-night, Aunt Julia.

—O, good-night, Gretta, I didn't see you.

—Good-night, Mr D'Arcy. Good-night, Miss O'Callaghan.

—Good-night, Miss Morkan.

—Good-night, again.

—Good-night, all. Safe home.

—Good-night. Good-night.

The morning was still dark. A dull yellow light brooded over the houses and the river; and the sky seemed to be descending. It was slushy[3] underfoot; and only streaks[4] and patches of snow lay on the

---

1. *properly* : accurately, correctly.
2. *shepherded* : conducted, guided.
3. *It was slushy* ['slʌʃi] : i.e. there was "slush" (a mixture of snow and water).
4. *streaks*   : long thin irregular lines.

roofs, on the parapets of the quay and on the area railings. The lamps were still burning redly in the murky[1] air and, across the river, the palace of the Four Courts[2] stood out menacingly against the heavy sky.

She was walking on before him with Mr Bartell D'Arcy, her shoes in a brown parcel tucked[3] under one arm and her hands holding her skirt up from the slush. She had no longer any grace of attitude but Gabriel's eyes were still bright with happiness. The blood went bounding[4] along his veins; and the thoughts went rioting[5] through his brain, proud, joyful, tender, valorous.

She was walking on before him so lightly and so erect that he longed[6] to run after her noiselessly, catch her by the shoulders and say something foolish and affectionate into her ear. She seemed to him so frail[7] that he longed to defend her against something and then to be alone with her. Moments of their secret life together burst like stars upon his memory. A heliotrope envelope was lying beside his breakfast-cup and he was caressing it with his hand. Birds were twittering in the ivy and the sunny web of the curtain was shimmering along the floor: he could not eat for happiness. They were standing on the crowded platform and he was placing a ticket

1. *murky* : dark, unclear.
2. *the Four Courts* : the Irish Law Courts across the river from Merchant's Quay.
3. *tucked* [tʌkt] : carefully placed.
4. *bounding* : moving forward energetically.
5. *rioting* ['raɪətɪŋ] : moving quickly and in an uncontrolled way.
6. *longed* : desired strongly.
7. *frail* [freɪl] : fragile, delicate.

inside the warm palm of her glove. He was standing
with her in the cold, looking in through a grated
window[1] at a man making bottles in a roaring
furnace. It was very cold. Her face, fragrant in the
cold air, was quite close to his; and suddenly she
called out to the man at the furnace:

—Is the fire hot, sir?

But the man could not hear her with the noise of
the furnace. It was just as well. He might have
answered rudely.

A wave of yet more tender joy escaped from his
heart and went coursing[2] in warm flood along his
arteries. Like the tender fires of stars moments of
their life together, that no one knew of or would ever
know of, broke upon and illumined his memory. He
longed to recall to her those moments, to make her
forget the years of their dull existence together and
remember only their moments of ecstasy. For the
years, he felt, had not quenched[3] his soul or hers.
Their children, his writing, her household cares had
not quenched all their souls' tender fire. In one letter
that he had written to her then he had said: *Why is
it that words like these seem to me so dull and cold?
Is it because there is no word tender enough to be your
name?*

Like distant music these words that he had
written years before were borne towards him from
the past. He longed to be alone with her. When the
others had gone away, when he and she were in the
room in the hotel, then they would be alone together.

---

1. *grated* ['greɪtɪd] *window* : window with iron bars across it.
2. *coursing* : flowing quickly.
3. *quenched* ['kwentʃd]: extinguished.

He would call her softly:

—Gretta!

Perhaps she would not hear at once: she would be undressing. Then something in his voice would strike her. She would turn and look at him. . . .

At the corner of Winetavern Street they met a cab. He was glad of its rattling noise as it saved him from conversation. She was looking out of the window and seemed tired. The others spoke only a few words, pointing out some building or street. The horse galloped along wearily[1] under the murky morning sky, dragging his old rattling box after his heels, and Gabriel was again in a cab with her, galloping to catch the boat, galloping to their honeymoon.

As the cab drove across O'Connell Bridge Miss O'Callaghan said:

—They say you never cross O'Connell Bridge without seeing a white horse.

—I see a white man this time, said Gabriel.

—Where? asked Mr Bartell D'Arcy.

Gabriel pointed to the statue, on which lay patches of snow. Then he nodded familiarly to it and waved his hand.

—Good-night, Dan,[2] he said gaily.

When the cab drew up before the hotel Gabriel jumped out and, in spite of Mr Bartell D'Arcy's protest, paid the driver. He gave the man a shilling over his fare. The man saluted and said:

—A prosperous New Year to you, sir.

—The same to you, said Gabriel cordially.

1. *wearily* ['wɪərɪli]: in a very tired way.
2. *Dan* : diminutive for Daniel O'Connell (1775-1847). He was considered affectionately as the 'liberator', because he won Catholic emancipation for Ireland in 1829.

She leaned for a moment on his arm in getting out of the cab and while standing at the curbstone,[1] bidding the others good-night. She leaned lightly on his arm, as lightly as when she had danced with him a few hours before. He had felt proud and happy then, happy that she was his, proud of her grace and wifely carriage.[2] But now, after the kindling[3] again of so many memories, the first touch of her body, musical and strange and perfumed, sent through him a keen pang[4] of lust. Under cover of her silence he pressed her arm closely to his side; and, as they stood at the hotel door, he felt that they had escaped from their lives and duties, escaped from home and friends and run away together with wild and radiant hearts to a new adventure.

An old man was dozing in a great hooded chair in the hall. He lit a candle in the office and went before them to the stairs. They followed him in silence, their feet falling in soft thuds[5] on the thickly carpeted stairs. She mounted the stairs behind the porter, her head bowed in the ascent, her frail shoulders curved as with a burden, her skirt girt tightly about her. He could have flung his arms about her hips and held her still for his arms were trembling with desire to seize her and only the stress of[6] his nails against the palms of his hands held the

---

1. *curbstone* : long stone dividing the road from the pavement.
2. *carriage* ['kærɪdʒ] : deportment, way of moving.
3. *kindling* : bringing to life.
4. *keen pang* : strong almost painful feeling.
5. *thuds* : indistinct heavy sounds.
6. *stress of* : (here) the pressure of.

wild impulse of his body in check.[1] The porter halted
on the stairs to settle his guttering[2] candle. They halted
too on the steps below him. In the silence Gabriel could
hear the falling of the molten[3] wax into the tray and the
thumping[4] of his own heart against his ribs.

The porter led them along a corridor and opened
a door. Then he set his unstable candle down on a
toilet-table and asked at what hour they were to be
called in the morning.

—Eight, said Gabriel.

The porter pointed to the tap[5] of the electric-light
and began a muttered apology but Gabriel cut him
short.[6]

—We don't want any light. We have light enough
from the street. And I say, he added, pointing to the
candle, you might remove that handsome article, like
a good man.

The porter took up his candle again, but slowly for
he was surprised by such a novel idea. Then he
mumbled good night and went out. Gabriel shot the
lock to.[7]

A ghostly light from the street lamp lay in a long
shaft from one window to the door. Gabriel threw his
overcoat and hat on a couch[8] and crossed the room

---

1. *in check* : under control.
2. *guttering* : dying (because the liquid wax has melted away on
   one side).
3. *molten* : very hot liquid.
4. *thumping* : pulsating violently.
5. *tap* : switch.
6. *cut him short* : interrupted him so as to stop him talking.
7. *shot the lock to* : bolted the door very quickly.
8. *couch* [kaʊtʃ] : piece of furniture (often with a low back and
   an arm at one end) on which two or more people can sit.

towards the window. He looked down into the street in order that his emotion might calm a little. Then he turned and leaned against a chest of drawers with his back to the light. She had taken off her hat and cloak and was standing before a large swinging mirror, unhooking her waist. Gabriel paused for a few moments, watching her, and then said:

—Gretta!

She turned away from the mirror slowly and walked along the shaft of light towards him. Her face looked so serious and weary that the words would not pass Gabriel's lips. No, it was not the moment yet.

—You looked tired, he said.

—I am a little, she answered.

—You don't feel ill or weak?

—No, tired: that's all.

She went on to the window and stood there, looking out. Gabriel waited again and then, fearing that diffidence was about to conquer him, he said abruptly:

—By the way, Gretta!

—What is it?

—You know that poor fellow Malins? he said quickly.

—Yes. What about him?

—Well, poor fellow, he's a decent sort of chap, after all, continued Gabriel in a false voice. He gave me back that sovereign I lent him and I didn't expect it really. It's a pity he wouldn't keep away from that Browne, because he's not a bad fellow at heart.

He was trembling now with annoyance. Why did she seem so abstracted? He did not know how he could begin. Was she annoyed, too, about something? If she would only turn to him or come to him of her own accord! To take her as she was would be brutal. No, he must see some ardour in her eyes first. He longed to be master of her strange mood.

—When did you lend him the pound? she asked, after a pause.

Gabriel strove [1] to restrain himself from breaking out into brutal language about the sottish [2] Malins and his pound. He longed to cry to her from his soul, to crush her body against his, to overmaster her. But he said:

—O, at Christmas, when he opened that little Christmas-card shop in Henry Street.

He was in such a fever of rage and desire that he did not hear her come from the window. She stood before him for an instant, looking at him strangely. Then, suddenly raising herself on tiptoe and resting her hands lightly on his shoulders, she kissed him.

—You are a very generous person, Gabriel, she said.

Gabriel, trembling with delight at her sudden kiss and at the quaintness [3] of her phrase, put his hands on her hair and began smoothing it back, scarcely [4] touching it with his fingers. The washing had made it fine and brilliant. His heart was brimming over with happiness. [5] Just when he was wishing for it she had come to him of her own accord. Perhaps her thoughts had been running with his. Perhaps she

---

1. *strove* (strive, strove, striven) : tried very hard.
2. *sottish* : stupid because habitually drunk.
3. *quaintness* : (here) unusual formality.
4. *scarcely* ['skeəsli]: hardly, only just.
5. *His heart ... with happiness* : so full (of happiness) that it could not all be contained.

had felt the impetuous desire that was in him and then the yielding[1] mood had come upon her. Now that she had fallen to him so easily he wondered why he had been so diffident.

He stood, holding her head between his hands. Then, slipping one arm swiftly about her body and drawing her towards him, he said softly:

—Gretta dear, what are you thinking about?

She did not answer nor yield wholly to his arm. He said again, softly:

—Tell me what it is, Gretta. I think I know what is the matter. Do I know?

She did not answer at once. Then she said in an outburst of tears:

—O, I am thinking about that song, *The Lass of Aughrim*.

She broke loose from him and ran to the bed and, throwing her arms across the bed-rail, hid her face. Gabriel stood stock-still[2] for a moment in astonishment and then followed her. As he passed in the way of the cheval-glass he caught sight of himself in full length, his broad, well-filled shirt-front, the face whose expression always puzzled him when he saw it in a mirror and his glimmering gilt-rimmed eye-glasses. He halted a few paces from her and said:

—What about the song? Why does that make you cry?

She raised her head from her arms and dried her eyes with the back of her hand like a child. A kinder note than he had intended went into his voice.

—Why, Gretta? he asked.

---

1. *yielding* [ˈjɪəldɪŋ] : submitting, surrendering.
2. *stock-still* : completely motionless.

—I am thinking about a person long ago who used to sing that song.

—And who was the person long ago? asked Gabriel, smiling.

—It was a person I used to know in Galway when I was living with my grandmother, she said.

The smile passed away from Gabriel's face. A dull anger began to gather [1] again at the back of his mind and the dull fires of his lust began to glow angrily in his veins.

—Someone you were in love with? he asked ironically.

—It was a young boy I used to know, she answered, named Michael Furey.[2] He used to sing that song, *The Lass of Aughrim*. He was very delicate.

Gabriel was silent. He did not wish her to think that he was interested in this delicate boy.

—I can see him so plainly,[3] she said after a moment. Such eyes as he had: big dark eyes! And such an expression in them – an expression!

—O then, you were in love with him? said Gabriel.

—I used to go out walking with him, she said, when I was in Galway.

A thought flew across Gabriel's mind.

—Perhaps that was why you wanted to go to Galway with that Ivors girl? he said coldly.

---

1. *gather* : take shape, form.
2. *Michael Furey* : Michael is the name of an archangel. Also, Nora (Barnacle) Joyce had a suitor called Michael Bodkin, who suffered a similar fate to Michael Furey. Compare the connotations of his surname with the flat, bourgeois existence of Gabriel Conroy.
3. *plainly* : clearly.

She looked at him and asked in surprise:

—What for?

Her eyes made Gabriel feel awkward. He shrugged his shoulders and said:

—How do I know? To see him perhaps.

She looked away from him along the shaft of light towards the window in silence.

—He is dead, she said at length. He died when he was only seventeen. Isn't it a terrible thing to die so young as that?

—What was he? asked Gabriel, still ironically.

—He was in the gasworks, she said.

Gabriel felt humiliated by the failure of his irony and by the evocation of this figure from the dead, a boy in the gasworks. While he had been full of memories of their secret life together, full of tenderness and joy and desire, she had been comparing him in her mind with another. A shameful consciousness of his own person assailed[1] him. He saw himself as a ludicrous figure, acting as a pennyboy[2] for his aunts, a nervous well-meaning sentimentalist, orating to vulgarians and idealising his own clownish lusts, the pitiable fatuous[3] fellow he had caught a glimpse of in the mirror. Instinctively he turned his back more to the light lest she might see the shame that burned upon his forehead.

He tried to keep up his tone of cold interrogation but his voice when he spoke was humble[4] and

---

1. *assailed* [ə'seɪld] : violently attacked.
2. *pennyboy* : messenger(-boy).
3. *fatuous* ['fætjuːəs] : silly, vacant and purposeless.
4. *humble* : deferential.

indifferent.

—I suppose you were in love with this Michael Furey, Gretta, he said.

—I was great with him [1] at that time, she said.

Her voice was veiled and sad. Gabriel, feeling now how vain it would be to try to lead her whither he had purposed, caressed one of her hands and said, also sadly:

—And what did he die of so young, Gretta? Consumption, was it?

—I think he died for me, she answered.

A vague terror seized Gabriel at this answer as if, at that hour when he had hoped to triumph, some impalpable and vindictive being was coming against him, gathering forces against him in its vague world. But he shook himself free of it with an effort of reason and continued to caress her hand. He did not question her again for he felt that she would tell him of herself. Her hand was warm and moist: [2] it did not respond to his touch but he continued to caress it just as he had caressed her first letter to him that spring morning.

—It was in the winter, she said, about the beginning of the winter when I was going to leave my grandmother's and come up here to the convent. And he was ill at the time in his lodgings in Galway and wouldn't be let out and his people in Oughterard were written to. He was in decline, they said, or something like that. I never knew rightly.

She paused for a moment and sighed.

—Poor fellow, she said. He was very fond of me

1. *I was great with him* : we were together a lot.
2. *moist* [mɔɪst]: slightly wet, humid.

and he was such a gentle boy. We used to go out together, walking, you know, Gabriel, like the way they do in the country. He was going to study singing only for his health.[1] He had a very good voice, poor Michael Furey.

—Well; and then? asked Gabriel.

—And then when it came to the time for me to leave Galway and come up to the convent he was much worse and I wouldn't be let see him so I wrote a letter saying I was going up to Dublin and would be back in the summer and hoping he would be better then.

She paused for a moment to get her voice under control and then went on:

—Then the night before I left I was in my grandmother's house in Nuns' Island, packing up, and I heard gravel[2] thrown up against the window. The window was so wet I couldn't see so I ran downstairs as I was and slipped out the back into the garden and there was the poor fellow at the end of the garden, shivering.

—And did you not tell him to go back? asked Gabriel.

—I implored of him to go home at once and told him he would get his death[3] in the rain. But he said he did not want to live. I can see his eyes as well as well! He was standing at the end of the wall where there was a tree.

—And did he go home? asked Gabriel.

---

1. *only for his health* : "if it were not for his health" (i.e. if his health had not prevented him).
2. *gravel* : very small stones.
3. *get his death* : "catch his death of cold", i.e. die of the cold.

—Yes, he went home. And when I was only a week in the convent he died and he was buried in Oughterard where his people came from. O, the day I heard that, that he was dead!

She stopped, choking with sobs, and, overcome by emotion, flung herself face downward on the bed, sobbing in the quilt. Gabriel held her hand for a moment longer, irresolutely, and then, shy of intruding on her grief, let it fall gently and walked quietly to the window.

She was fast asleep.

Gabriel, leaning on his elbow, looked for a few moments unresentfully on her tangled[1] hair and half-open mouth, listening to her deep-drawn breath. So she had had that romance in her life: a man had died for her sake.[2] It hardly pained him now to think how poor a part he, her husband, had played in her life. He watched her while she slept as though he and she had never lived together as man and wife. His curious eyes rested long upon her face and on her hair: and, as he thought of what she must have been then, in that time of her first girlish beauty, a strange friendly pity for her entered his soul. He did not like to say even to himself that her face was no longer beautiful but he knew that it was no longer the face for which Michael Furey had braved[3] death.

Perhaps she had not told him all the story. His eyes moved to the chair over which she had thrown

---

1. *tangled* ['tæŋgld] : untidy and disordered.
2. *for her sake* : because of her.
3. *braved* ['breɪvd] : challenged, met with courage.

some of her clothes. A petticoat[1] string dangled[2] to the floor. One boot stood upright, its limp[3] upper fallen down: the fellow[4] of it lay upon its side. He wondered at his riot of emotions of an hour before. From what had it proceeded? From his aunt's supper, from his own foolish speech, from the wine and dancing, the merry-making when saying good-night in the hall, the pleasure of the walk along the river in the snow. Poor Aunt Julia! She, too, would soon be a shade with the shade of Patrick Morkan and his horse. He had caught that haggard[5] look upon her face for a moment when she was singing *Arrayed for the Bridal*. Soon, perhaps, he would be sitting in that same drawing-room, dressed in black, his silk hat on his knees. The blinds would be drawn down and Aunt Kate would be sitting beside him, crying and blowing her nose and telling him how Julia had died. He would cast about[6] in his mind for some words that might console her, and would find only lame[7] and useless ones. Yes, yes: that would happen very soon.

The air of the room chilled his shoulders. He stretched himself cautiously along under the sheets and lay down beside his wife. One by one they were all becoming shades. Better pass boldly into that other world, in the full glory of some passion, than

---

1. *petticoat* : underskirt.
2. *dangled* : hung downwards moving slightly.
3. *limp* : without rigidity or firmness.
4. *fellow* : companion (i.e. the other boot).
5. *haggard* ['hægəd]: extremely fatigued.
6. *cast about* : search.
7. *lame* [leɪm] : weak and unsatisfactory.

fade and wither[1] dismally with age. He thought of how she who lay beside him had locked in her heart for so many years that image of her lover's eyes when he had told her that he did not wish to live.

Generous tears filled Gabriel's eyes. He had never felt like that himself towards any woman but he knew that such a feeling must be love. The tears gathered more thickly[2] in his eyes and in the partial darkness he imagined he saw the form of a young man standing under a dripping tree. Other forms were near. His soul had approached that region where dwell the vast hosts of the dead. He was conscious of, but could not apprehend, their wayward[3] and flickering[4] existence. His own identity was fading out into a grey impalpable world: the solid world itself which these dead had one time reared and lived in was dissolving and dwindling.

A few light taps[5] upon the pane[6] made him turn to the window. It had begun to snow again. He watched sleepily the flakes, silver and dark, falling obliquely against the lamplight. The time had come for him to set out on his journey westward. Yes, the newspapers were right: snow was general all over Ireland. It was falling on every part of the dark central plain, on the treeless hills, falling softly upon

---

1. *fade and wither* ['wɪðə]: gradually lose vitality and fall into decay.
2. *thickly* : abundantly.
3. *wayward* ['weɪwəd]: conforming to no fixed rule or principle, erratic.
4. *flickering* : vacillating, repeatedly flashing up and dying away quickly (like a candle).
5. *light taps* : distinct sounds made by something striking lightly.
6. *pane* [peɪn]: the glass of the window.

the Bog of Allen[1] and, farther westward, softly falling into the dark mutinous Shannon[2] waves. It was falling, too, upon every part of the lonely churchyard on the hill where Michael Furey lay buried. It lay thickly drifted[3] on the crooked crosses and headstones,[4] on the spears[5] of the little gate, on the barren thorns.[6] His soul swooned[7] slowly as he heard the snow falling faintly through the universe and faintly falling, like the descent of their last end, upon all the living and the dead.

1. *Bog of Allen* : a large peat lowland southwest of Dublin.
2. *Shannon* : when one crosses this river, one arrives in the west of Ireland.
3. *drifted* : blown into piles.
4. *headstones* : upright stones (placed at the head end) to mark a grave.
5. *spears* [spɪəz] : the vertical poles of the gate which have points on the end (and so look like spears).
6. *crooked crosses ... thorns* : notice the biblical allusions.
7. *swooned* ['swuːnd] : entered into a state of rest and inactivity.

Characters

1. Fill in the table below, placing adjectives from the list opposite the names of the characters they describe.

fussy	graceful	protective	bitter	feeble	
frank	musical	sinister	snobbish	moribund	
grinning	hospitable	talkative	nervous	brisk	bland
jocular	sensitive	slow proud	eager	mysterious	

CHARACTERS	ADJECTIVES
Lily	
Gabriel	
Gretta	
Aunt Kate	
Aunt Julia	
Mr Browne	
Miss Ivors	

2. What purpose does Freddy Malins serve in the story?

3. What purpose does Mr Browne serve in the story?

Structure

1. The structure of "The Dead" has been described as built around three intimate conversations between Gabriel and different female characters. Fill in the chart below.

SETTINGS	THE LITTLE PANTRY	THE DANCE FLOOR	THE GRESHAM HOTEL
Gabriel talks to			
on the subject of			
Afterwards, Gabriel feels			

2. According to the critic C.C. Loomis, '"The Dead" follows a logical pattern; we move from the general to the particular, then to the universal.'
    Where are the two turning points in the story (the point of transition from general to particular and that from particular to universal)? If you disagree with Loomis's view, explain your disagreement and give your own view of the structure.

3. The closing scene of "The Dead" is very different from the rest of the story. Foreshadowing (when something hints at what is to come) provides many small links between the story of the party and the closing scene. Make a list of examples of foreshadowing. One example has been provided.

DETAILS FROM EARLY IN THE STORY	EVENTS FROM THE END OF THE STORY
Kate and Julia say that Gretta must be 'perished alive' (p. 210).	Michael Furey dies of cold

Symbolism

Mark the crucifixion images in the final paragraph of "The Dead". Why are they there?

Narrator

1. How does the narrative style of the last three paragraphs of "The Dead" differ from that of the rest of the story? How does it differ from the usual narrative style of *Dubliners* as a whole?

2. Read the last sentence of the story and comment on its use of alliteration, assonance, repetition and imitative form.

Themes

1. Describe the epiphany or epiphanies in "The Dead".

2. Discuss the treatment of the ideas of Irish nationalism represented by Miss Ivors in the story.

3.   '– Goloshes! said Mrs Conroy. That's the latest. Whenever it's wet underfoot I must put on my goloshes. To-night even he wanted me to put them on, but I wouldn't. The next thing he'll buy me will be a diving suit.'

   This quotation is one instance of the imagery of protection from and exposure to water or the weather that runs through *Dubliners*. Find and discuss two other examples in "The Dead" and two or three from earlier stories.

General Questions on *Dubliners*

Characters

1. Several characters in *Dubliners* experience shame and humiliation. Make a list of these characters, then compare and contrast two instances. What causes the feelings of shame? What results from them?

2. Many characters in the stories can be seen or see themselves as outsiders. Make a list of these characters, noting in each case what makes him or her an "outsider".

3. The stories of *Dubliners* are linked in many ways: by themes, images, symbols, characters and situations. Give two or three examples of the linking of characters from different stories through shared attributes or situations.

Structure

Joyce said that the stories of *Dubliners* fell into four categories: childhood, adolescence, maturity and public life. Comment on this overall structure.

Narrative Technique

Describe the variety of narrative techniques in *Dubliners*.

Themes

1. Discuss the representation of the Catholic Church in _Dubliners_ as a whole.

2. Discuss the use of music in _Dubliners._

3. Discuss the theme of paralysis (both physical and moral) in _Dubliners_ as a whole.

4. From time to time I see in publishers' lists announcements of books on Irish subjects, so that I think people might be willing to pay for the special odour of corruption which, I hope, floats over my stories. (James Joyce, _Letters_)

    Discuss "corruption" in _Dubliners._ Why should it be considered an "Irish subject"?

5. Discuss the representation of England and British rule in _Dubliners._

Idioms and phrasal verbs used in the text

Rewrite the sentences below, replacing the italicised phrases with formal English equivalents.

Idioms

1. I *am not long for this world*

   _____

2. Let him learn to *box his corner*

   _____

3. we *ran the gantlet*

   _____

4. he had never *gone for her*

   _____

5. she had been *laid up* for a day

   _____

6. Is she *game for* that?

   _____

7. it's *a mug's game*

   _____

8. it was *no go*

   _____

9. he came home *in the small hours*

   _____

10. the girl has to *bear the brunt*

    _____

11. he had *sown his wild oats*

_____

12. she had *made a clean breast of it*

_____

13. I'm going to *have my fling* first

_____

14. The kitchen was *spick and span*

_____

15. so long as you didn't *rub him the wrong way*

_____

16. It *cost a pretty penny*

_____

17. they could *ride roughshod over her*

_____

Phrasal verbs

1. I'll *pull it off*

_____

2. ... only one reparation could *make up for* the loss

_____

3. Once you are married you are *done for*

_____

4. They were always *falling out*

_____

NOTES

NOTES

NOTES

NOTES

Notes

NOTES

NOTES

NOTES

NOTES

NOTES

NOTES

NOTES